The Golden Mean

SUNY Series, The Margins of Literature
Mihai I. Spariosu, Editor

The Golden Mean

James S. Hans

STATE UNIVERSITY OF NEW YORK PRESS

Production by Ruth Fisher
Marketing by Bernadette LaManna

Published by
State University of New York Press, Albany

Printed in the United States of America

For information, address the State University of New York Press,
State University Plaza, Albany, NY 12246

Library of Congress Cataloging-in-Publication Data

Hans, James S., 1950-
The golden mean / James S. Hans.
p. cm. — (SUNY series, the margins of literature)
ISBN 0-7914-1831-6 (acid-free). — ISBN 0-7914-1832-4 (pbk. : acid-free)
1. Good and evil. 2. Aesthetics. 3. Excellence. 4. Moderation. 5. Literature—Philosophy. 6. Literature and society. I. Title. II. Series.
BJ46.H36 1994
111′.84—dc20 93-19242
CIP

10 9 8 7 6 5 4 3 2 1

For Heather

Contents

Acknowledgments

I would like to thank Wake Forest University for a leave and for other assistance that made the publication of this book possible.

1

The Three Goods

One of the advantages of living in an era of reappraisal like our own is that we can see how cultural values have been shaped by the desires and misunderstandings through which people have construed their lives. For the past century and more we have become increasingly adept at discerning the ruses our ancestors used to convince themselves that the world was more congenial to human interests than it now appears to be; we have been less inclined to see that those misunderstandings were often derived from truths that elude us today because we have decided that all values are nothing more than cultural constructs, devices to constrain and channel behavior that might otherwise get out of control and undermine the order upon which society is based. The tendency has been to accuse anyone who finds value in the thought of earlier eras of nostalgia, of a desire for a time or an origin that never existed. This inclination has been helpful in keeping us more critical than we might otherwise be, but it also has its own terrible bias built in: the assumption that almost anything that derives from the Western past must, by definition, be false and pernicious.

While it is often hard to argue with the notion that social values are created out of a desire to escape the fundamental truths of existence, one wonders how the species could have survived as long as it has if it were so habitually prone to self-delusion. It may be that our delusions are only now catching up with us, that our time on the planet has been relatively brief for a species; in that case it would not be surprising that we have been capable of producing vast delusions at the same time that we have thrived, at least for several millennia. But even if it is true that humans are particularly susceptible to delusion, we do have some grounding in the activities of the planet, and it would be even more surprising if there were no wisdom to be gained from the thousands of years we have been attempting to figure out our place in the scheme of things. One of the problems of our era of reappraisal, however, is that there is far too little space for the kinds of questions that would help us discern the relationship between the ruses that have led to serious misunderstandings of our place in the world and the truth that is also to be found in the same location.

An interesting example of the ways our values develop is the manner in which the distinction between the two kinds of good has evolved: the good of performance, of a job well done, and the good of morality, of what is right and wrong. One might imagine a time when the two were the same, when the word *excellence*, or the Greek word *arete*, covered both areas without hiding an ambiguity. Although we might think that the lack of distinction between our two kinds of good demonstrates Greek misunderstanding or self-delusion, it is just as likely that they perceived something more completely than we do. The excellent performance of an activity is as much an ethical act as the choice to avoid doing something that would cause harm to another, and it makes sense to see the two as fundamentally related, even if we are not inclined to do so. We have erroneously stripped the excellent performance of moral value even as we have overstated the degree to which our commitments to restraint in the social arena are a function of good and bad, of right and wrong. We moralize in places where the early Greeks did not, and they moralize in places where we do not.

If we assume that the two kinds of good do not employ the same word by accident, then we need to reconsider their relationship more seriously than we have so that we can see how our desires have clouded an earlier sense of the good and discern the ways in which our reappraisal of the Greek manner of construing things allows us a better vantage point on our own times as well. The good of performance and the good of right and wrong are not mistakenly associated by the early Greeks, nor is it wrong to see them as an expression of the same human impulse. Yet when we consider the effects of separating the two, the results have been astonishing, even if we only think of the most obvious examples. On the one hand, we live in societies whose rewards are dispensed almost exclusively on the basis of the good of performance; on the other, we expect those who perform well to lead exemplary moral lives as well. In spite of such expectations, we insist that there is an essential distinction between the way the word *good* is used when it comes to performance and when we think of moral right and wrong.

We are not inclined to think of a self-made billionaire as one who expresses virtue through the economic decisions that he or she makes, for we see economics as a system devoid of moral considerations. We believe the billionaire simply has an acute understanding of certain basic phenomena and is willing to place himself at risk on the basis of that knowledge. If he is right, the payoff is enormous, but it has nothing to do with good and evil. It is simply that which accrues to one who has learned how to exploit his relationship to the social flows about him. His "private life" is another matter, one that has nothing to do with his ability to perform well as an entrepreneur. The billionaire might be held to the standards of the community if his wealth is dependent on purchases other people make, but this fact has less to do with the moral good of performance than with the desire of communities to keep excess from pushing the social network off center.

At the same time, we repeatedly undergo the morality play of athletics and athletes who excel at their activities and are expected to be exemplary citizens as well. If economic achievement is not thought of as ethical in any way, neither is athletic performance, but if Michael Jordan leads anything less than a straightforward middle-class life, he is said to be failing to live up to the ideal that is demanded of him as a star athlete. But why should we expect his moral life to be in any way related to the quality of his athletic performance, particularly when our values refuse to acknowledge the significance between these two kinds of good? It is not enough to say that Michael Jordan is in the public eye and is someone young kids look up to as a role model, for even if that is true, it fails to address the issue. There is a community standard in play here, the problem of Oedipus, if you will: great athletes like Jordan are given riches beyond their wildest dreams, yet they are also expected to live ordinary lives and fail to do so at their own peril. The wrath of society can quickly turn a cultural icon into a symbol of social shame, and those who find themselves in the public domain must learn to live with the potential cruelty that accompanies godlike status in a community. But that is still another kind of good that according to our own scheme of things should have nothing to do with the good of right and wrong. Why, then, do these contradictions continue to plague our public discourse?

Michael Jordan is the best basketball player of his time, and even that doesn't begin to cover the distinction of his performance; it is not simply that he scores more and has more assists and is more essential to his team than any other player; it is also that the manner in which he does these things is inimitable, is so striking that one can immediately detect his way of shooting a basket or making a steal. And it is not just that he is more eager or quicker; there is something unquestionably special about his behavior on the court that will forever alter the way that people think of basketball. But how is this *good*, and what does it have to do with right and wrong? Jordan has physical talent, and his consummate expression of the body is an aesthetic good: one finds it fitting that he should be able to articulate the possibilities of the body in the way that he does, and he provides us with satisfaction when he does so. Excellence. The perfect measure of the body in flight. Grace. All of these words apply to what Jordan does, and there is good in what he accomplishes, for it seems wholly appropriate that he should be able to express himself in the ways he does. This, we might say, is the pure good of being, to borrow from Wallace Stevens, the pleasure that is always found when one fully occupies the space available to one with consummate skill. But it has nothing to do with morality. It is secular, not sacred, and the way we have drawn the distinction between secular and sacred prevents Jordan's kind of excellence from being properly related to the other good, the one of right and wrong.

One might think that the pressures upon those who excel to hold to the normal course of right and wrong is simply a mistake, a reflection of a Puritan heritage that was inclined to construe in moral terms things that weren't moral at all. If that heritage saw moral good in economic success, we have come to distinguish between the two domains now; we ridicule the facile ways in which our ancestors convinced themselves that they were members of God's elect because they were so well off and saw their sacred status fully reflected in their secular achievements. Yet that same tendency to see the secular expression of excellence as a reflection of sacred excellence is in play today when we expect Michael Jordan to teach the children well, to show them how to be good people. This could be a mistake, a part of the linkage between sacred and secular that we have so far been unable to cast off, but it might also be one of the vestiges of an earlier way of thinking about things that allows us access to the relationship between the two kinds of good.

Why should Michael Jordan or any other practitioner of excellence feel the pressure to be morally good? Why shouldn't he be allowed the extravagance of his own *arete*? Shouldn't he be able to define his own sense of good and evil? Are the athletes and movie stars of our era Nietzschean overmen who reveal to us the world beyond good and evil? There are any number of them who think so and who are inclined to assume that the rules of ordinary society don't apply to them. And they may be right, except for those times when our resentment of their extravagance prompts us to pull them down, to bring them to a level beneath us in order to compensate for the time they spent above us as gods. Certainly the fundamentalist strains of our society are inclined to vilify the practices of these "great" figures in precisely these terms, conjuring a future in which all of us will end up behaving like the superstars of our era because we have chosen them as exemplary figures. The fundamentalists believe that because we would like to live beyond good and evil but lack the courage to do so, we celebrate figures who provide us with images of such a life. But this argument fails to make the proper connection between the excellence of Michael Jordan and his exemplary status. We certainly didn't choose to make him exemplary because of his desire to live beyond good and evil, for by all accounts his excesses are rather minor and uninspiring, just what one would expect from someone with his background. And he lacks the charisma that would make us think that it is thrilling to be Michael Jordan and to live beyond good and evil. No, the fundamentalists have it wrong.

What the fundamentalists have right, however, is that there is a connection between the excellence of Michael Jordan on the basketball court and the exemplary life he should lead. He should be a practitioner of *arete* on the court and in his daily life as well, and if he is not, then he fails properly to understand the genius of the movements of his body. And if he doesn't learn to lead an exemplary life on his own, he will be taught by the negative reactions that will follow from his excesses. True, some exemplary figures like to revel in scandal, are proud of the way they can throw their excesses in the face of the bourgeoisie, but even these figures suffer the pressure of opprobrium and must find ways of dealing with the violent negativity that can come their way when society becomes outraged. If one is pushed into the public domain because of one's excellence, one learns how to develop a persona that conforms to the social behavior that is expected of one, even if only by regularly violating the common standard of right and wrong.

One of the problems with the good of *arete* is that it can mislead, can convince one that the chief virtue of the practice of excellence is that it allows one to have one's own way. The powerful emotional effects that attend the expression of excellence can lead one to believe that the real reason why one enjoys one's excellence so much is because one can ride above all the petty concerns of everyday life and exist momentarily on a godlike level where one's will is all that matters. This problem is intensified in a culture like ours that fetishizes the self and localizes the accomplishments of selves within a private realm apart from any context that might give that self occasion for expression. In such a situation, it is all the more likely that one will come to think of the "thrill of victory" as the expression of joy at making others submit to one's will. This emphasis on the self and its singular importance is one of the main reasons that athletes and others in the public spotlight often lose their way. Not that the tendency to mistake the power of a context for the power of a self hasn't always been a human dilemma, for it is present in Oedipus and Agamemnon, and even in Odysseus. One loses sight of the situation that allows one to express oneself as one wishes and tumbles into extravagance that invariably demonstrates how little one knew about the origins of one's own excellence.

❦

Michael Jordan's physical accomplishments are intrinsically related to a conception of the good, yet we cannot seem to find a point of entry into that domain. Part of the reason for our difficulty lies in our history, in our scrupulous attempt first to link virtue to social success and then to separate them, first to link the excellence of sport to the good of the community and then to strip the expressions of the body of any relationship to the good whatsoever. One could, like Nietzsche, blame the Christians for depriving the bodily domain of its glory and reducing life to an ascetic mode of nihilistic denial, and there is some truth to this. If we have chosen to see the body as a degraded instrument of our own unseemly origins, we can hardly expect to find it also as that which allows us to express the good. In other words, we can reward physical accomplishments, but we cannot link them to moral good because the body itself is evil. As social success becomes more and more linked to economic success, we are faced with the quandary of how to deal with a tradition that also finds money to be the root of all evil. We handle this by separating the economic domain from moral considerations, perhaps the most astonishing act ever accomplished in Western civilization. People have complained for years how scandalous and erroneous it is for us to assume that science is value-free and to act as though there are disciplines that escape society's natural valuing tendencies, but it has been a long time since we have seriously entertained the notion that the economic domain is quintessentially the place of values. To be sure, we talk about *market* values and assume benignly that somehow the magic of the market will indeed evolve the values we want. But market values are no different than any other kind of social values, and any system that both grants priority to the market and denies that it has anything to do with morality is deeply wrong.

Unfortunately, the tendency to see the economic world as beyond good and evil is even more prominent today than it was a generation ago, largely for two reasons: one, the decline of the communist regimes has left the erroneous impression that capitalism is the consummate expression of human social behavior, a mistake so egregious that it staggers the imagination; and two, the great success of Japan and other Eastern nations at our own economic game has made us more and more inclined to define everything in the social world in purely economic terms. Quality of life, whatever that once meant, now becomes exclusively a function of standard of living, which is defined in terms of take-home pay. These pressures have combined to give the economic system a kind of omnipotence previously unimaginable, truly beyond good and evil, truly beyond the constraints of social practice. Our main priority has become the need to feed the economic engine, to increase the gross domestic product, an activity that purports to have nothing to do with good or bad beyond the fact that it is better to have more gross domestic product than less. In the United States, the result of these shifts has been that the only difference between political parties and candidates is in the degree to which they feel the need to restrain the "behavior" of the market, and even there the difference is so slight as to be almost irrelevant.

Once we stripped the body and the economic system of the link to the good of right and wrong, we created a schizoid world in which the most fundamental of secular activities, those that manifest themselves through the display of the body and the practice of economy, had nothing at all to do with the sacred, with the world of good and evil. When we severed the two in this fashion, we lost our ability to understand the ways in which the good of excellence is related to the good of right and wrong. It could be that even at the origin of the word *good* there was insufficient understanding of how the two kinds of good are related; this is something we can never know. But our lack of understanding of the origins of the word should not keep us from probing more deeply into this relationship than we have, and one of the ways of doing this is to ask what Michael Jordan's consummate abilities on the court should have to do with a sense of right and wrong. Even better, we could ask why it might offend us to think of Jordan in the way his detractors want us to imagine him: an incredibly egocentric individual who has problems with his golf game and his penchant for gambling. Why should this image of Jordan bother us in the least, and why should it diminish his accomplishments on the court?

If we assume for the purposes of argument that Jordan is egocentric and that he gambles relatively large sums of money (to us) on golf games, are these facts related to the way we should think of his basketball skills? Not really, although we might wonder why there isn't some transfer of knowledge from the physical capabilities that make him such a great player to the social realm where the question of behavior arises. In the best of cases, the skills of the body can contribute to our understanding of other domains, much as nature in general regularly instructs us in that which we need to know. We have long forgotten what Emerson stated early in his career, that nature is a discipline, and we have also forgotten how to make use of the discipline with which it provides us:

> In view of the significance of nature, we arrive at once at a new fact, that nature is a discipline. This use of the word includes the preceding uses, as part of itself.
>
> Space, time, society, labor, climate, food, locomotion, the animals, the mechanical forces, give us sincerest lessons, day by day, whose meaning is unlimited. They educate both the Understanding and the Reason. Every property of matter is a school for the understanding,—its solidity or resistance, its inertia, its extension, its figure, its divisibility. The understanding adds, divides, combines, measures, and finds nutriment and room for its activity in this worthy scene. Meantime, Reason transfers all these lessons into its own world of thought, by perceiving the analogy that marries Matter and Mind.[1]

Emerson's language here is clogged by Kantian distinctions between Reason and Understanding that don't fit today, and it is also true that in a real way "nature" has ceased to exist for us in the late twentieth century, but these remarks demonstrate how it continues to be a part of our lives even after we have lost sight of it, for it is indeed nature that disciplines us into the distinctions through which we make sense of life. We begin with the fundamentals, learning about the properties of matter, discerning solidity, resistance, inertia, extension, and so forth; and we transfer these notions to the level of understanding in terms of division, combination, measurement and the like, which in turn Reason makes use of by "perceiving the analogy that marries Matter and Mind."

The terminology has its pitfalls, for Matter and Mind do not remain discrete for us the way they did for Emerson, and Understanding and Reason are no longer faculties of the mind, but these facts are less important than the notion of nature as a discipline, as that which gives us "sincerest lessons" into the way things are. The material world out of which all our distinctions finally come is the basis for that which disciplines our thought and action in every domain, regardless of how much we think our behavior remains unconstrained by the properties of matter and inertia, of extension and solidity. And if this is true of nature, it is equally true for that most obviously natural aspect of our existence, the body, which is also a site of sincere lessons into the discipline of living organisms and what they can and cannot do. We may not take its effects as didactically as Emerson does, but they have precisely the effects he claims for it, and we lose sight of this at our own peril.

In Michael Jordan's case, the discipline of nature is obvious. First, he demonstrates to both himself and others the outer limits of what the body can do in certain situations. His grace and the movements he is capable of express both the wonders of the human body and just how far it can go. Although these motions come "naturally" to him, surely he is as aware of the way they are shaped by the discipline of nature as we are, just as at times he too is surprised to find what his body has done. Each new move, each twist of the arm as he loops under the basket and waits to the last second before he commits himself to shooting from the left or the ride side, before he decides to dunk or bounce it lazily in off the backboard, provides a further sense of the extensions of which the body is capable, the measure of its capabilities, and we learn by watching even as Jordan learns by doing. This "good" of the body in action gives one "sincerest lessons" in what bodies can and cannot do, and that is as much a part of the good and bad of life as it is a measure of excellence. Morality has its origins in this discipline rather than in the metaphysical codes that come from another world altogether, although much of the discipline of nature directly relates to the morality that has developed within the major religions of the West and the East.

Like Michael Jordan, each of us is disciplined into an ongoing sense of what the world is like and what its possibilities are, just as we are disciplined into an understanding of what our own bodies can and cannot do. That our bodies are more adept at expressing themselves one way rather than another becomes obvious over time, even in a society that claims we can all do whatever we set our minds to. Our bodies tell us otherwise: we are only inclined by simple physical disposition to be able to do some things well, even though there is no reason why we can't make use of the lesser capabilities the body also provides us with. Although we are given to thinking that at best we learn these lessons early on in life and then forget them, in fact we are making adjustments in these natural and bodily disciplines all the time. At the very least, we spend relatively few decades learning how most fully to express that which our body is, should we pay attention to it, and then we spend many more decades learning how to adjust to its increasingly diminished capabilities. We tend to think that the "lessons of the body" have been learned by 18 and that is that, but those lessons are never over, and the adjustments we must make to them are never ending. This is the most rigorous of disciplines, and it is one that is moral at heart because it both literally and metaphorically makes apparent to us the ways in which limit, distinction, and choice are built into and out of a discipline that always exists outside of our own invention. We didn't *decide* to have the body we have, although we can choose to allow it to express itself in some ways and not others; we didn't *choose* to be the body we are, although we can again emphasize some of our features rather than others. The discipline of nature and the body is such that it regularly brings us into contact with that which we most need to know, which is what we should be devoting our attention to at any given moment.

Michael Jordan's actions on the basketball court teach us these lessons as well, just as they do for him. Games like basketball have many "sincere lessons" built into them, but we have chosen to emphasize the less interesting ones. We have our Vince Lombardi quotes about how "Winning is the only thing," and we have other clichés that cover the "thrill of victory" and the "agony of defeat," and we can talk about the "poetry in motion" that is on display when someone like Michael Jordan glides through the air, but we have no proper language to talk about the nature of the contest itself, the *agon* through which the dynamics of every game play out. If, for example, the Chicago Bulls are demonstrably the best basketball team in the NBA in 1992, why is it that they lose at all? If their players and the team as a whole are significantly superior to other teams, why don't they go through the season undefeated? Well, on any given night any team in the league can beat any other team. But why is that? Why should a miserable team with personnel that don't come together as a unit be able to defeat players with much greater skill and cohesion? Because the *agon* itself on any given occasion develops in ways of its own that no player on the court and no coach on the sideline can determine. This too is one of the sincerest lessons of the discipline of nature.

In a recent series, for example, the Cleveland Cavaliers and the Boston Celtics split six very close games, and one would have expected the seventh and deciding game to be as close as the others. Instead, the Cavaliers came out and blew the Celtics off the floor. For all practical purposes, the game was decided in the first quarter, and the last three quarters were beside the point as far as the outcome was concerned. As with any individual game in the league, one could come up with explanations. The Celtics were an older team, and perhaps they were just tired out. Of course if they had won we would have heard about veteran toughness and experience and how it often compensates for slight declines in stamina and physical ability. And in all honesty one could easily enough imagine a series that ended with the Celtics blowing out the Cavaliers after six tight games. We have our clichés for both outcomes, but we tend not to see that the clichés themselves often are beside the point.

To take another angle, we could say that the Cavaliers won as handily as they did because "they wanted it more," though it is hard to believe that the players on the Celtics didn't want it at least as much given their knowledge that there wouldn't be many playoff opportunities left for them. Still, we will say that the Cavaliers wanted the series more, or that they were "hungrier" for victory than the Celtics, having never made it into the next round of the playoffs before. And there might be some truth to such utterances, just as it might well be that the Celtics were tired out from the six difficult games that preceded the final one. At the same time, one can as easily imagine all this talk about the hungrier ballplayers who "wanted it more" to have been determined by events that had nothing to do with human will. Indeed, I would suggest that most often the things that decide such cases have little to do with the motivations that humans bring to the game: after all, Michael Jordan wanted to win the NBA championship for many years before he finally did in 1991, and no amount of hunger or desire made that possible for him until other factors came together. And if the quality of the personnel around him and the caliber of the coaching staff were essential factors, so too were other things that had nothing much to do with desire or hunger. We say that those who win a major game wanted it more, but that only covers half of it and is a little like saying that the survival of the fittest can be demonstrated by the fact that, by definition, those who have survived were most fit or else they would not have survived.

It could be that the Cleveland Cavaliers came out for their seventh game and everything "clicked." The shots went in, the game plan they had established flowed smoothly, they were able to move with grace on the court, and the other team didn't get off to quite the same engaged level of play. And it could be that this is what led to the blowout and demonstrated the great hunger that the Cavalier players had. It certainly wouldn't take away from their skills or their desire to say that both skill and desire were aided by intangible things that were related to this specific game and no others. Nor would it undermine our confidence in the value of these battles to come to the conclusion that the dynamics of the individual game are beyond human will, that indeed, at their best such games are the consummate expression of the elaboration of the discipline of nature and the body as they unfold according to a prechoreographed dynamic that is based on the arbitrary rules of a game we have created for our own enjoyment. We certainly didn't invent basketball to obtain sincere lessons into the discipline of nature, but that is what the game provides us. The fierce desires that are in play on the court are interesting in their own right, but the *agon* that takes place as the music of the game unfolds on its own and the ways in which those desires respond to the unfolding of the dynamic of the game are far more interesting finally than what any individual player might do, although our own tendency is to single out the superstar and ignore the dynamic that makes him what he is.

Having said as much, however, I must return to another aspect of the discipline of nature that Michael Jordan must also have learned in order to become the great basketball player he is: he had to work hard. For better or worse, one of the most significant developments in the sports of the late twentieth century is that the discipline that is necessary to compete at the highest levels has never been greater. As always, there are dissolute players, but the efforts that go into maintaining the body of an athlete are more rigorous today than they ever were, and Michael Jordan is no exception in this regard. He has had to work long and hard and has had to discipline his life in such a way that it focused on the body and the needs it would have for the competitive level that Jordan wanted to reach. This is only another way of expressing desire or hunger as the terms are used of athletes, and Jordan's great feats on the court are as much a function of this hard work as they are derived from his innate capabilities or the demands of the game itself. In any given year, there are a number of players who come into the game with great potential and never master that potential for reasons that seem to have mostly to do with hunger, desire, or something more fundamental still in the human disposition. One thinks, for example, of a player like Ralph Sampson, someone with an astonishing combination of gifts for a man his size, a player who was always more in idea than he was, finally, in fact. Why Ralph Sampson never came into his own is no more to be explained than Michael Jordan's overwhelming success is, though desire, commitment, and disposition do have much to do with these particular outcomes.

Michael Jordan brings discipline to his life *and* his body, and without these he would never have been capable of what he has done. The hard work that he has brought to bear on his skills is definitely a *good* in the sense of good and bad. He is, after all, supposed to be a role model for children precisely because his skills alone are not enough. What would be the point of having a role model who was exemplary exclusively as a result of something he was born with? If Jordan or any other athlete is to be exemplary, it is because they are supposed to teach children the "sincerest lessons" about the nature of desire, hard work, commitment, and the ways in which they combine to allow one to "be all that one can be." *That* is the good that Michael Jordan is supposed to put on display every night when he suits up, and it is also the goodness that his everyday acts are supposed to reflect. It is not an accident that great players like Jordan are besieged by requests from dying children who just want to touch or meet the holy icon before they die: there is something sacred about what Jordan can do, and when he fails to live up to the other qualities that go along with being a sacred figure, his reputation begins to tarnish a bit.

Our own morality places a schizoid burden on a figure like Michael Jordan. On the one hand he is a sacred figure to many precisely because his gifts defy the homilies of our own lives. Hard work and self-discipline are not enough to account for his gifts, even if they have everything to do with Jordan's ability to explore those gifts fully over the course of a long career. Michael Jordan is special because of gifts he had no hand in. The discipline of nature unfolded within the body he was given to provide a human with extraordinary skills. Children want to see him on their deathbed not because he has worked hard but rather because he is touched by the magic of God, has been given a special gift that no one else possesses. True, even then he required parents who were capable of recognizing and nurturing his skills, for without that he would have come to nothing. The work of his parents and their own discipline had to combine to provide him the opportunities that allowed him to make his way as he did. A great many events had to come together properly to make Michael Jordan into what he is, but in the end it is his grace, his theological grace on the court, his magical body, that makes him special to kids.

By definition, however, what makes Jordan extraordinary is what keeps him from being exemplary. He is an example only of those special few who are possessed of great gifts and the good fortune to be able to find outlets of expression for those gifts. We could say that the morality to be found in the exemplary life of Jordan is that he suggests to children and others that they can be like him, but surely that doesn't get at his special charm either, for a great many kids doubtless love to play at being him on their own backyard court without any hope at all of being like him one day. And if there is ego involved in this, as there doubtless is—most everyone would love to be great, to be distinguished, to be memorable—I would argue that it is the magic that gave Magic Johnson his name that the children want. And this is not a magic to "be all that one can be," or a magic to be famous; it is instead the magic of grace, the charm of sublimity, the warmth of the perfect moment when everything in the world is as it should be and we know that life is as good as it could possibly be. *That* is what children want; that is what *adults* want, and

Michael Jordan gives them a taste of that every time he takes flight.

I need to emphasize that this gift of sublimity is a moral phenomenon that has as much to do with right and wrong and good and evil as the Ten Commandments. Michael Jordan is being good when he enacts one of his marvelous plays, not just because his act convinces us of the good of life but also because that act demonstrates what the good is all about: being wholly in accord with that which is, being supremely in tune with the discipline of nature, being a consummate expression of the nature of things from one's place within its flows. This is the most important good, out of which the other goods flow, and Michael Jordan is as significant a manifestation of this good as is any minister or "ethicist." Indeed, one might think that Jordan is a *better* example precisely because his grace is so obviously on display and because it so powerfully charms us into thinking that there is a way to be that is good and appropriate and *fitting*. The origin of morality is to be found here, in the sense of what is fitting, in the context through which we come most fully to understand the discipline of nature and the ways in which it can bring charm to our own lives, if we are able to understand its laws. This is the highest morality in the land, or at least the origin of it, and Michael Jordan probably teaches it better than any other figure at the moment. It is this morality to which dying children respond, quite rightly, for they know grace when they see it and are happy to behold it for what it is rather than expect it to be something more in accord with their own petty lives.

❦

The morality of grace is not sufficient in human communities because not all humans find ways of expressing themselves gracefully, so we insist that our great humans provide the other kind of exemplary life as well: they must demonstrate the good of hard work, of adhering to the social codes, of being nice to their parents and respecting others while being humble enough to tell us regularly that they themselves are not responsible for their significant difference from us. We demand this good of Michael Jordan too, and he does a fair job of providing it. He *does* work hard and demonstrate the virtue of intense self-discipline. He does evoke for us the exemplary democratic myth: a boy from a modest social background strives to develop his skills, and with the help of his parents, his coaches, and his community, he rises to the status of a superstar, one whose force upon people's lives is far in excess of the origins from which it came. Whether or not an athlete like Jordan should be asked to demonstrate these things to the populace is something worth thinking about, but the reasons why he is called upon to do so are not hard to find. The good of grace in our culture is thought to be of theological origin, and the theological domain provides us with the rules for being good and for avoiding evil that are essential to the disposition of fates within a community. Therefore, those who are possessed of grace must also display these clear distinctions between good and evil that society depends on for its ongoing maintenance.

There is a dilemma here, however, for the demands on Michael Jordan to be exemplary with his grace are different in kind from those that insist he be good and show others how to be good in everyday life. It is not that there shouldn't be a link between the two kinds of good; it is not that Jordan shouldn't be fully capable of demonstrating how his grace on the court is related to the disposition of good and bad in his life, for he should. As Emerson made clear, the discipline of nature gives us lessons in Matter and inertia, and these are translated into categories like division and distinction by the Understanding; these in turn should be translated into the ideas of Reason. There should be a transference from the material to the rational, or to go the other way, there should be a transference from grace to everyday life. The charm of the court should lead to a good everyday life as well. And there is no reason to think that this link is faulty in the least. Our sense of good derives from the lessons that nature teaches us through its discipline, and we either adhere to those lessons or stray and lapse into the bad. But inasmuch as we have gone out of our way to avoid these linkages, we can hardly expect our graceful superstars to intuit them along with their movements on the court.

Which brings us back to the infelicities in Michael Jordan's life. If his humility in front of the cameras ("I'd like to thank my teammates, my coach, my mom and dad") is just an act, if he is really a totally egocentric individual who demands to be the center of attention, where has his grace gone? If he is reduced to blowing large sums of money on his own vain notion that he is a serious golfer, where has his gift gone? Why can't he properly subscribe to the basic middle-class virtues and avoid these petty sins? First, it should be said that in this respect he is no different from those middle-class folks whose morality he is supposed to represent. Betting on golf is hardly an unusual or particularly tawdry thing to do as far as the middle class is concerned, any more than betting on basketball games is, or buying lottery tickets, or going to Atlantic City or Las Vegas. The only things that distinguish Jordan's acts in this respect are the sums of money involved and the fact that the money seems also to be connected to people who lead less than exemplary lives.

But there are doubtless any number of good businessmen and bankers who associated with people like Michael Milken and Ivan Boesky, and we don't condemn them because they had modest associations with these people. And given Jordan's wealth, thousands of dollars on a golf match is commensurate with the tens or hundreds a more typical individual might put in play. In this sense, Jordan is little different from the minister who has been caught in an affair: the problem is not that he is doing things that his flock avoids but rather that he is doing precisely what they *are* doing—it is just that his special status is such that those who have affairs expect him to avoid these human pitfalls. Those who have grace are supposed to have the sense not to lapse into human frailty, to become silly, to let down their self-discipline and be sucked in by other people's eagerness to lie to them. All this is true enough, yet it seems as though Michael Jordan should not have to be the purveyor of these codes simply because he is in the public spotlight.

One of the complaints one hears from athletes and other people whose lives unfold in the public domain is that they don't believe it is their role to be exemplary. They certainly feel the pressures of society to conform their behavior so that kids will look up to them and want to grow up to be just like them, but many feel that these demands have nothing to do with their physical gifts and their display in whatever context they appear. They come to resent the consequences of stardom and complain about the ways in which society insists that they be one kind of thing rather than another. On what basis, they ask, can society demand this of me just because I can hit a baseball or throw a punch well? They didn't ask for the role of moral spokesperson, and they are not happy about having to live up to it. Much of this has to do with the difficulties of living a public life in which one's acts are under constant scrutiny. Some individuals move effortlessly into this world that insists on a public persona that conforms to the mores of those who write the stories and put the features on television, but there are always those who insist that although they wanted money and fame, they never had any interest in being a manifestation of the moral good and are unwilling to provide that persona for the public. One might even think that these figures are more honorable than some, for they resist the hypocrisy that insists they be something in public that they don't feel themselves to be and don't want to be in the least.

One can certainly sympathize with someone whose life has gotten out of control as a result of a misunderstanding of the nature of fame, for few who seek it realize that there are procrustean demands that go along with being a public idol. If one becomes a creature of the people, one must submit to their will, and invariably they demand that one subscribe to the same norms they are forced to abide by. We may not think that it is good that social mechanisms force themselves upon extraordinary individuals in this way, but however one chooses to look at the reasons behind the pressures society places on the Michael Jordans of the world to be extraordinary and yet not deviate one jot from the behavior of the average working person, they are part of the dynamic that is related to the manifestation of excellence in the public domain. One excels, and that is good, and that good should lead to a broader sense of the good in one's everyday life. If one doesn't achieve that sense on one's own, society will demand that one subscribe to its morality or else. Its notions of good and evil may be quite arbitrary, or they may have to do with traditions that have a basis only in a specific culture, but whatever drives the moral energies of the populace usually comes to bear on those who are public figures.

An athlete like Michael Jordan thus finds himself in the midst of *three* different kinds of good. He begins with the simple grace of excellence, with the aesthetic good of his gift, and that may or may not be related to the specific pragmatic goods of everyday life: hard work, self-discipline, self-control, and adherence to some general principles that society as a whole finds morally upright. But those two goods are linked to the *social* good as well, a good that may be pure convention, that, as Nietzsche would have it, may be driven purely by *ressentiment*, for if on the surface society only demands of its great figures that they behave like everybody else (even as it demands that they behave extraordinarily as well), there is less moral good in this than might appear. We know that people resent those who seem to have it better than they do, who appear to be relieved of the constraints of normal life, and this resentment is often directly proportional to the excessiveness of the talent or the special nature of the person involved. The community values might well convey a sense of social outrage at acts that are beyond the bounds of propriety, as though good and evil are at stake, and that may well be true, but there is also decidedly evil at stake; the poison in the people's heart that enviously wishes the great one to become less than he or she is. This good has less in common with the other two goods in that it is good exclusively in a normative way. People will tolerate only so much excess, and then someone will have to pay. This is the divine judgment of Ananias, the wrath of God exerting itself through the people as the extravagant one is stoned.

One might question whether this is a good at all, for its resentful character suggests an origin in evil rather than good, and this distinguishes it from the good of excellence or the pragmatic good that helps one dispose of the measure of one's everyday life in a clear and meaningful way. That people appropriate for themselves the wrath of God when they feel they can no longer bear their resentment seems not to be good, and perhaps it is not. Perhaps this concept of the good has been put in play within religious systems precisely to cover up the lack of good involved. Instead of admitting to themselves that their resentment drives them to acts of persecution every now and then, humans invent religions that dispose of these energies in a way that makes them seem to be good, necessary, and fitting. If these are divine judgments rather than manifestations of envy, people have less trouble expressing themselves in such resentful ways, and the Judeo-Christian tradition has much to do with the power of these hostile energies. We could say that they are not good energies at all, then, but rather evil forces we displace into a godlike context in order to justify them. In this case, our religions have been disguises for our own resentments, cloaks we put around our evil to hide it from ourselves and from others.

Still, the notion of divine retribution is a powerful one, and perhaps it is not quite so easily dismissed, even when we know the ways in which the dynamics of interpersonal relations can lead to retribution against those who violate the codes of the tribe. If God was invented to deal with these forces, and if He suggests an appeal to a higher good and a more powerful morality when such retribution comes into play, we cannot reject this as a site of the good simply because we have come to doubt the invention. Nietzsche may have been right in arguing that there is a master morality and a slave morality, and that the slave morality of *ressentiment* is pernicious in its effects because it cuts the great humans down to size and strips them of their wonder. But the sheer persistence of this phenomenon would suggest that Nietzsche hasn't gotten to the bottom of the problem. It may be that the slave morality is in some respects truly evil at its origin, and it is certainly true that the right of divine judgment that societies appropriate for themselves every now and then has evil energies in it. But can we so easily dismiss this morality by scornfully claiming that only weak people are driven by it? That its good is really an evil to be contrasted to the goods of excellence and the disposition of everyday life in a coherent way? I want to agree with Nietzsche here, want to condemn this code as the opposite of the good, as the expression of evil. Societies should not be so insistently normative that they demand payment from those who violate their borders in nonvolatile ways.

But even if we don't want to call this normative morality *good*, it still has everything to do with the good, at least indirectly, and perhaps directly as well. At the very least, our awareness of these demonic forces and their seeming inevitability—there has yet to be a human community that doesn't make use of the furies of resentment to contain its own excesses and to restrict its impulses, and none is likely to be forthcoming—prompts us to invent codes that keep these forces from spinning out of control. We have yet to do a decent job of this because we are reluctant to confess our complicity in demonism and are still content to clothe ourselves in the self-righteousness of the divine right of God. But perhaps the good does come from our assessment of resentment and its negative effects and our desire to build a life and a culture that is outside of its sway. Surely the invention of democracy was motivated by a desire to remove the politics of resentment from society, and even if our political system has yet to do this, it was based on the good and the idea that resentment should not be a motivating principle in politics. In order to avoid the furies of resentment, of evil, we could say, we invent strategies for the good that will keep them out of play. And if this normative sense of the good cannot be separated from the evil at its origin, it is still a good that disposes of things in the everyday world in essential ways.

It is worth emphasizing that the idea of a nonresentful human being is inconceivable. Given this, the idea of a non-normative theory of the good is equally inconceivable. There may be overlapping senses of the good, which is precisely the view I am articulating here, but there is no getting beyond the *ressentiment* that is an intrinsic part of the species and thus no way to escape from a morality that is at least partially predicated on these demonic forces. Whether we celebrate this good or revile it is finally beside the point, for it will have its day regardless of whether we pay attention to it or not. The only way around this region of the good is to invent an idea of the human that erases the toxins of resentment, and whereas that can be done, it has not seemed to eradicate the impulse itself. We can imagine a multicultural world of benign tolerance, or a feminist world in which the pure good of woman is allowed finally to express itself, and thus tame the testosteronic evils of the male, but such possibilities are both silly and pernicious. They are fictions that cover up their own resentment. Women will not rescue us anymore than the increasingly polyglot nature of our communities will. Women *may* help us to face those aspects of human nature from which we have run for millennia, and indeed have already done so. But there is simply no way around the human phenomenon of resentment: if there is memory, there is resentment; if there is self-awareness, there is self-appraisal that leads to resentment. This is not a cultural phenomenon at all, for it is to be found in every human community that ever occupied a space on the planet.

One of the things often held against Nietzsche's work is that it declares the end of the regime of *ressentiment* even as it is riddled with the same impulse. How can Nietzsche be offering us anything more than another disguise for our own resentment when he has not been able to escape his own? This contradiction seems to be a fatal flaw, and it also may be that this flaw is related to Nietzsche's inability to deal with his own desire for divine retribution against those who failed to appreciate the value of his work or life. But anyone who has invented a concept like the overman to demonstrate the great—and perhaps impossible—difficulty of overcoming the forces of *ressentiment* surely knows well enough that the demons of the human world are not to be dismissed with words or paper shields. That Nietzsche himself could not escape from their intoxication any more than we can is no testament against his work but rather a fundamental affirmation of it. One may think of resentment as a disease from which the species suffers, but if it is only a disease, then it is potentially eradicable, and perhaps we have only to wait for our scientists to discover a cure. That such a cure is not likely to be forthcoming is simply the result of what I have already stated: resentment is a product of memory, of self-awareness, of our ability to measure our place within time and to recognize ourselves as temporal creatures, and as such the only way to excise it is to remove our memory. And if modern society has indeed foreshortened memory in amazing ways, the end of memory is also the end of the species as we know it. Without it as a distinguishing feature, we would have to be named otherwise, and "overman" wouldn't suffice. We would be the last man instead.

Like it or not, our conception of the good must be related to the normative forces of resentment as they express themselves in the human community. Like it or not, Michael Jordan must humble himself before his lord—that is, us—if he is going to be able to continue in his role as a superstar. If he does not, we shall ruin his life as we strip a large portion of it from him by insisting that he be what we make him out to be. These sacrifices are part of the trade-off that celebrities undergo: they lose their selves in order to become our idealized selves, but we cut them down to size if we feel that they begin to take our idealized visions of them seriously. They must be that self we demand of them, yet they must also be an everyday person with the humility we are all forced to express in order to cover up our resentment. Michael Jordan must be seen to be grateful to his teammates because Michael is tacitly thanking *us* and admitting his dependence on *us* when he tells us that he could not perform his amazing feats without them. Perhaps this is unfortunate, and perhaps this is not the way it should be. Perhaps Michael should just be allowed to be Michael, if he could remember what he was like before he began to be what we wanted to make of his great gift. Perhaps.

Even if it has its origins in the evil of resentment, the normative good is also intrinsically related to the second of our goods, the one that orders everyday life in such a way that an individual is devoted to the good rather than the bad. In theory, Michael Jordan should be able to derive from his excellence on the basketball court an ethic that would make his everyday life sound: he could deduce principles in the one domain that would have applicability in the other. And no doubt at one time he did that. If we keep in mind, for example, that Jordan's background is a humble one, we can assume that for years his public expressions of humility about his gift were sincere: any person who could not make the cut for his high school basketball team and who then went on to become the dominant force of his era in the highest realm of basketball would surely be circumspect about his gift. His humility was genuine, we might think, particularly given the teachings of his parents. But, we might hypothesize, he lost sight of that humility after several years of having his way, of being worshipped by everyone who spoke to him. He could not escape from the flattery, and over time it convinced him that he *was* better than others, exemplary in every way, rather than simply having the gift of grace on the basketball court.

Jordan's loss of humility would in turn make him less concerned with the disposition of his everyday life; even though he would continue to make public assertions about the necessity for his fellow players and their help, he would increasingly come to disbelieve them himself. Having moved away from the codes that brought him to where he was, he might find the social corrective useful; perhaps it would remind him of the truly humbling nature of his gifts. Perhaps the normative nature of those who would condemn him for arrogance would give Jordan the perspective he would need in order to appraise once more the order he should bring to his everyday life. This is not necessarily what people had in mind when they began to complain about his arrogance and started talking about the people he associated with, yet those impulses of resentment cannot be separated from the conception of the good life, either for Jordan or for those who relished slicing him up a bit. Resentment cannot be justified in this way, but it can still supply a corrective that is useful to those who suffer its vengeance, as many people who have fallen in public esteem would recognize. Whether one is a televangalist who lost sight of himself and fell from the grace of his television parish or an athlete like Michael Jordan or even Mike Tyson, these falls from grace are instrumental in getting one to focus on the relationship between one's gifts and the disposition of everyday life. In this way, *ressentiment* is deeply intertwined with the human achievement of a good life.

❦

One of the most significant factors in the disposition of the three kinds of good that we have identified is that they are reflections of impersonal forces. Michael Jordan's athletic gift is not a function of God's personal attention to him, nor is it a product of hard work, however much it can shine only as long as Jordan continues to discipline his energies. The resentment that rushes forth to meet him every now and then is also an impersonal force, for even if the individual expression of it is as unique as his gift—everyone has his or her own special reasons for being resentful about life—still *ressentiment* itself is always a social force, and it is one that is not dependent on its particular manifestations. It is a function of the species and a regulative mechanism within all social systems, and those who express its furies are no more in control of them than those who make use of the gifts they have been given. I emphasize this impersonality because we live in a world in which the idea that humans construct themselves has yet fully to die out. Indeed, it seems to thrive most powerfully at the cultural and intellectual centers of our society. Too many individuals are still convinced that our natures are so thoroughly constructed that there is nothing that cannot be added to or subtracted from them if only we set our minds to it. The idea that we undertake these personal projects to mold ourselves in ways that we find fitting will doubtless never die because it has such great appeal, because it always conjures for us the possibility of another, better life than the one we currently have. But Michael Jordan is a *gift*; he didn't make himself that way, nor did we. He had to take advantage of his opportunities, and he had to work hard, and he had to have some luck as well. But those are the elements in a life that determine what one will do with a gift; they do not create the gift itself. Likewise, people do not become resentful by an act of will. It would be nice if they did, for then their resentments would be more easily eradicable. But gifts and *ressentiment* are in place in the human community in ways that have nothing to do with the lives we construct. The way we construe our relationship to the gifts that have come our way and the resentment that is a part of our life may seriously influence how we make use of what we have been given, but they have nothing to do with the origin of gifts or resentment.

I also need to emphasize the impersonal nature of these forces—these *good* forces that work for the good—because many people have concluded that without universal statements about right and wrong moral anarchy can be the only result. If something is not universally true, the argument runs, then it can only be one more justification in an endless series of disguised displacements of self-interest and will to power. These tedious assertions all glide by the fact that however we construe their origin, neither the gifts an individual has nor the resentment that is also an expression of the person are dispensed in a relativistic way. Morality is never relativistic in the larger scheme of things precisely because these forces are impersonal: they don't care about the American people or Michael Jordan or anyone else. Humans either attend to the disposition of these elements in societies, or the societies themselves unwind. Morality is not derived from universal law or divine fiat but is found in the impersonal disposition of the three kinds of good.

We might find it troubling that the gifts of life are a function of impersonal forces, but when we think about it, most of us would admit that this seems to be the case. Even if we seek to link them to specific origins like genetic background, still there is no accounting for why one person's skills should exceed another's, even when the parental heritage contributes to the exception one becomes. There are many, many parents who are physically gifted, but there is only one Michael Jordan, and only hundreds of people whose skills are sufficient to get them a place in the NBA. That Michael Jordan should turn out to be as exceptional as he is cannot be attributed to anything but the impersonal mechanisms of the universe. In his case things fell out in such a way that he had significant talents that he was also capable of disciplining, and the result is the best basketball player in the NBA. Most of us think that only seriously deluded people would conclude from their gifts that the world had been waiting just for them, that everything had led up to them and their special nature. Likewise, we might erroneously want to take credit for whatever makes us special, or we might want to attribute our good fortune to a higher power, but in the end there seems to be no personal origin for the disposition of individual lives.

The same can be said for the social forces that accumulate around particular resentments that become collective. Michael Jordan has been fortunate in that his "sins" have been so small that the *ressentiment* of the people has not gathered around him, but if it did, this would not necessarily be due to any great mistake on his part. As we have seen in too many cases of a prominent individual pilloried in the press, society demands victims every now and then, and it will have them. Whether they be Michael Jordan or Donald Trump or Mike Tyson is less of matter of choice than of the things in the air at the particular moment, though the arrogance of Trump and Tyson made them readier candidates for public pillorying than Jordan, who has continued to assert his humble vision of his gifts in spite of reports to the contrary. He may *think* he is better than the rest of us, but he has not been foolish enough to say as much in public, as Trump regularly did, or as Tyson repeatedly did with his actions. When society brings its forces to bear on the exceptional, it takes its hardest swipes at those who have declared their freedom from its constraints, but it forces even those like Jordan to bring their public persona into line with what we demand. It is not that we have anything against him; it is just that he must conform to the rhythms of our life or else we will withdraw the adulation we have thrown his way.

If the gifts of life and resentment are impersonal forces, though, the disposition of everyday life must also be accounted for: Michael Jordan's gifts define one part of his good, the resentment of the community expresses another part—or at least a limit to—another element of his good, but what about the ways in which those forces contribute to the pragmatic order of Jordan's everyday life? Surely that is the most personal of domains, the one where the impersonal forces of the other goods find their individual expression. We wouldn't expect that the work Jordan does to shape his everyday activities would have anything to do with an impersonal kind of good, for he is the one who is doing the choosing. But if we assume that he orders his life on the basis of a good he derives from a combined sense of his grace on the court and the social pressures of resentment, his notion of what to do or how to shape his decisions is based upon what Milan Kundera has called the "laws of beauty": his sense of what is right and fitting in his daily life is based upon motifs, rhythms, patterns that he has discerned with intensity in his best moments on the court or in his worst moments in the press. These "laws" would tell him how best to link the rhythms of his daily life to the flows of the world he participates in most intensely when he is performing one of his looping layups while he threads his way through three focused opponents. In this respect, the forces that operate in his life are truly impersonal, are hardly relativistic or idiosyncratic at all. To the extent that Michael Jordan finds a comfortable way of ordering his pragmatic activities in the world, he will have made choices on the basis of the impersonal force of the laws of beauty as they manifest themselves in his particular context. He will have taken his physical grace and found a way to establish an equivalent pattern in his everyday life. And he will find it fitting precisely because it corresponds to a pattern that exists outside his ego or his desire for power and prestige.

The three goods are a function of impersonal forces, of the unique curve that life has taken in the human precinct as it modulates itself through each particular individual. If the word itself weren't used up by the controversy that has surrounded it in recent decades, we might say that the impersonal forces of the good are what Emerson was talking about when he spoke in his essay on "Nature" about the "currents of the Universal Being" that circulate through us all. Stripped of its metaphysical connotations, this is a phrase that finds its echo in Kundera's laws of beauty, the shaping forces of the universe that find their specific application in the human corner of the world through the good of beauty, the dynamics of *ressentiment*, and the pragmatic disposition of these forces in our everyday lives. All of us can choose to ignore the curve of life as it swings in our direction, just as we can therefore make choices that are based entirely on self-interest. There is nothing in the scheme of things that says we must adhere to our ongoing sense of the curve of the world as it filters itself through us. But there *is* a curve of the world, and it bends its patterns in our direction in such a way as to provide for us the necessary patterns for life.

One of the most intriguing things about our discourse on these matters is that we seem unable to get beyond simple-minded notions of the forces that drive individual lives. If some of us are inclined to see humans as totally constructed, others are just as insistent that they be absolutely determined by the forces of God. Few are willing to recognize that the many elements that go into the curve of the universe as it bends through us are more than constraining enough to provide the impersonal forces to which we either attend or ignore at our peril. Individuals can be inattentive to what their senses have told them about the relational nature of the universe and about the need to pattern their behavior on the basis of these relations, but they always do so at a cost. At its most basic, the laws of beauty reveal themselves as rhythm, and anyone who has thought at all about the pleasing moments of his or her life knows that they depend on rhythm. If Michael Jordan, on the top of his game "gets into a rhythm" in which everything seems to go in, this is not just a figure of speech. He is for the moment supremely a part of the rhythmical pattern that unfolds on the court. We have no trouble conceding that these sublime moments are based on rhythm as it expresses itself through us—on the basketball court, in music, or through our prose—but we have a harder time recognizing that we seek the same thing in our everyday life.

Yet we regularly talk about the need to establish a pattern of life, and when we are out of sorts we are told to "get with it," where "it" would presumably be the pattern in which we might find ourselves. We know that the discipline Michael Jordan needs on an everyday basis in order to play good basketball depends on a rhythm all of its own, one that insists on the need to keep the body at the peak of its powers, but also one that allows other interests to find their place within the pattern of life. Over time all of us develop a "way of life," and that way is most pertinently realized not in the things we own, or the people we see, or the places we go; but rather in the way these particular phenomena are measured out on a daily basis, in the way we pattern these relations with the other elements of the universe, in the way these patterns reveal how the impersonal forces of the universe express themselves through our own best skills and interests. We can choose to ignore these patterns or to adopt those of another whose life we think is superior to ours, or we can just wander from moment to moment. But we all know at the best moments of life and during the most pleasing of everyday moments that we are indeed in the swing of things, in the midst of a pattern that manifests the curve of life and its good as it filters itself through the particular place within which we are.

Another way of getting at a fuller sense of the three goods is to compare them to a trio to which they bear a superficial resemblance: Freud's id, ego and superego. First, it is worth noting the emphasis that Freud places on the dynamics of the individual psyche: id, ego, and superego are impersonal forces in a way too, for each of us is constituted by them—as far as Freud is concerned—but the individual tussle with these internal forces is that which Freud is most interested in, inasmuch as he is seeking to found a comprehensive vision of psychology. The three goods, however, are not forces of a psyche; they exist independent of any internalized human state and are not a function of their particular display in any person. We participate in them without possessing them. We cannot say "*My* good" like we can say "*My* id." And "*my* superego" is no more mine than it can be possessed by anyone else. Freud's psychology is all about relations, but it is also about specific possessions, and even if his work is in the loosest sense devoted to a scientific exposition of the laws of human psychology, for the most part this comes down to the laws of social communities and *ressentiment* as they filter themselves through the particular individual's needs and desires.

The three goods are not a function of our needs or desires. Instead of having an id that expresses our deepest libidinal wishes, we have a sense of grace and beauty that is filtered through particular modes of expression, some of which are sexual, some of which are purely aesthetic in nature. We do not have a superego that internalizes the pressures of resentment as they manifest themselves on the domestic scene and in society as a whole. Instead, we have an awareness of the rhythms of human relations that demand a limit to the expressions of self-interest as a result of our inevitable need to keep relations among things within the bounds of acceptability. And instead of having an ego that mediates between these two forces, we have an ongoing ethic that is based on our sense of what is fitting, that is derived from those Stevensian "sounds passing through sudden rightnesses"[3] that evoke for us the pattern we seek to establish in our everyday dealings with the world. This is far from a compromise between our purely self-interested libidinal forces and the stern demands of the father, a way of construing human behavior which assumes that all of us would be pure libido if we had the chance. Rather, it assumes that in the best of cases we learn how to live the life that has been given to us; we discern how to assume our place within the patterns of life; we become one of the "sounds passing through sudden rightnesses" through which the rhythms of the universe display themselves at the human locations on the planet. This is not a matter of *settling* for something while desiring something more; it is a question of *settling into* those patterns that make us feel most at home in the world. And this feeling of being at home is *not* a function of being relieved momentarily of the blows that human resentment metes out to us; it is *not* a function of giving up some of the joy of life in order to escape from the resentments of others. Instead, it is a process of learning best how to graft one's gifts onto the flows of the universe, nothing more and nothing less.

The problem with Freud's psychology, useful as it is, is that it is too human; it begins with Freud's particular conflicts rather than with the larger scheme of things out of which those conflicts come. Of course humans have great difficulties with social order and with the expression of their libido; of course many desires are mediated through the relations we establish with our parents and with the conflicts they involve us in merely as a matter of being who they are; and of course we spend a lifetime working through these patterns without ever wholly escaping from them. But to start here is to miss the links these relations have with the larger world around them. For psychology to have value for us, it must be rooted in the world beyond the human into which the human is always subsumed. Whereas it will continue to be useful to understand these relations in chemical, biological and physical terms, these ways of construing the fundamental elements of the world of which we are a part are insufficient as a guide for our behavior. They all reveal pattern, which is the essential point, but we get too easily lost in the minutiae: we become preoccupied with the role of serotonin in psychotic behavior or the role of endorphins in ecstatic states. We lose the pattern, the rhythms out of which the human context flows and through which it manages to express both the best and the worst of itself.

By reducing all of human psychology to a domestic drama, Freud sold the human short. He forced us to narrow our conception of ourselves so much that we saw ourselves simply playing out the same middle-class tale he found in his own life. Not that that tale isn't to be found within us, for it surely is. But to see the path to health as a compromise between competing forces within us, or to construe it as accepting the reality principle as Freud defines it is to lose sight of the greatest wonder of the human world: we truly are capable of knowing reality, and it is not something we need to *accept*, again a term that implies a sense of loss and degradation, but rather something we need to embrace, to establish firmly in our everyday life. The reality principle is not a function of the domestic drama that goes on in our heads but rather the patterns that are established in everyday life as a result of the three goods.

Our tradition of construing the flows of the world through the self that we see ourselves as finds its culmination in Freud, and we should be grateful that he unfolded the absurdity of this way of conceiving of human activity with such mastery. One can only conclude from Freud's view that humans are silly, are incapable of assuming themselves into a kind of maturity. We know that Freud's reality principle is in effect based upon a Romantic nostalgia for a world in which we would be able to express our libido fully, a place in which there would be no superego to constrain us. And we can also see why this nostalgia leads him to see the acceptance of the reality principle as a compromise, as a mature exchange of the libidinal impulses of the child for the mediated desire of the adult: "I'll give you modest pleasures in return for a willingness to forego your feelings of omnipotence." This strain makes Freud's vision a *sad* view of humans, for we spend most of our lives trying to get to grips with or forget an original loss. The domestic tragedy is not really a tragedy at all because its dynamics are never sufficiently expanded to embrace the impersonal forces from which they have been derived.

In the end, Freud is driven by a kind of Romantic self-pity that blinds him to the very wonders in his midst. In this respect we can see that although his ideas depend to a large degree on Nietzsche's thought, he probably lost sight of this influence and seriously reduced the forces at work in Nietzsche's texts: he moved from Greek tragedy to closet drama because the Greek vision was too much for him, too impersonal, too devoid of the middle-class need for goals and strategies for success. Nietzsche's origin of the gods is far more interesting than Freud's finally because of its chilliness, because of its indifference to the domestic farce; it insists that the great joys of life are not libidinal but rather a function of the currents of the universal being, of which libido is only one current rather than the central one. Freud gave up the major joys of life in order to keep the great tragedy a little less tragic than it is. He reduced the cold indifference of the universal flows out of which our sense of good comes to the need to compromise between the desires of the child and the power of the father. Not a bad life, one supposes, but hardly one that conjures up the great potential of the species either.

The virtue of Freud's work is that it provides a wonderful story about conflict. Freud had read his Hesiod and knew that the beginning was bloody and that we were still trying to eat our children and devour our parents, and there is no more profound way of getting at the conflicts in life than through these great early myths of the origin of the human community. In a world determined by the interplay of the three goods, we are always in the midst of struggle, we are almost always slightly off true, and the result is conflict and befuddlement at why life must involve so much difficulty. That we must suffer more rather than less as we age seems the grossest of injustices, as it surely is from a context that assumes the fair play of the universe. But the fact is that more problems do come with age, and suffering is part of the way that the goods play themselves out from within our lives. The only question is why the dynamic of the good must unfold as much through conflict as through the rhythmical expression of beauty that is more obviously related to our innate sense of the good.

If Freud reduced the flows of the universe to melodrama, how are we to think of those flows and the conflicts they involve us in as we try to imagine the world otherwise? Certainly much struggle in the human world is simply a function of misperceiving. Freud might have thought that our troubles stemmed from refusing to accept the reality principle, but often it is more that we have difficulty seeing just what that reality is. We do have desires and self-interest, and even if they are in some respects an expression of the real, they are also impediments to our sense of things because too often we cannot properly distinguish self-interest from they way things are. Confucius said that it was hardest for a person to judge his enemies and those he loved, and we know this to be true because we have the most invested in our enemies and those we love. It is often more difficult for us to see them as they really are than it is for us to see people about whom we don't care greatly. So too with the rest of our engagements with the world: sometimes the deeper our connections to them, the harder it is to discern them with clarity of vision. In this respect we are not experiencing conflict so much as misperception: we only got part of what was going on, and the result was discord. A good bit of the suffering in the human world is a result of these kinds of misperception, and such problems never disappear because our vision is never perfect and the world is always changing, thereby demanding continual reassessments of that which we have already perceived.

But the worst conflicts in the human world have to do with the suffering that comes to temporal creatures who realize themselves to be temporal creatures. There is no getting around the sorrows of life, for they will surely come, and in many ways they are an enduring part of everyday existence. One of the virtues of having children, after all, is that they make one acutely aware every day of the nonrepeatability of a human life. One is sorry to see the wonderful child of five move on to the equally wonderful child of eight, not because she isn't as charming at eight as she was at five but because those charms are different and the other ones can never be reclaimed, not even by another child, whose wonders will be different and whose life will unfold in different ways. These are the deaths we live through every day if we are aware of how fleeting each stage of life is, and they cannot be willed away any more than they can be adequately explained by Freud's domestic vision of life. His father only wants his children to behave; he doesn't appreciate those moments when they refuse to do so, nor does he note that childhood is indeed charming, captivating, heartbreaking in its simplicity, yet even more heartrending in its ignorance. These are the kinds of things Freud's stern father never really saw because he was only interested in preserving order, in keeping the peace, in keeping his own dogs chained.

The proper life, the one informed by the three goods, has sorrow as an everyday companion, and that sorrow is in the best of cases devoted to the things that can never be again. Outside of the human community there may or may not be sorrow—we hear stories of herds of elephants stamping their feet on the ground at the death of one of their members that warm us because they make us feel less lonely and broaden the reach of suffering to make us more rather than less like the other animals—but for us the good is partially a function of the sorrow we carry around with us as we cast our glance backward in order to move better into the future. Even if the universe doesn't construe itself in that way, the rhythm of life is based on these sorrows because the waste of the richness of things is almost more than we can bear. The death of loved ones is unquestionably the most powerful of sorrowful contexts, but we also arrive at an age when we lament the passing of particular days in spring, or particular smells that will never return, or interesting developments that have unexpectedly turned up after many decades and doubtless won't return again. It is easy to be sentimental about such things: I have watched two robins bring three chicks into the world from the beginning of the nest to the final flights of the young, and it has been a rare privilege; I was sorry to see them go off, just as I will be when my daughter leaves home. But the sorrow comes not from sentimentality, nor from humanizing the robins outside my window and turning their acts into yet another domestic story, but rather from the fact that these things happen as they will. If the positive side of the impersonal nature of the good is that it is something that can be relied upon because it exists outside of the control of individual humans, the negative side is that its impersonality means that there is no telling what it will throw our way or if it will throw anything at all. We relish what comes our way all the more because we realize that things might just as well have been otherwise, that we ourselves might have been part of an "otherwise" that never came about at all. These expressions of the good are sorrowful precisely because of the impersonality of the workings of the universe, but they are still good, and they are so essential to the elaboration of our patterns within the world that we can ignore them or run from them only at great cost: the reduction of the patterns of the world to a middle-class drama that seeks to contain those forces in order to make them personal, predictable, and controllable.

❦

One comes back finally to the grace of Michael Jordan on the basketball court. *Grace* is a word whose origins are filled with many related flavors, all of which can be found as much in Michael Jordan as they can be in any other expression of the sublime: there is the sense of favor, charm, and thanks to be found in the Middle English, the pleasing and grateful located in the Latin, and the sense of sighing in Old High German that is linked to the Sanskrit sense of praise. It embraces on the one hand "elegance or beauty of form, manner, motion, or action," "a pleasing or attractive quality or endowment," "favor or good will," "the freely given, unmerited favor and love of God," "the influence or spirit of God operating in humans to regenerate or strengthen them," and "a virtue or excellence of divine origin."[2] As with the word *good*, we have trouble locating the precise region of grace, for it spreads from the theological context to the expression of physical movement to the beautiful in general. And as with *good*, this is not an accident, for all these phenomena are related and constitute the origin of our fundamental sense of what is good about our life. Those times when we discern most fully the patterns through which our sense of things takes shape are unquestionably the equivalent of the "freely given, unmerited favor and love of God," and one of the virtues of most religions is that they make one humble in the face of one's grace. Many of us may no longer be inclined to attribute our gifts to God, but all of us have some sense that whatever our gifts might be, they are unmerited, are a function of processes beyond our own control. People lose sight of this fact more quickly than any other as they learn to accommodate themselves to their gifts, becoming confident that it was really their hard work that made their grace display itself the way it does, but the gifts are unmerited, are a bonus given to the living by the fates. To take credit for them is the gravest of errors, as everyone from Oedipus to the most recently fallen public figure can attest.

We feel the favor of the universe through our grace, and it is through the manifestations of elegance in our lives that we learn to celebrate the value of life itself. Without those charmed moments when things are as they should be, we would constantly be contesting the worth of what we have been given. probing the value of this gift that often seems a curse. The grace of movement, of flow, of the rhythmical movement of breath, is that which attunes us to the splendor and the goodness of the world. Whatever "pleasing or attractive quality or endowment" we may have, we experience the charm of life through it and give praise to the world by our full expression of it. Michael Jordan's grace on the court constitutes a moral act, an exemplary locus for the articulation of the wealth of the world, so much of which is on display in just one twist of his body as he moves toward the basket. Without a sense of grace, life becomes unworthy, tainted by the sense of cursed bread, and we who live comfortably ignore this at our own peril when we contemplate the poor who have grown up without our comforts.

We have recently experienced a resurgence of violence in the rioting in Los Angeles, and although one could hardly be shocked by this turmoil given the abandonment of so many people over the previous decade, one could be distressed by our way of accounting for these acts of abandon. On the one hand, one heard endless accounts of the riots that focused almost exclusively on the economic devastation they had wrought. There were stories about how many had been killed, but the primary concern was always over how many jobs were lost, how much property had been ruined, how many personal fortunes went up in smoke. These are important matters, but the commentators spoke of them as though they were relevant to those who did the rioting, as though they measured their lives by such economic considerations in the first place. At the very least, we lost sight of the fact that we created an entire subculture whose way of life had nothing to do with the mechanisms of the economic world that govern our own lives. Our sense of the good life was virtually inconceivable to these people, rendering absurd any account of economic devastation.

The lives of too many of those in the ghetto lack grace, are devoid of the charm of life that would give them a sense of goodness that would link them to our far more comfortable world. We have forgotten King Lear's most desperate assertion that our basest beggars are in the poorest thing superfluous, some excess through which the pleasurable can manifest itself. We know this well enough when we talk about how soiled the lives are in the ghetto, how filled with despair they are, yet we fail to link this to the need for grace that all people have. Even worse, in doing so we cause whatever charm there is to be melded onto *ressentiment*, thereby prompting it to mutate into a form of pleasure that is increasingly devoid of any sense of positive value. It is not an accident that the moves on the basketball court that are most evidently a display of will to power—those dunks that claim dominance over the other, asserting one's godhood over the lessers around one—come from ghetto basketball. It is not enough merely to express grace in motion, or even to get the ball into the hoop. Rather, the good of grace must be stuffed through the net with violence so that it is undercut by the display of mastery. These too are acts that display grace in a way, but they also show what happens to it when it is mixed with the resentment of one whose only moments of pleasure must also be devoted to pushing others down.

The same thing could be said for the other expressions of the charm of life in the ghetto: drugs and guns. Both provide their bearers with the sense of pleasure that can be acquired through the gifts on display on a basketball court, but they are not gifts, and they do not provide a liberation of movement but an enslavement of it. People will seek out "the influence or spirit of God operating in humans to regenerate or strengthen them," and if they cannot find a way of obtaining it through freely given gestures of the body or mind, they will find it in drugs or guns. Both are intoxicating, and both take the pleasure of the good and twist it into something that tortures the self and turns it into a monster-god who can ecstatically dispense life and death at his own whim. Lives need grace, *demand* grace, and if we create societies in which great numbers of people are kept from even the slightest movements of charm, we can expect drugs and guns to follow. Riots will always be lurking somewhere underneath the surface waiting for the moment to express the other side of grace: the Dionysian violence that overturns all in a final expression of *ressentiment*.

Michael Jordan's grace on the court regenerates or strengthens because it allows us to affirm life, to feel that it is good, to discern ways in which things are clearly fitting even when they are not in our everyday lives. His grace provides an expression of rhythm that we can find ways of employing in our own lives, and it demonstrates the locus of the pragmatic good to be found in the most commonplace of activities as well. As Stevens asserted when he mentioned the subjects about which modern poetry should speak:

> It must
> Be the finding of a satisfaction, and may
> Be of a man skating, a woman dancing, a woman
> Combing her hair.[4]

The "finding of a satisfaction" is the moment of grace, the origin of our knowledge of the good, but it can be found in anything that provides such moments in everyday life. One doesn't need exotic places or exceptional contexts to realize the charm of things; it can be found in skating, in dancing, in combing one's hair. The pattern itself is less important than the lesson of pattern, the movement that provides a locus for that which is fitting in our lives that allows us to sense what is and is not appropriate to what and where we are.

It is true that the Old Testament God was not given to finding the origin of the good in such grace; that is a New Testament phenomenon in every respect. The Old Testament God was a creature of *ressentiment*, a purveyor of the economic motif par excellence: He established the rules, He demanded compliance, and He also insisted upon sacrificial acts that conveyed His mastery over us. He possessed the gift of life and insisted on dispensing it on His own terms, as we see when we note His distress at the possibility that Adam and Eve might become immortal like Himself. One can't get away from the fact that He declares "the man is become as one of us, to know good and evil: and now, lest he put forth his hand, and take also of the tree of life, and eat, and live forever" he must be sent from the garden. The charm of life hangs on that tree, just as the knowledge of good and evil does, and they are linked to that fruit, to the sensuous pleasure of taking nutrition that sustains and regenerates Adam and Eve and enhances life for them. As with Hesiod's account of the beginning, we have here a story that places the origin of morality in the expressions of resentment, in the fears of the other becoming like us, of usurping our special place in the world. And inasmuch as we always enter a world in which we are vulnerable, in which there will always be things more powerful than us to put our lives at risk, we cannot avoid the morality of resentment, but we can choose whether to build our own sense of the good of life out of *ressentiment* or out of the grace that is found in all of the charming moments of life.

When we consider the history of the West, perhaps the most striking thing about it is how assiduously we have resisted the possibilities to be found in locating the origin of the good in the charm of movement, in the grace of rhythm, in the flow of pattern. Longinus discovered greatness there, and arguably the early Greeks did as well, but we seem to have moved farther and farther away from an ethic that places the pragmatic and resentful ethics in a context that is determined by the goodness of grace. Every now and then a writer like Schiller will declare that we are most fully human only when we play, but our ethic continues to be based on resentment rather than beauty. That is what has prompted us to separate the three goods as though they were entirely different things: the grace of beauty is the pure expression of emotion, devoid of links to the good or the true; the pragmatic disposition of the ethical life is simply a matter of mastering commandments whose origins precede us and need not be considered; and the ethic of resentment we learn on our own as soon as we begin to think of the flows of the world in terms of self-interest, in terms of whether or not we are getting our rightful share of the riches of the world. That these goods are all grounded in the good of beauty, in the expression of grace, remains almost inconceivable, and only when it becomes the regulative thought of our lives will we be able to put the normative pressures of resentment into their proper context. At that point, Michael Jordan's fluency on the court will be readily understood for what it is, a consummate expression of the good of the world in all of its richness and intensity.

2

The Straight and Narrow

Most of the ethical systems that have been devised by humans have some conception of what Christianity thinks of as the straight and narrow path. We are regularly told throughout the Bible that the journey to God is arduous and requires great self-discipline and that we therefore must learn early on how to keep ourselves in check. Whether it be the middle path of an Eastern religion, Aristotle's golden mean, the golden rule of reciprocation, or the straight and narrow upon which one focuses, one sees that humans have decided that the good life is finally determined by the rigorous adherence to a code that leaves little room for error. If one wants grace, one abides by the code, stays on the path, moves along the known but difficult location for the fitting life.

As with our sense of the good, however, this middle path is often confusingly manifested in several ways that seem unrelated at best and incompatible at worst. The work that an athlete undertakes to hone his or her skills or the discipline that an artist imposes on his or her craft is one kind of straight and narrow, for without it, the individual's capabilities wouldn't be able to develop completely. The everyday schedule of a typical middle-class life is in turn its own kind of straight and narrow: it is rigorous in its disposition of one's energies, and straying from it can often lead to all kinds of disruptions. Whether one intends for the daily regime to be a middle path through which one makes one's way in life or not, the routines we establish often have this effect over time, particularly when they work well and help us to make the best use of our time. Likewise, the work ethic upon which so much of our society is based depends on a rigorous implementation of a regime designed to achieve certain ends: sometimes work is an end in itself, but more often one establishes goals in order to achieve the ideal life of wealth and success; one stays on the middle path in order to increase the quality of one's financial life and achieve the status one is taught to strive for. Physiologists in turn tell us that the best life is a *regular* one in which the flow of daily existence is regulated predictably: one is more likely to be at one's best if one goes to bed at the same time every night and rises at the same time every morning. If one wants to be fully attentive, this is the middle path through which acuity is achieved.

In the ethical domain there are any number of expressions of the straight and narrow. Most pertinently, there is a set of prescriptions one must follow on a daily basis if one is to remain among the holy. These rules are for the most part proscriptions: virtue is to be achieved more by *not* doing things than by undertaking specific activities. One should pray, and one should be charitable and generous, but often the largest sway comes from the avoidance of sins: don't murder, covet, curse, and so forth. The golden rule of reciprocity is yet another way we have of characterizing the path of righteousness: if one does unto others as one would have them do unto oneself, one learns how to develop a way of life that is consonant with the good. This may not seem to be an expression of the necessity of a straight and narrow way of life, but inasmuch as we would prefer to be treated with respect and integrity ourselves, we would impose a serious regime upon our acts were we to choose to live by the golden rule. More important, the rule is the simplest expression of reciprocity one could imagine, and the need for the rhythm of reciprocity, the pattern of give and take out of which the relations of human communities are constituted, is that which prompts one to adhere to a stable and seriously constraining set of rules.

But there is also the Eastern expression of the middle path or the straight and narrow, and its character differs from this Western emphasis on proscriptions and prescriptions. It may be based on moderation, but it also tends to construe that moderation in positive ways rather than negative ones. If everything is best done in moderation, that is not because we have a need to constrain our behavior to keep it from getting out of hand, or to prevent it from going in a way toward which it is in some respects inclined; it is rather that knowledge of the good is only possible as long as one rigorously adheres to the constraints of the *real.* One's discipline comes not from an artificially imposed regime that is designed to prevent one from doing things but rather from a careful attempt to see things as they are. For me the best assertion of this kind of middle path is to be found in Confucius's famous statement about order:

> The ancients who wished to preserve the fresh or clear character of the people of the world, would first set about ordering their nation life. Those who wished to order their national life, would first set about regulating their family life. Those who wished to regulate their family life would set about cultivating their personal life. Those who wished to cultivate their personal lives, would first set about setting their hearts right. Those who wished to set their hearts right would first set about making their wills sincere. Those who wished to make their wills sincere would first set about achieving true knowledge. The achieving of true knowledge depended upon the investigation of things. When things are investigated, then true knowledge is achieved; when true knowledge is achieved, then the will becomes sincere; when the will is sincere, then the heart is set right (or then the mind sees right); when

> the heart is set right, then the personal life is cultivated, then the family life is regulated, then the national life is orderly; and when the national life is orderly, then there is peace in this world.[1]

For Confucius, the middle path is the way to the sincere will, that which is required of humans who seek to achieve "true knowledge." The goal of this ethic is not the normative goodness of Christianity but rather the goodness that comes from knowing what is the case: one doesn't come to the good life by practicing the abstinence of this and the restriction of that; rather, one comes to see what is and acts accordingly. Doubtless restraint is as much a part of the Confucian ethic as it is of the Christian one, but the good is arrived at by a discipline that focuses on seeing only what is.

One could argue that the sincere will ends up being as prescriptive in its own way as the Christian commandments or the more elaborate regulations of most denominations, and there is some truth to this. Surely a confucian who had a sincere will would understand the golden rule and would practice a careful reciprocity. Surely such an individual would also maintain decorum in sexual affairs and would avoid the egregious sins of sloth, pride, and so forth. But the confucian would achieve these effects through an acquisition of knowledge, through an attempt to understand the fundamental nature of things. The proscriptions he would undertake would be more related to his disciplining of his desires and delusions: the individual would work assiduously to keep from succumbing to lures of ease and false hope, of uncontrolled desire and envy, in order to see only what is there and nothing more. As we well know, we constantly see the world through our desires for another one that would be more accommodating of our needs, and the fiercest discipline is required to avoid seeing something that is not there because we wish it to be.

For Confucius, order is achieved by a willingness to investigate that nature of things. One who has a sincere will undertakes such an investigation, guided by a heart that is "set right." Personal cultivation, then, is a result of accepting the order of what is, of adhering to the straight and narrow of a vision uncluttered by desire, and such personal cultivation leads to the order that all life should be based on. If human communities are lacking in order, Confucius argues, that is because they derive from humans who are unwilling to investigate the nature of things, to discipline their wills in order to make them sincere. As with Stevens' snow man, when one contemplates the nature of things "in the distant glitter / Of the January sun," one must work hard "not to think / of any misery in the sound of the wind"[2] because we tend to anthropomorphize our local environment and fill it with human emotion that doesn't apply. The discipline to see only what is there, the discipline to be "nothing himself" and discern "Nothing that is not there and the nothing that is" (9), is one that we are not ordinarily trained in; our religious sensibility tends to be informed by laws whose origins are not supposed to be questioned by us even as society encourages us to imagine a world saturated by our own desire and filled out with expressions of ourselves.

There are other kinds of straight and narrow as well, although one might think of them as ethical frameworks that have gone awry. Most simply, an ethic is a sense of order, something all humans have a need for, and the straight and narrow order for each of us is on display in the regimes we establish to make ourselves comfortable in the world, the little superstitions we create to make the world right for us. We tend to do things in the same way over and over again because it makes us feel good to do so; it gives us the impression that we are in control of whatever situation is at hand. Whether it be the behavior we establish to begin and end the day or the patterns we use to integrate ourselves into uncertain social situations, we develop protective routines that bear the character of a straight and narrow path that we assume will bring us the life we desire if only we adhere to them. In extreme cases, these regimes are pernicious, as we see in obsessive-compulsive individuals whose lives depend so much on the repetition of meaningless routines that daily life becomes an endless round of washing hands or crossing oneself or starting out on the left foot. Likewise, autistic people who insist that things go according to their order or else strenuously rebel give us some sense of what happens when the superstitions of life take control: someone who demands that one make only right turns in a car and who screams unceasingly every time a left turn is made has not found an order in the world but has rather imposed one on it. This is true to a lesser extent with most of our superstitions, but we generally minimize their intrusion into our observations and thus don't trade the comforts they bring for delusions that keep us from seeing the nature of things.

Nevertheless, it is worth emphasizing that the little rituals we establish do bring us comfort of a sort, do establish a minor form of grace that more or less goes unnoticed in everyday life. If we perform the same routines when we wake up every morning, we don't say to ourselves at the end of them "Now I feel at home in the world, now I feel as though my rhythms are consonant with those around me," but that is certainly the intent underlying the regime, and its comfort is derived from its tacit display of a common pattern that has helped orient us to the world every morning we have made use of it. In some respects, we could say that the difficulties in the way of a confucian knowledge of what is are most often found in our unreflected use of these routines to impose a pattern on the world that is artificial at best and unreal at worst. That the pattern is artificial is in itself not a bad thing as long as one focuses on the nature of pattern itself rather than assuming that the specific elements that compose it are in some way real. Rather, because we tend to remain unaware of the ways we have already ordered our world through the imposition of these regimes, we are incapable of discerning the straight and narrow that allows us to see the true from the middle path that excludes the real altogether. Our wills lack sincerity, and the result is a buffered life that may have its comforts but is also increasingly devoid of interests that would allow us gracefully to express ourselves.

One of the virtues of the confucian path to order and the good life is that it is predicated on the idea that the good can be firmly rooted in a life only when it is allowed to emerge on its own as a result of one's intense inquiry into the nature of what is. Rather than imposing a regime on the life that will allow the person to attain goodness, one achieves it by looking ever more carefully into the nature of things and thereby discerning the patterns that exist, consequently establishing within one's life the patterns that sustain and enliven. Given the emphasis on the need for intense and regular inquiry in the confucian way, one is less likely to be lured into delusion by one's desire for this or that element of the world because one has discerned the nature of things for oneself. If one has a regime imposed upon oneself from the outset and is expected to grow into its significance, one may or may not arrive at the wisdom to appreciate the nature of the proscriptions that led one there in the first place; one might say "Now I know why I was supposed to do that," but one might just as well never learn the reasons underlying the discipline. Many of the most zealous adherents of disciplines are content never to assume themselves into the larger meanings of their regime; they remain satisfied by the fact that an order has been imposed upon things that makes them feel more at home in the world, and that is more than enough. If this is a distinction between inductive and deductive processes of learning, the inductive has the virtue of binding the order to a level of insight that isn't necessary in the deductive regime.

The limitation of Confucius's way is that it depends on a collective group of people who are willing to undertake the rigors of an inquiry into the nature of things. It assumes that people are inclined to want to cultivate their personal life and to achieve order and therefore doesn't account for the fact that many people are not the least bit interested in doing so. Ironically, the man who lived in the midst of an authoritarian regime built an ethic on the basis of the equivalent of inductive reasoning about the world even as we who live in democratic systems that depend on our taking up the responsibility of investigating things with a sincere will seem to find fewer and fewer people who are willing to embrace the challenge. So the democratic system becomes more and more authoritarian, more and more devoted to prescriptions and proscriptions, more and more focused on the imposition of order on people whose inclinations lead them away from any interest in the larger social order. We suffer from the effects of inappropriately conjuring the nature of the straight and narrow, and given our inability to convey to the populace the need for a sincere will, we impose a straight and narrow on them both through the rule of law and through the increasingly emphatic disposition of our lives in brutally economic terms.

Most people who have given thought to the direction of their lives would agree that some equivalent of the straight and narrow is necessary for a fulfilling existence. The problem is that we have confused so many different kinds of straight and narrow that we no longer have a clear idea of what is at stake in any given situation. One of the virtues of games, after all, is that they allow these disciplines to display themselves with clarity. Michael Jordan's moves on the court are seldom ambiguous, and the straight and narrow of his discipline has clearly definable results that everyone can see. In everyday life one sense of the middle path dissolves into another; we remain uncertain of the motives that prompt us in a given situation and are left unconvinced of the sincerity of our own wills—understandably so given the discipline that is necessary to keep us from seeing what we want to see. It is always the work of a lifetime to keep knowledge of the world separate from desire, and it would seem that there are few who succeed in doing so throughout the course of their existence.

❦

One of the virtues of literature is that it makes these facts clear to us in all their complexity even as it demonstrates the necessity for a straight and narrow kind of life.

One of the most powerful recent expositions of the middle path is found in Toni Morrison's novel *Beloved*, where the character of Baby Suggs reenacts our ethical dilemmas for us even as she echoes the miraculous nature of Jesus. Her credo is simple: "'Everything depends on knowing how much,' she said, and 'Good is knowing when to stop.'"[3] The difficulty of living by that credo is another story, or rather the story of *Beloved*. And although the novel is a story of slaves and ex-slaves and the abuses they suffered at the hands of white people—stories so degrading that they shame us all—still in the end those facts are only another aspect of that which counsels one about how much and about knowing when to stop. The result of slavery in this context is that people choose not to live in order to avoid the pain of their degraded status. Paul D. closes up his heart to life and love after the horrors he suffers through, and most of the characters are among the living dead. Knowing when to stop means knowing how much life to let in, how much pain to keep out.

Baby Suggs thus has as her chief ethical criterion the simple statement that good is knowing when to stop, nothing more and nothing less, and she is not speaking specifically about abiding by commandments or doing the Lord's work or staying within the givens of one's society. Her statement's universal applicability comes from the fact that it must be interpreted afresh in every context by every person every day. Baby Suggs cannot say *what* is enough, cannot tell others when to stop; they must figure that out for themselves. She can only assert that the good life is predicated on knowing how much is enough, how much is just right, whatever the context might be. The virtue of her statement is that it embraces the three goods alike without discrimination: it doesn't assert that the good of grace is different from the good of pragmatic life or the good of resentment. In all cases where the word *good* is employed, the goal for humans is to discern how much is enough: what will properly fill out the event without excess?

Baby Suggs is a central figure in the lives of the characters in the novel, and her golden mean is only the most obvious example of her powers. She is also a common person in the best sense of the word, and she is at pains to remain so even as others want to distinguish her from the crowd:

> Accepting no title of honor before her name, but allowing a small caress after it, she became an unchurched preacher, one who visited pulpits and opened her great heart to those who could use it. In winter and fall she carried it to AME's and Baptists, Holinesses and Sanctifieds, the Church of the Redeemer and the Redeemed. Uncalled, unrobed, unanointed, she let her great heart beat in their presence. When warm weather came, Baby Suggs, holy, followed by every black man, woman and child who could make it through, took her great heart to the Clearing—a wide-open place cut deep in the woods nobody knew for what at the end of a path known only to deer and whoever cleared the land in the first place. In the heat of every Saturday afternoon, she sat in the clearing while the people waited among the trees. (87)

Although her gifts entitle her to much prestige, she is "untrained" in the conventions of the church, so she becomes an "unchurched preacher" who simply does what she does. Equally important, though the community itself would like to "title" her, she refuses to lift herself above them, so the most she will accept is the "caress" of the word *holy* after her name. Thus, she is called "Baby Suggs, holy," and that is more than recognition of her special talents in the eyes of the people to whom she ministers.

Baby Suggs' mission, however, is not to spread the message of God so much as to open "her great heart to those who could use it." Significantly, her powers stem less from any particular dogma than from her character: "Uncalled, unrobed, unanointed, she let her great heart beat in their presence." She doesn't tell them how to live their lives, doesn't fill them with the wrath or the glory of God. Instead she lets her great heart beat in their presence, fills them with her goodness and wisdom, all of which can most succinctly be reduced to the statement that good is knowing how much. We are not told where Baby Suggs gets her wisdom because there is never any way of accounting for such things, as her own humility in the face of what she does attests. She had simply made it to Cincinnati and freedom, and "because slave life had 'busted her legs, back, head, eyes, hands, kidneys, womb and tongue,' she had nothing left to make a living with but her heart—which she put to work at once" (87). So "Baby Suggs, holy, loved, cautioned, fed, chastised, and soothed" (87), and 124, the place where she lived, was a "cheerful, buzzing house" (86) that provided a place for her to minister to the needs of people who had suffered mightily. Her everyday role in the community is thus the most important one, and it involves putting her heart to the best uses she can find for it.

But Baby Suggs is also a preacher of great power, and she has a site for her ministrations in this regard as well. She takes "her great heart to the Clearing—a wide-open place cut deep in the woods nobody knew for what at the end of a path known only to deer and whoever cleared the land in the first place." Here in this clearing on warm Saturday afternoons she would bring the people together and let her heart fill them with her wisdom and her sense of life. She would pray and exhort the people to come alive, and they would, in fairly traditional ways, but eventually her power would spread and the boundaries between people would slip away: "It started that way: laughing children, dancing men, crying women, and then it got mixed up. Women stopped crying and danced; men sat down and cried; children danced, women laughed, children cried until, exhausted and riven, all and each lay about the Clearing damp and gasping for breath. In the silence that followed, Baby Suggs, holy, offered up to them her great big heart" (88). Like most people, her flock is constrained by the roles everyday life imposes on them, and these limits are further exacerbated by the slave past out of which they have come: they have truly learned how not to live. In the Clearing, however, on these sacramental occasions, they are given the opportunity to express themselves, first within the confines of their roles, and then within whatever context suits them. If they want to cry, they can; if dancing seems the best way to express themselves, that is fine, too. At the edge of the community and the law that has forced them to submit in all sorts of demeaning ways, they can have this special time each week when they are allowed to be human: in the Clearing it is alright to be human, it is not too much to be so. Back in their own lives being human would be too much, would be an excess that they are unwilling to accept.

Given the powerful celebration of human life that takes place in the Clearing every Saturday, it is not an accident that Baby Suggs' sermons would also speak of the here and now and of the life these people must live in the midst of their great suffering. Instead of counseling them to forget about their lives and the awful things that have happened to them, instead of encouraging despair and a focus on the next life, Baby Suggs heretically speaks to them of the wonders of their bodies and the planet of which they are presently a part, even if they should prefer to forget about their abused bodies and the tired planet. Her sermon rings with the force of God, yet it is not the least imbued with the sentiments of one whose main goal is to get the children of God to stay on the straight and narrow of the Ten Commandments. Indeed, her fundamental heresy is to tell them "that the only grace they could have was the grace they could imagine. That if they could not see it, they would not have it" (88). The tangibility of Baby Suggs' message is its most important feature, and her claim on a secular grace of the kind we have already discussed powerfully commands her parishioners to pay attention to the one life they truly know they have.

Likewise, Baby Suggs' sermon puts the power of grace into the people's hands, for they themselves are responsible for imagining whatever grace it is that they will eventually achieve. It must be a grace that can be seen, much as the greatness of Baby Suggs' heart is on display every day, and it must be a grace that is vividly brought to life by the one who imagines it. That this message speaks of the need independently to achieve grace is significant, for it moves the people away from the subservience they have suffered ingloriously for years. That it is also acknowledged to be grace, a gift, unmerited, uncalled for, unplanned, and holy even if its expression is sacrilegious in the eyes of the church, is more important. Baby Suggs calls them to the gifts they can claim if only they have imagination and a willingness to live in the midst of the horrors they have suffered.

The theme of Baby Suggs' sermon is not surprising, for it too calls the people to a greater sense of themselves and a richer claim on the world of which they are a part:

> Here, . . . in this here place, we flesh; flesh that weeps, laughs; flesh that dances on bare feet in grass. Love it. Love it hard. Yonder they do not love your flesh. They despise it. They don't love your eyes; they'd just as soon pick em out. No more do they love the skin on your back. Yonder they flay it. And O my people they do not love your hands. Those they only use, tie, bind, chop off and leave empty. Love your hands! Love them. Raise them up and kiss them. Touch others with them, pat them together, stroke them on your face 'cause they don't love that either. *You* got to love it, *you*! And no, they ain't in love with your mouth. Yonder, out there, they will see it broken and break it again. What you say out of it they will not heed. What you scream from it they do not hear. What you put into it to nourish your body they will snatch away and give you leavins instead. No, they don't love your mouth. *You* got to love it. This is flesh I'm talking about here. Flesh that needs to be loved. Feet that need to rest and to dance; backs that need support; shoulders that need arms, strong arms I'm telling you. And O my people, out yonder, hear me, they do not love your neck unnoosed and straight. So love your neck; put a hand on it, grace it, stroke it and hold it up. And all your inside parts that they'd just as soon slop for hogs, you got to love them. The dark, dark liver—love it, love it, and the beat and beating heart, love that too. More than eyes or feet. More than lungs that have yet to draw free air. More than your life-holding womb and your life-giving private parts, hear me now, love your heart. For this is the prize. (88-89)

Although it could be argued that this is a sermon from resentment, as the repeated assertions that "They don't love your eyes; they'd just as soon pick them out" suggest, the gist of Baby Suggs' remarks moves in another direction. Resentment is present throughout, at least insofar as a recognition of the measure of one's value in a community is an expression of it, for there is no denying that the ex-slaves are treated as less than people. The whites do *not* love any part of them in any sense. For them to have a heart that related to the blacks, they would have to see them on equal terms, and that is not going to happen. So it is fitting for Baby Suggs both repeatedly to mention this unfortunate fact of their lives and to move away from it as well. As we have already seen, the good of resentment comes from the way in which it establishes the context through which we are to construe the positive aspects of our lives. These ex-slaves cannot depend on any good coming from the larger society of which they are a part, and that knowledge should in turn give shape to what they do in life to make good for themselves. The facts of discrimination are always unpleasant and degrading, but they should not keep one from finding a place for the good in one's life.

So instead of playing the understandable resentment of her people for all it is worth, Baby Suggs uses it to exhort them to love what they have: their bodies, their hearts, their lives. And as powerfully as Walt Whitman had done earlier, she urges them to embrace *all* of their bodies, including the "dark, dark liver," the "life-giving womb," and the "life-giving private parts." These are not shameful, hidden elements of being to be disguised and ignored. Indeed they are an essential part of the good of these characters' lives. If Whitman brashly asserted that the scent of his armpits' aroma was finer than prayer, Baby Suggs here is claiming the same thing, and insistently so. Her cadences, her repetitions, keep her audience focused on the double point: both that they are to love what they have, chiefly this fleshly world of which they are a part, and that every part of that fleshly world is worth loving, not just those aspects that are deemed appropriate by polite society. The emphasis on the need to love the flesh may be heresy, but it is also the rhetoric that can spur these people to love what little they have at their disposal. They are clearly not destined for riches and comfort in the world, and social prestige outside of their own little community is no more possible than it would be for them to be God. Given the bereft nature of their circumstances, what are they to love if not the bodies they have and the physical world in which they are rooted? This may be heresy, but for Baby Suggs the sacraments of life have to do with the body and not the soul, and the consolations she offers her parishioners are not of the spirit at all but rather the body in all of its rich fleshliness.

The caress of "holy" behind Baby Suggs' name is the stroke of a sound, of an act of praise to her for her ministrations, of her love for her own body and for the bodies of others. She knows that life comes most richly to those who acknowledge their bodily status even if everything in their lives counsels them to do otherwise. And she revels in all of the body's attributes, lovingly gazing on the hands that are abused by the whites: "Love your hands! Love them. Raise them up and kiss them. Touch others with them, pat them together, stroke them on your face 'cause they don't love that either." Baby Suggs urges her audience to make use of the wonders that are available to them in those aspects of their being that they take for granted. Even something as simple as a hand is cause for just praise. It is beautiful in its own right, and it allows one to touch, to pat, to stroke, and to do so many other things that it is hard to imagine how one could so easily ignore it. The same can be said for the mouth, the liver, and every other aspect of the body. Ignored, hidden, abused, unexplored, the body remains the wonder it always is and calls one to the joy of life in its decrepitude.

In the end, however, Baby Suggs emphasizes that the heart is the "prize," is that which most makes life worth living, for it allows one to do what Baby Suggs is doing for others: to celebrate life with them without regard for the discriminations that seek to diminish the quality of their existence and prompt them to think otherwise of what one can do. The body by itself has wonders that we ignore and that we should revel in, but like the rest of human life, it takes on full value only when it is imbued with a heart, only when it achieves relations with others, only when it expresses itself in communion with something beyond the threshold of its own skin. The prize of the heart is that which makes life holy and keeps the flesh from being merely that through which we fulfill our appetites. It is the principle of generosity that redeems the body and the life, removing it from the self-interest that so many would ordinarily be inclined to see in Baby Suggs' exhortations to love the body.

In our own day, when the emphasis on self-interest is so intense that books on the best seller list come with titles that speak about the art of "self-love" as though masturbation were a sacramental act, it is easy to miss Baby Suggs' point, for we are inclined to see the pleasures of the body as purely self-serving and the body itself as the one instrument of pleasure that is always available to us. One has books on self-love only when the love of others seems an increasingly remote possibility, perhaps even a possibility that has been deliberately discarded. But if Baby Suggs emphasizes the need to love the body, she is not talking about the same kind of self-love to which our own age is committed. It is rather a love of the body as a body rather than as *my* body; it is a love of the possibilities of life rather than a crabbed assertion of autonomy achieved desolately in the quiet of one's own room. Linking the love of the body to the prize of the heart demonstrates this more than anything else. It is *not* self-love that the heart calls out for but for a love of life as expressed through the relations we establish with other people and with the earth in general. Baby Suggs declares the virtuous life to be one that embraces heart and body as one, that affirms life in the midst of the horrors that are done to one every day.

At the same time, we must remember that the cardinal rule of Baby Suggs' ethic is that one should know how much is enough. If she is called upon repeatedly to sermonize about the wealth that is available to the people in their hearts and bodies, she is telling them that they don't have enough of what they need. *Enough* is something they haven't yet achieved, something they haven't measured up to. They don't yet love the body and the heart sufficiently. They have been dulled by life and called to inattention in order to forget their pain and have thus fallen on the short side of enough. Ordinarily when someone claims that good is knowing what is enough, we assume that the problems of life concern excess, going too far rather than not far enough. One becomes a hedonist or revels in self-pity or is driven by the furies of resentment, we might think, and these forces need to be restrained. That is too much, we might say. Enough is enough. The good life is knowing when to stop.

But Baby Suggs' idea of the good also embraces the *not enough*, and it is that to which her sermons are devoted. She is such a powerful force within the community in part because she can bring the people to life in the Clearing. During the week their lives are dulled expressions of abuse, and they deliberately choose a nonlife to hide from their pain. In the Clearing, however, they are allowed to be human for a time. They can be reminded of everything that is within them that cries out for articulation. They can cry and dance and laugh in ways they cannot within society because that would make them more vulnerable to the people who have power over their lives. So they shut themselves in, and on Saturday afternoon Baby Suggs exhorts them to come to life. And if we can assume she doesn't mean for her exhortation to work only on Saturdays, still the fact that she can bring the people to life in the Clearing is the chief manifestation of her powers. Her sermon doesn't tell the people to come alive only on Saturday: it maintains a love of the body and the heart all the time. But at the very least Baby Suggs keeps their spirits alive by reminding them on Saturday that they do indeed have joy and life within themselves that need to be brought out, that need to be expressed, if only in the Clearing on Saturdays.

The people do not allow themselves enough. They do not know how much is enough, and as a result they live hollow lives. They value Baby Suggs for reminding them of the richness of life, but they need constantly to be reminded of the fact that they are alive; they rely upon the sacramental moments in the Clearing to bring praise to their lips in the same way that communicants rely upon the bread and the wine to remind them of the life they lose sight of during the week. Holiness is to be found in the proclamation that life is good in the face of an existence that constantly challenges that notion, and Baby Suggs is the one in the community who takes upon herself the cause of holiness, the love of the heart that transforms life into something worthy of our constant attention. Neither too much nor too little, the holiness of Baby Suggs appropriately measures out the wonder of the lives the people have and calls them to heed that which is all around them every day. In so doing, she tells them to be more even as she reminds them that too much is as bad as too little.

As an ethical principle, the notion that "good is knowing how much," is thus devoid of the prescriptions ordinarily found at the center of the straight and narrow path. If there is a morality to be found in Baby Suggs' sermonizing, it has nothing to do with rules of conduct or with rituals to focus one's mind on the sacred. Baby Suggs tells no one how to live. She only shows them what to love and to know how much is enough. As the emphasis on the body suggests, her ethic is an aesthetic one at least as much as it is religious: good is nothing more or less than knowing how to let grace express itself through one, regardless of the means of expression. Good is knowing how to move far enough into life to experience the grace that is available to all of us in some way or another without going so far as to move beyond grace into self-indulgence, oblivion, or collective hysteria. Inasmuch as the borders that determine what is enough differ from individual to individual, there is nothing more to be said. One can exhort others to discern the parameters of their own good, but one cannot tell them what those parameters are.

In asserting that Baby Suggs' good is an aesthetic good, I am saying nothing more than that its specific rootedness in a context is that which differentiates it from a religious good, which tends to be abstracted from the contexts of this world precisely in order to be able to provide more specific guidelines for the good life. Inasmuch as most religious systems are predicated on the universality of their specific principles, they can succeed only by denying the individual contexts of the lives they purport to address. Thus, it is no accident that they also tend to devalue the body and the physical world in general, for these are the elements of life that are rooted in specific ways and demand unique responses from those who are so rooted. An aesthetic good finds goodness in the presence of beauty, and that is a central mark of its grace; but grace is to be found in the presence of beauty only because we know what is good always from within a specific site within the scheme of things through which we momentarily discern the rightness of things and approve of what we find. The Judeo-Christian tradition is generally less interested in our specific affirmations of the value of life and the body and the heart; it is more concerned with an ethic that bypasses our rootedness in one way or another. The heresy of Baby Suggs is in this respect deeply rooted. Her refusal to exhort anything more than a love of the body and the heart and to come to know what is enough is a reflection of an aesthetic good that overrides any unversalizing ethic that subordinates the individual to a higher good. The good to be found is never *higher*; it is always right in our midst wherever we might be.

❦

If "good is knowing what is enough" is the perfect formulation of the ethic that Baby Suggs proclaims in *Beloved*, however, the events of the novel demonstrate the great difficulties to be found in that statement, for the plot revolves around the fact that Sethe killed her baby to keep it from being brought back into slavery. The very passage that introduces us to Baby Suggs' ethic is caught on both sides by Sethe's horrific act. We are told that "Before 124 and everybody in it had closed down, veiled over and shut away; before it had become the plaything of spirits and the home of the chafed, 124 had been a cheerful, buzzing house where Baby Suggs, holy, loved, cautioned, fed, chastised and soothed" (87). We learn about the good of knowing what is enough only after it has been long gone, after the richness of life has been overtaken by the ghosts of the past that have brought life to an end at 124. Likewise, Baby Suggs' sermon is presented to us as a memory, for we are told that "Sethe wanted to be there now. At the least to listen to the spaces that the long-ago singing had left behind. At the most to get a clue from her husband's dead mother as to what she should do with her sword and shield now, dear Jesus, now nine years after Baby Suggs, holy, proved herself a liar, dismissed her great heart and lay in the keeping-room bed roused once in a while by a craving for color and not for another thing" (89). Morrison informs us so powerfully of Baby Suggs' declaration of grace long after it has died, long after Baby Suggs herself has given up, and long after she has died as well. Her carefully calibrated devotion to life in the midst of resentment has turned rancid and become nihilistic:

> "Those white things have taken all I had or dreamed," she said, "and broke my heartstrings too. There is no bad luck in the world but whitefolks." 124 shut down and put up with the venom of its ghost. No more lamp all night long, or neighbors dropping by. No low conversations after supper. No watched barefoot children playing in the shoes of strangers. Baby Suggs, holy, believed she had lied. There was no grace—imaginary or real—and no sunlit dance in a Clearing could change that. Her faith, her love, her imagination and her great big old heart began to collapse twenty-eight days after her daughter-in-law arrived. (89)

Four weeks after Sethe appeared in town, the white man came to reclaim his lost property, and rather than giving it back to him, Sethe chose to end its life. Thus life at 124 closed down, Baby Suggs turned on her grace and declared it all a lie. *Ressentiment* overtook her, and she spent the rest of her life without heart, with only the occasional expression of interest in a particular color that might catch her fancy.

In order to understand the desperation that drives Baby Suggs to abandon all in the face of her grief, we need to look more carefully at the circumstances of the horrible deed Sethe did, for it is directly concerned with knowing what is enough and with questioning whether or not life is full of grace even in the midst of slavery. At the same time, the specifics of the event make it impossible for us to dismiss it as exclusively a function of white racism, however central that is to what happens. For one of the most striking facets of the novel is the way in which Morrison introduces the end of life within the community. We might expect the origins of Sethe's act to be found across the border in slave country, as in some respects they clearly are, but in an equally important way they are in evidence right there in Cincinnati within the black community, and they are located in the midst of a moment of grace. Even more important, the original act had little specifically to do with Baby Suggs herself, though it was a response to her exhortations about grace and the prize of the heart:

> It was Stamp Paid who started it. Twenty days after Sethe got to 124 he came by and looked at the baby he had tied up in his nephew's jacket, looked at the mother he had handed a piece of fried eel to and, for some private reason of his own, went off with two buckets to a place near the river's edge that only he knew about where blackberries grew. He walked six miles to the riverbank; did a slide-run-slide down into a ravine made almost inaccessible by brush. He reached through brambles lined with blood-drawing thorns thick as knives that cut through his shirt sleeves and trousers. All the while suffering mosquitoes, bees, hornets, wasps and the meanest lady spiders in the state. Scratched, raked and bitten, he maneuvered through and took hold of each berry with

> fingertips so gentle not a single one was bruised. Late in the afternoon he got back to 124 and put two full buckets down on the porch. When Baby Suggs saw his shredded clothes, bleeding hands, welted face and neck she sat down laughing out loud. (135-36)

Stamp Paid was inspired by the presence of the baby and her mother to go pick some blackberries. This was a gesture of the heart, the kind of thing about which Baby Suggs had preached, for clearly it was difficult to acquire those berries. Stamp had to walk six miles, slide down a ravine, suffer "mosquitoes, bees, hornets, wasps and the meanest lady spiders in the state" and generally scratch himself up as well. He did this "for some private reason of his own," and he was the only one to be able to do it, for no one else knew where the blackberries were.

Whether that private reason had to do with an interest in the mother or the charm of the baby, Stamp Paid was smitten by generosity and was compelled to undertake a reciprocal act. From his perspective the berries provided the perfect response because they "tast[ed] so good and happy that to eat them was like being in church. Just one of the berries and you felt anointed" (136). Again, as with Baby Suggs and her sermon about the flesh, Stamp has found the spirit of life in these berries, feels anointed when he eats them, and his actions therefore are the equivalent of bringing a sacrament home to Sethe and Denver and Baby Suggs, a celebration of life that has to do with them as well as their escape from slavery and Stamp's part in their delivery. A perfect act of love.

As one would expect, Baby Suggs is moved by Stamp Paid's act, however silly he looks after his adventure in the brambles, and like many kind gestures, Stamp's in turn prompts Baby Suggs to undertake one of her own. Although they worried about the effects of the berries on the baby, they let her taste them, and "the baby's thrilled eyes and smacking lips made them follow suit, sampling one at a time the berries that tasted like church. Finally Baby Suggs slapped the boys' hands away from the bucket and sent

Stamp around to the pump to rinse himself. She had decided to do something with the fruit worthy of the man's labor and his love. That's how it began" (136). One act of generosity deserves another, so Baby Suggs heads to the kitchen to make some pies. "That's how it began," we are told, though just what that "it" is remains something of a mystery. It could refer to the feast the community had, or it could point to Sethe's acts and the death of her baby. One way or the other, these events had their origin in Stamp Paid's act of heart and had nothing to do with Baby Suggs herself.

Accident and generosity, then, play a significant role in the crisis of the story, and the initial fortuity of Stamp Paid being touched by the baby leads to another chance event, equally insignificant in the overall scheme of things, except for the fact that it leads to the end of life at 124. Baby Suggs "made the pastry dough and thought she ought to tell Ella and John to stop on by because three pies, maybe four, were too much to keep for one's own. Sethe thought they might as well back it up with a couple of chickens. Stamp allowed that perch and catfish were jumping into the boat—didn't even have to drop a line" (137). One spontaneous act leads to another, as we are made to think that the pie dough turned into more pies than Baby Suggs had planned, which prompted her to want to share the excess with John and Ella, which led Sethe to suggest that they could have an entire meal if they cooked a few chickens as well, which inspired Stamp to say that he could catch perch and catfish with no trouble at all. The moment is charmed by the magical presence of more food than anyone knows what to do with, and the result is that they all want to share their bounty with their neighbors. The sacrament of the berries leads to a transformation of their lives at 124 instead of at the Clearing on a Saturday afternoon.

It turns out that "From Denver's two thrilled eyes it grew to a feast for ninety people. 124 shook with their voices far into the night. Ninety people who ate so well, and laughed so much, it made them angry. They woke up the next morning and remembered the meal-fried perch that Stamp Paid handled with a hickory twig, holding his left palm out against the spit and pop of the boiling grease; the corn pudding made with cream; tired, overfed children asleep in the grass, tiny bones of roasted rabbit still in their hands—and got angry" (136-37). A gesture for one person led to a reciprocal gesture that spread to several more, and before it was all over ninety people were entertained at a feast the magnitude of which was striking to all involved, given the poverty of their lives and the severely limited means they all had at their disposal. Given that, we are surprised when Morrison doesn't even let her account of the event get through the third sentence before she tells us that they "ate so well, and laughed so much, it made them angry." We would not expect anger to be the result of generosity, and inasmuch as everyone had a wonderful time, we are not inclined to see the event as an occasion for resentment of any sort. Indeed, it is the kind of blessed event that allows one briefly to overcome the bitterness of everyday life and simply celebrate the moment without regard for the hardness that occupies such a large space in one's mind.

But no, the celebrants were angry. They were hung over with excess the next morning and upset by the way they had carried on the day before. Their anger becomes the most insistent factor in their disposition, an anger that clearly should be directed either at themselves or at no one, for neither Baby Suggs nor anyone else forced them to eat and revel to excess; no one commanded them to violate their own sense of appropriate behavior. If they did so, they were clearly carried away by the spirit of the event, and no one can be blamed for that; indeed, one usually doesn't look to affix blame to a context in which one's life is momentarily charmed: one takes it for what it is and moves on. But for people whose lives were bearable only by a deliberate act of numbing, for people who narrowed their lives as much as possible in order to minimize the pain of their existence, coming back to life in such a celebration was too much, reminded them of a life they didn't have, prompted them to note the difference between their normally crabbed existence and the great bounty and joy of the feast. They couldn't bear the discord and the loss, and so they responded with anger.

Morrison emphasizes the intensity of the people's anger through repetition. It is mentioned twice in the paragraph above, nestled carefully within the richness of the feast, and it comes up insistently again in the further exposition of the feast that quickly follows:

> Baby Sugg's three (maybe four) pies grew to ten (maybe twelve). Sethe's two hens became five turkeys. The one block of ice brought all the way from Cincinnati—over which they poured mashed watermelon mixed with sugar and mint to make a punch—became a wagonload of ice cakes for a washtub full of strawberry shrug. 124, rocking with laughter, goodwill and food for ninety, made them angry. Too much, they thought. Where does she get it all, Baby Suggs, holy? Why is she and hers always the center of things? How come she always knows exactly what to do and when? Giving advice; passing messages; healing the sick, hiding fugitives, loving, cooking, cooking, loving, preaching, singing, dancing and loving everybody like it was her job and hers alone. (137)

In lives made deliberately small, a house "rocking with laughter, good will and food for ninety" is simply too much. It not only makes them angry—it makes them furious. And because they are unwilling to face their own complicity in the circumstances of their lives, they cannot deal with their resentment; they would have to acknowledge that they played a part in the smallness of their lives as well. They have been blighted by the white man and may have been forced into lives of poverty as a result, but their current situation is also a specific choice of their own: they *choose* to remove themselves from life. Thus, when it comes back and reminds them of its joy, they are angry and need someone to pin their resentment on. Someone has sinned, has exceeded the bounds of propriety, has failed to know what is enough, and they must either blame themselves or find another origin for their anger.

Baby Suggs is the likely choice for a victim because to the other people in the community she seems to have led a charmed life. Of course they feel this way because she has brought so much to them, because her great heart has cheered them and roused them back to life. But when they are feeling badly about themselves, they turn their gratitude into resentment and construe the facts in a crazy way. They ask "Where does she get it all, Baby Suggs, holy?" as though she has much more than they do. They wonder "Why is she and hers always the center of things?" as though they had no part in making her such an important force in the community. And having sensed excess within themselves, they begin to question Baby Suggs' own ability to know what is enough: "How come she always knows exactly what to do and when?" Baby Suggs, holy, a humble woman who only did what she could to let her great heart have some positive effect upon others, is suddenly seen in a new light, is now construed as someone who is arrogant: "Giving advice; passing messages; healing the sick, hiding fugitives, loving, cooking, cooking, loving, preaching, singing, dancing and loving everybody like it was her job and hers alone." Who, finally, is *she* to think that she *deserves* all these roles? Who is she to be so instrumental in the community that seemingly nothing can be done without her? These things may stem from her loving, from her great heart, but the people are not interested in that. What they now see is a woman who has arrogated too much to herself and not enough to them.

The steps in these turns of resentment are predictable enough by now, for we have seen them in our own culture as far back as Oedipus. Once the people's resentment is turned away from their own complicity in the accidents of fate and what they do with them, they need a victim, someone to blame for what is wrong with the time, and the leader of the community is the most likely spot to look. So what is good becomes bad, what is holy becomes profane. The ministrations of a great heart become the actions of a proud woman usurping a role for herself she has no business occupying:

> Now to take two buckets of blackberries and make ten, maybe twelve, pies; to have turkey enough for the whole town pretty near, new peas in September, fresh cream but no cow, ice *and* sugar, batter bread, bread pudding, raised bread, shortbread—it made them mad. Loaves and fishes were His powers—they did not belong to an ex-slave who had probably never carried one hundred pounds to the scale, or picked okra with a baby on her back. Who had never been lashed by a ten-year-old white-boy as God knows they had. Who had not even escaped slavery—had, in fact, been *bought out* of it by a doting son and *driven* to the Ohio River in a wagon—free papers folded between her breasts (driven by the very man who had been her master, who also paid her resettlement fee—name of Garner), and rented a house with *two* floors *and* a well from the Bodwins—the white brother and sister who gave Stamp Paid, Ella and John clothes, goods and gear for runaways because they hated slavery worse than they hated slaves. (137)

The miracles of the previous evening are now seen in a different light: instead of a feast for everyone that materialized out of nothing, now the wonders come from a woman who is pretending to be Jesus. She undertakes her own feeding of the 5000 and expects them to be eternally grateful for what she has done for them. The people quickly move from thinking highly of Baby Suggs to faulting her for arrogance to accusing her of hubris, of trying to steal the place reserved for Jesus. No human has a right to work miracles, and if one attempts them, she must be put back in her place. The furies of the gods demand this kind of justice, or rather the furies of a resentment that cannot find its proper place within the people's lives, and so the town determines that Baby Suggs has more than overstepped her place: she has attempted to exceed the bounds of humanity altogether.

Equally predictably, the assertions of hubris come together with a general vilification of Baby Suggs as a person. Now suddenly it is important that this ex-slave "had probably never carried one hundred pounds on her back." Now it is significant that she "had never been lashed by a ten-year-old whiteboy as God knows they had." And now it is worth emphasizing that Baby Suggs was bought out of slavery rather than having escaped it. Somehow this demeans her in their eyes, even though they were never troubled by it before. It seems undignified that she was bought out of slavery by her own son and driven all the way to Cincinnati by her former master. Even worse, the man rents a house for her that has "*two* floors *and* a well." This excess is not proper, and it is certainly not deserved, so the people's anger at Baby Suggs seems increasingly justified. Once they decide to interpret the important events in her life in a negative light, they can turn all of them into a manifestation of excess, and of an excess from a woman whose main exhortation to them was that good was knowing what was enough. Clearly *she* had not learned these lessons herself, so who is she to be telling them about moderation and the straight and narrow?

Furious with themselves for coming momentarily back to life, the people displace their anger onto Baby Suggs, confident that they have now found the origin of their ills, the site that has contaminated their well with water too rich for the living. Their hostility permeates the air, and Baby Suggs is wise enough to catch its drift as soon as it comes her way:

> The scent of their disapproval lay heavy in the air. Baby Suggs woke to it and wondered what it was as she boiled hominy for her grandchildren. Later, as she stood in the garden, chopping at the tight soil over the roots of the pepper plants, she smelled it again. . . . Baby Suggs, holy, looked up. The sky was blue and clear. Not one touch of death in the definite green of the leaves. She could hear birds and, faintly, the stream way down in the meadow. . . . Nothing seemed amiss—yet the smell of disapproval was sharp. . . . Baby Suggs leaned back into the peppers and the squash vines with her hoe. Carefully, with the blade at just the right angle, she cut through a stalk of insistent rue. Its flowers she stuck through a split in her hat; the rest she tossed aside. The quiet clok clok clok of wood splitting reminded her that

> Stamp was doing the chore he promised to the night before. She sighed at her work and, a moment later, straightened up to sniff the disapproval once again. Resting on the handle of the hoe, she concentrated. She was accustomed to the knowledge that nobody prayed for her—but this free-floating repulsion was new. It wasn't whitefolks—that much she could tell, so it must be colored ones. And then she knew. Her friends and neighbors were angry at her because she had overstepped, given too much, offended them by excess. (137-38)

There has been a change in the tone of life in the community that Baby Suggs can sense in the midst of her ordinary activities, and as she goes about her business she observes the state of things, noting that all outward appearances remain the same. Stamp Paid is quietly chopping wood, the "sky is blue and clear," Sethe is doing work with the beans, the leaves were as green and full of life as they could be, the birds, the stream, the dog, the voices of Buglar, Howard and the crawling girl are all exactly as they were before: "Nothing seemed amiss—yet the smell of disapproval was sharp."

As Baby Suggs goes about her work she probes for the source of the change in tone, and this leads her to thoughts about her relationship to the community. We are told that "She was accustomed to the knowledge that nobody prayed for her—but this free-floating repulsion was new." And knowing the smell of whitefolks' repulsion, she realizes that it doesn't come from them. Then it occurs to her that "Her friends and neighbors were angry at her because she had overstepped, given too much, offended them by excess." Baby Suggs has noticed the special way she is treated by the community in the lack of prayers for her. She doesn't need their prayers, presumably, because she ministers to them. One doesn't pray for one's betters but only for those who are worse off, and so Baby Suggs has accepted the fact that in some ways she is not treated as well as the rest of the people because she has such a great heart. In giving more to them than they give to her, she can expect less in return. They sense that she is above them, and so in some respects she becomes less than human, an object of unconcern. They diminish her in the same way we lessen all our great figures by reducing her to the gifts she brings to them and stripping her of her own human need. Baby Suggs, holy, realizes the change of state that comes with the "holy" that is appended to her name, and she has accepted this loss of humanity as the price to be paid for who she is.

But it is one thing to be treated as less than human because people think one is more than human, and another thing to be the object of the "free-floating repulsion" Baby Suggs feels in the air. Realizing this, she looks for a reason for the change in sentiment toward her and comes to the conclusion that she has offended them by giving them too much. Whether she was previously aware of the fact that it is possible to give too much is not clear, but we do know that Baby Suggs comes to realize that a great heart must also be held in check, must learn how much is enough in each particular context in which it finds itself. Wisdom involves exuding greatness of heart to other people and warming them with one's sense of the richness of life, but it also demands that one know how much life each person can take before resentment and the surrounding lack of life overcome the festive feelings of joy that accompany too much of a good thing.

So Baby Suggs, holy, takes upon herself this burden too, just as Christ did, and accepts the hostility of her community: "Baby closed her eyes. Perhaps they were right" (138). Having discerned the origin of the scent of disapproval in the air, she comes to the conclusion that she should reappraise what she gives with that great heart and what she withholds. And perhaps the true test of wisdom is indeed to be found in this furthest extension of the straight and narrow and the golden rule. Just as we saw that Baby Suggs' rule also spoke to the "not enough" of people who deliberately diminished their lives as well as to the "too much" of those who regularly exceeded the bounds of the good, so finally the novel allows us to discern the good to be found in resentment. For if *ressentiment* is a horrible thing and is responsible for much of the evil in the world, it is also the mark of the good in that it reminds the wise that the principle of knowing what is enough applies to the expression of goodness as well. The overflowing of a great heart can be too much for one with a small heart, can so overwhelm the person as to ruin his or her life. Wisdom is knowing how much grace each life can bear and dispensing it accordingly. It is understanding that each individual has a specific capacity for the richness of life as well as for misery, and both must be calibrated if one is to treat the person as a distinctive human being. Given the fact that there are few manifestations in life of an *excess* of goodness, people fail to understand that there can be too much of it as well. And in accepting responsibility for the people's repulsion, Baby Suggs admits that she has overstepped the bounds and will have to take this into account in the future.

Unfortunately, as the accidents of fate go, Baby Suggs does not get a chance to work through her new understanding of the limits of good, for in the same breath she takes in this knowledge, she smells something worse than the scent of disapproval. That smell was readily recognizable to her, and she tracked it down without trouble, but the new scent is different in kind: "Suddenly, behind the disapproving odor, way way back behind it, she smelled another thing. Dark and coming. Something she couldn't get at because the other odor hid it" (135-136). The dark and coming thing that is in the air is the white men coming for Sethe and her babies, but Baby Suggs cannot figure out what the odor is because it is covered up by the air of disapproval. Even though she remains some literal distance from the community's disapproval at this moment, still the odor is so strong as to mask the more pernicious smell of white men tracking down an escaped slave. And so the white men come, and Sethe kills her baby in order to keep it from being degraded and enslaved. Inasmuch as Baby Suggs makes it clear that she cannot sniff out the white men because of the hostile odor exuded by the blacks, the community's revulsion over its own acts directly contributes to the horrors that follow. It may not be right for whites to do what they do to the blacks, but in this case they wouldn't have had the opportunity—and Sethe wouldn't have killed her baby—if the blacks had not been so consumed by self-loathing over their acts of excess on the previous evening.

Even more, the bad odor the community exudes is not the only thing that keeps the knowledge of the white men from being transmitted to 124. As Stamp Paid makes clear when he is thinking about how to tell Paul D about the why and wherefore of Sethe's acts, there was premeditation in their silence as well:

> Stamp Paid looked at him. He was going to tell him about how restless Baby Suggs was that morning, how she had a listening way about her; how she kept looking down past the corn to the stream so much he looked too. In between ax swings, he watched where Baby was watching. Which is why they both missed it: they were looking the wrong way—toward water—and all the while it was coming down the road. Four. Riding close together, bunched-up like, and righteous. He was going to tell him that, because he thought it was important: why he and Baby Suggs both missed it. And about the party too, because that explained why nobody ran on ahead; why nobody sent a fleet-footed son to cut 'cross a field soon as they saw the four horses in town hitched for watering while the riders asked questions. Not Ella, not John, not anybody ran down or to Bluestone Road, to say some new whitefolks with the Look just rode in. . . . Nobody warned them, and he'd always believed it wasn't the exhaustion from a long day's gorging that dulled them, but some other thing—like, well, like meanness—that let them stand aside, or not pay attention, or tell themselves somebody else was probably bearing the news already to the house on Bluestone Road where a pretty woman had been living for almost a month. (156-57)

Here we have two blows, the one indirect, the other more deliberate. Both Stamp Paid and Baby Suggs are "looking the wrong way" when the white men come down the road because they are working on the smell of the community's revulsion. Thus, they face in the wrong direction to get a proper sense of the real danger than is coming their way.

But Stamp Paid also realizes that the community is making Baby Suggs pay for being so special, for having such a great heart, by an act of omission. To get back at her they don't do anything when they ordinarily would. Instead of sending someone down to tell Baby Suggs and Sethe that white men are coming, they choose silence instead. It was not inattention or preoccupation with their own darker side that kept them from acting but rather "meanness," the kind of meanness that is not visible because it can be accounted for in other ways. It might be that the people's vision was clouded by their feelings of revulsion over the excesses of the feast. Their anger at Baby Suggs might have further muddied the waters, and the turmoil within them over displacing their own self-loathing onto someone who didn't really deserve it might also have contributed to the fact that they were not as focused on the danger of the situation as they should have been. But if *meanness* wasn't also to be found in their hearts—that smallness of people whose impoverished lives had inadvertently been revealed to them by the great feast that brought them back to life—they would have been more than capable of attending to the situation and warning Sethe of the white men. Their training in catching the "righteous Look" was something that "every Negro learned to recognize along with his ma'am's tit. Like a flag hoisted, this righteousness telegraphed and announced the faggot, the whip, the fist, the lie, long before it went public" (157). Given the powerful nature of their feelings when it came to the self-righteousness of the whites who were on the path to right the wrongs done to them by a slave who had escaped, no self-distress would be powerful enough on its own to overcome the immediate and intense feelings the people would get on seeing these men.

So the community deliberately contributed to the events that ruined the lives at 124 and allowed the ghosts to take over. They might not have planned on Sethe trying to kill her babies, but they had to know that something bad was going to happen. In effect they willingly allowed the prospect of Sethe's return to slavery out of spite over Baby Suggs' generosity. That was their way of getting back at Baby Suggs for her generosity, and the totally inhuman nature of this act, this willingness to let one of their own become reenslaved because of their petty feelings about themselves, staggers the imagination, however much it is also a typical—even an everyday—act. White resentment and black resentment come together at this moment to destroy the roots of a community that had only recently come to life, that had some prospects if only it could get past its own *ressentiment*, could learn how much is enough.

❦

Baby Suggs' great heart was her undoing. It brought life to the community, but it also escaped its proper borders, and the results were tragic. The boundaries of Baby Suggs' goodness are best exemplified in the novel through the two sites in which her message takes on its most powerful manifestations: the sermon in the Clearing and the feast at 124. "Too much" seemed to apply only to the energies of life on display at 124; in the Clearing it was acceptable to come to life for a few hours because everyone realized how localized and rarefied that site was. Any attempt to translate the situation to a more secular context, however, risked overturning all the boundaries people had put in place to contain their misery and restrain their contact with the horrors of their lives. Just as "too much" is a different value in every individual's case, so too it operates according to a variable scale in communal contexts as well, and one has to calibrate when and where to let those sacred forces display themselves. Failure to heed this wisdom risks the dissolution of the community.

Morrison doesn't necessarily draw these conclusions in the novel, so the reader is forced to conclude either that there is nothing more to be said or that Baby Suggs' wisdom should have extended into these realms as well. Nor does Morrison explain the lapse in Baby Suggs' wisdom when it comes to turning on her own faith, for again the most important moment for the community is not when Sethe kills her baby but rather when Baby turns away from her own sense of grace and declares that "'Those white things have taken all I had or dreamed . . . and broke my heartstrings too. There is no bad luck in the world but whitefolks'" (89). When she decides that no grace exists, that she lied to herself and others, she breaks faith with her own ministry, but she also fails to account for the role of her own people in the awful events at the center of the novel. It remains true that whitefolks have taken all she had or dreamed of having, and they would have done so even if—especially if—Sethe hadn't sought to kill her children. But if a lesser light like Stamp Paid can figure out the part in these events that the blacks played, surely Baby Suggs should have been able to do so as well. Her failure to acknowledge her own complicity in the matter, however small, reflects the self-righteousness the whites possess that is finally based on resentment. Are we to assume that Baby Suggs is indeed blind to the community's complicity? Or does Morrison deem it irrelevant? Or does she lapse here by making a much richer character reduce everything to the whites? If so, why does she do such a masterful job of painting all the ambiguities of the situation and do so well at fleshing out the character of Baby Suggs?

The more likely conclusion to draw is that Baby Suggs' heart breaks as a result of the disaster, and having lost faith in her own sense of grace—how could one imagine grace of any kind in the midst of all that blood?—she retreats into a lesser vision herself and restricts her life to an even smaller flow than most of the rest of the community. Now she will let in only an occasional interest in color and nothing else. The powers of the whitefolks, their willingness to enslave others with self-righteousness, are capable of overwhelming the strongest of characters, and the demise of Baby Suggs' hope thus represents the true power of the whites over the blacks.

The question of Baby Suggs' loss of grace affects Sethe powerfully as well, for once she is ostracized by the community, the only place she could go for comfort would be to Baby Suggs. If 124 becomes the playground for ghosts, that is at least as much because Baby Suggs gives up on life as because the rest of the people in town turn on Sethe. Even in this situation, though, we have complications that are both predictable and enigmatic. One might think that the horror of Sethe's deed—killing a child being equivalent to parricide or incest—would be more than enough to make her an exile in life. Such deeds poison communities, and it is best to avoid the potential pestilence by quarantining the origin of the evil. But the community has a further problem with Sethe, and that concerns her reaction to her deed: it may have been horrible, but it was even worse that she made no attempt to apologize for it, to do penance for it, to make herself abject in the face of the Lord and his people. And again there is an ambiguity in the text which at first confuses us, for on the one hand the deed itself overwhelms all, and on the other it is the putative sin of pride that keeps people away from 124.

The crime of the murder and the crime of pride are acknowledged together seriously for the first time only briefly toward the end of the novel when Ella is about to intervene in the life of the house because the tangible ghost of Beloved threatens the inhabitants. We are told that "Whatever Sethe had done, Ella didn't like the idea of past errors taking possession of the present. Sethe's crime was staggering and her pride outstripped even that; but she could not countenance the possibility of sin moving in on the house, unleashed and sassy. Daily life took as much as she had. The future was sunset; the past something to leave behind. And if it didn't stay behind, well, you might have to stomp it out" (256). Although Sethe was shunned because of her deed, quite clearly her pride "outstripped even that"; the people expected something from her that she wasn't willing to give, a humbling before them that acknowledged the gravity of what she had done. Yet incredibly, here we find a self-righteous woman talking about how she didn't "like the idea of past errors taking possession of the present" when the ghosts have been haunting

124 for years. Why didn't Ella's belief that such errors shouldn't overwhelm the present prompt her to sweep those ghosts out of the house long ago?

We could say that it would have required too much of Ella to overcome the ghosts. As she admits herself, "Daily life took as much as she had," and there was no energy left to confront such formidable opponents. Everyday existence expended all her resources, for it always demands as much as people have, and yet most of us do not suffer under the burdens that Ella and the community had to bear. No doubt it was all she could do to get through the day, and we shouldn't expect more of her. But then why doesn't she explain how her belief isn't capable of addressing the forces in 124, that she has a belief that she lacks the strength to apply in that context? In fact she does reveal why she decides to intervene in the life of 124 at this late date, and her account is simple: "As long as the ghost showed out from its ghostly place—shaking stuff, crying, smashing and such—Ella respected it. But if it took flesh and came in her world, well, the shoe was on the other foot. She didn't mind a little communication between the two worlds, but this was an invasion" (257). Here Ella suggests that the real problem is not with other people's errors but only with the way those errors might affect her. Again, the statement is ambiguous, for it suggests that the ghost of 124 must be dealt with now because it has taken on flesh, but it also asserts that the real problem is not its fleshly nature but that it has escaped the house and threatens Ella's domain as well. Beloved *has* taken over 124, and she poses a threat to the rest of the community too, but the powers of this fleshly ghost have nothing to do with a credo that asserts that the errors of the past should not take possession of the present. That vision of things should have caused Ella to intervene years before she does. Something is lacking in her explanation, an assertion that smacks more of self-justification than anything else, even if there is truth to it.

Having taken on a fleshly guise, the ghost of Beloved threatens to overrun the community. She has all but sucked the life out of her mother Sethe, and she threatens to spread her evil elsewhere as well. These facts come to light chiefly because Denver goes in search of help; she sees that Beloved will not be satisfied until she has taken Sethe's life in return for the loss of her own, until the error of the past and its resentment has final sway over the present. So Ella acts and thirty women go down to 124 and intervene, though even here, the past almost repeats itself, with Sethe ready to undertake yet another ritual murder that is this time prevented by the people. The townsfolk prevail almost by accident, however important it is that they finally decided that they had to deal with the problems of 124. And whereas it is good that Ella finally takes it upon herself to deal with the errors of the past, her own error remains hidden here. It is still *Sethe's* error she is referring to and not her own. That mistake remains hidden, as it will even after Beloved departs.

No, Sethe was a proud woman, a woman who refused to accept the humiliation that was her due given the staggering nature of her crime. She never repented, never explained, and all these years later this is the barrier that separates her from the rest of the community. The people cannot countenance her pride, and until she submits to their will, they will have nothing to do with her. Knowing what is enough requires a balancing of the scales, redressing the evil of the past by admitting one's part in it, and Sethe refuses to do that. Sethe's explanation of her crime *does* take on an unearthly quality, for she certainly doesn't react the way we would expect her to. In fact, her explanation doesn't measure up to the public act that is expected of her, as we see when many years later she asserts yet again her feelings about her crime:

> Sethe knew that the circle she was making around the room, him, the subject, would remain one. That she could never close in, pin it down for anybody who had to ask. If they didn't get it right off—she could never explain. Because the truth was simple, not a long-drawn-out record of flowered shifts, tree cages, selfishness, ankle ropes and wells. Simple: she was squatting in the gar-

> den and when she saw them coming and recognized schoolteacher's hat, she heard wings . . . And if she thought anything, it was No. No. Nono. Nonono. Simple. She just flew. Collected every bit of life she had made, all the parts of her that were precious and fine and beautiful, and carried, pushed, dragged them through the veil, out, away, over there where no one could hurt them. Over there. Outside this place, where they would be safe. And the hummingbird wings beat on. (163)

To say that Sethe thought it was better for her babies to be safe in death than enslaved and alive is only to cover part of her gist, for if that is the kernel of her motivation, there are qualifications that need to be made. First, most pertinently, as we would expect, this is hardly something Sethe cogitates about while the white men ride up. Instead, "she heard wings. Little hummingbirds stuck their needle beaks right through her headcloth into her hair and beat their wings" (163). Whatever was going on in her mind was not exactly thought at all, nor would we expect it to be under such a threatening situation. Hummingbird wings said "No, nono, nonono," and that was all there was to it. She simply "Collected every bit of life she had made, all the parts of her that were precious and fine and beautiful, and carried, pushed, dragged them through the veil, out, away, over there where no one could hurt them. Over there. Outside this place, where they would be safe." The beating wings tell her that this is what she should do, and it is as simple as that.

Indeed, it remains as simple as that all these years later when she once more tries to tell Paul D what her reasons were. People demand an explanation from a woman who attempts to murder her children, and this is the best she can do, knowing full well by this time that "she could never close in, pin it down for anybody who had to ask. If they didn't get it right off—she could never explain. Because the truth was simple, not a long-drawn-out record of flowered shifts, tree cages, selfishness, ankle ropes and wells." We are asked to believe as readers the same thing that the people around Sethe are required to accept: that things were that simple, and that in the traditional sense there is no more reason behind Sethe's actions. More importantly, there need not be any more reason behind them than this. Sethe knows that there is nothing more to be said, and that people either get it or they do not. And the people of her community do *not* get it.

Sethe is even more straightforward about the situation in the conversation with Paul D that follows. He tells her that her "'love is too thick,'" as though she has smothered her children, the one in death, the other in life, and she responds simply that "'Love is or it ain't. Thin love ain't love at all'" (164). Paul D doesn't comprehend what she says, though, so responds "'Yeah. It didn't work, did it? Did it work?" (164), fully expecting a confession of sins from her, but to his astonishment she replies "'It worked'" (164). He cannot understand how Sethe could begin to imagine that her acts worked with all the devastation in her life that they have wrought, but again her answer is simple: "'They ain't at Sweet Home. Schoolteacher ain't got em'" (165). For Sethe, this alone means that it worked, not that it was right to do so necessarily, but that it worked.

Paul D occupies the conventional ethical space in this dialogue, so he comes up with the most compelling argument against Sethe's position: "'Maybe there's worse'" (165). He acknowledges the horror of having to return one's children to slavery, particularly after one has had a few weeks of relative freedom to contemplate what that means, but by any ordinary standard slavery is preferable to death, and the mother who lets her children return to its confines is unquestionably morally superior to the mother who tries to kill her children to keep them "safe." But once again, Sethe explains: "'It ain't my job to know what's worse. It's my job to know what is and to keep them away from what I know is terrible. I did that'" (165). A different kind of ethic is being proposed here, one that is not based on the moral absolutes of tradition but one that weighs the particular context and seeks to determine what is appropriate for that specific situation. For better or worse, within that contextually defined space, Sethe determined that it was better for her children to be safe and dead than alive and enslaved. She may have arrogated to herself the power of God to dispense life and to take it away, but she doesn't see it that way, and she certainly doesn't see her act as a selfish one, as her thoughts on the matter reveal. She wasn't trying to do what was best for herself but rather for her children. From her perspective, we might disagree with her actions, but we cannot gainsay her ethic; therefore, there is nothing more to be said.

Nevertheless, Paul D takes up the role of conventional morality once more and makes the only argument that follows: "'What you did was wrong, Sethe." And he insists that there had to be "'Some other way'" besides killing her own children (165). Sethe knows of no other way, though, and doesn't feel that she has done wrong. Quite clearly she doesn't believe that she has violated any absolute standard. She has simply done what the situation has demanded of her, difficult though it was for her to accomplish, horrifying though it was in its consequences. If she has failed to humble herself in the eyes of the community, if she has refused abjectly to ask for their forgiveness and support, then, as Ella and Paul D would think, she must be a proud woman who feels no need to explain her actions or apologize for them. She has taken on the role of a God who can do what He wants to do without having to justify His ways to man. And this is a great wrong in the eyes of the community, understandably so. More than understandably so, for one cannot have mothers killing off their babies, in whatever context, to keep them away from slavery or anything else. The goal of a community is to provide order and to promote life, and it cannot be expected to tolerate Sethe's acts. To do so would cause it to violate its most fundamental provision: Thou shalt not kill, whether it be the father or the child one is killing.

Within the normative ethic, Sethe's act was evil, bestial even, as Paul D suggests when he nastily reminds Sethe that she has two feet rather than four, a statement that doubtless bears resemblance to many of the things she has heard since she committed her act. But at least Paul D is honest enough to recognize his own excess, to realize that he has gone too far for reasons that have more to do with him than with Sethe: "Later he would wonder what made him say it. The calves of his youth? or the conviction that he was being observed through the ceiling? How fast he had moved from his shame to hers. From his cold-house secret straight to her too-thick love" (165). Paul D has shamed himself with Beloved even as he has tried to make a place for himself with Sethe, yet he hasn't told Sethe about this nor explained to himself how such a thing could happen. He might argue that his sin was a common one and hardly in the same category as killing one's children, but instinctively he realizes that his own dirtied scroll leaves him little room for moral arguments with this woman. Even worse, he concedes that he has projected his own sense of shame, of having been bestial, onto Sethe and refused to see her position at all. From shame to shame in an endless circle: the real problem with Sethe, the real reason for her exclusion, is that she brings shame to the surface, forces others to confront their own degraded acts.

Nevertheless, one can well understand why Sethe's refusal to see her act as anything other than the proper response to a given set of circumstances would be construed as a prideful act by the community. It is unquestionably a violation of their standards, and the explanation for that violation is insufficient given the gravity of what she has done. Unlike Oedipus, after all, she didn't unintentionally kill her child; she deliberately undertook the act with a full awareness of the possibilities open to her. In this respect, her action is even more tragic than Oedipus', for his obliviousness of what he has done could be construed as a partial justification for his horrible crime, or at least a partial explanation. For Sethe there is no such exculpation: she knew what she was doing and thought that it was the appropriate thing to do. Her remarks make it quite clear that she would do it again if the same set of circumstances presented themselves to her: that is precisely what it means for her not to be apologetic about her crime. It was the only thing to do, however much it ruined her life and blighted the environment of 124.

What the community cannot recognize is that Sethe's seeming pride, her unwillingness to refuse the responsibility of her act, does not mean that she sleeps at night without concern for what she has done, even if that fact should be obvious to all. Ghosts inhabit 124 and make a ruckus that everyone knows about. If people stay away from the house because Sethe refuses to do any penance for her sin, they also stay away because they want nothing to do with those ghosts. But what are the ghosts other than Sethe's shame for what she has done? Her situation is tragic precisely because on the one hand she will not and cannot revoke what she has done and would do it over again, and on the other she is endlessly bedeviled by the ghosts of her act that haunt her throughout life. All this is made most obvious when Beloved comes fully back to life, for Sethe willingly lets Beloved devour her. Her guilt is overwhelming, and she is quite willing to give her dead daughter her life if that is what is required. She would no more deny that right to Beloved than she would ever be purged of the shameful after-effects of what she has done. She is as shamed by her act as any human would be. The only difference is that she will not retract the act to save her soul. She will not deny who she is or the appropriateness of the act she as a person undertook at a certain point to preserve life by killing it. No one has paid more than Sethe for her crime, and anyone who hears the ghosts knocking around in 124 should know that to be true. To her credit, Sethe has not buried her ghosts but has allowed them to hover about her. She has chosen not to repress her deed—as an ordinary person would do—but rather to live with it and all of the shame that involves.

Sethe's choice is both clear and not really a choice at all. The normal course would be to pay for her sins, to make peace with the community and herself by an act of contrition, by a request for forgiveness and support. Through such an act she would be able to bury the "errors" of the past and keep them from infecting the present. This is the ordinary way of dealing with the "sins" of life and their shameful residues within us. Barring that, she can take her act for what it was, assess it and decide that it was the right thing to do at the time, and then willingly live with the ghosts of her shame that others would have banished by their act of abjection. The divide between these two possibilities is so large that it is easy to see why Sethe could never begin to explain her motivations: because in the one case the act has everything to do with motivations and in the other it has nothing to do with them. Conventional morality says that one does this or that bad thing for this or that reason, and one determines in the end that the motivation was bad and the act was bad and one does some kind of penance. Sethe, however, lives by a different ethic, one that measures situations in terms of knowing what is enough, and for her there was no moral good or bad here, no hard choices between lesser evils and greater goods; there was a situation that demanded from her what she gave it; the murder of her child. That was neither good nor bad in conventional terms but simply what the context imposed upon her. She took it upon herself to do what was appropriate for her in the place where she found herself, and then she willingly agreed to live with the consequences of her act regardless of the cost.

From Sethe's perspective, in other words, conventional morality always only enters into such situations *after* the event, after whatever is to take place has occurred. One doesn't evaluate such things in terms of choices and lessers and greaters; one acts on the basis of one's assessment of a situation, and the consequences of that action are gauged in terms of good and bad, lesser evil and greater good once everyone sees the outcome. To borrow from Confucius again, the sincere will acts on the basis of its knowledge of what is, and that in itself is good. That the action itself violates the fundamental mores of one's community and demands recompense is another issue altogether, though Sethe is willing to pay the community's price as well. She accepts the burden of its resentment as simply another ghost that inhabits the house.

Although Sethe requires grace, at the same time she ultimately needs the intervention of Denver and the community if she is going to be kept from being swallowed by Beloved. Forced off into the awful corner of her own autonomy as a result of her act, she suffers her isolation willingly and lives with her shame as best she can. But in the end she would be totally consumed by it without an act of grace, of generosity of spirit, of the heart that seemingly died the day Baby Suggs gave up on her own vision. One can attribute the act of grace in this case to Denver's concern for her mother, or one can look to Ella and the community for the moment that allows the errors of the past to be forgotten, but in either case the motives are not as simple and pure as one might imagine. This is most obvious in the case of Ella and the community, for they clearly had abandoned Sethe because in their eyes she was too prideful to admit her sins when their real reasons for casting 124 adrift had as much to do with their own shame as they did with Sethe's. Just as Paul D quickly projects his own shame on to Sethe's awful act, so too does the community. The only difference is that Paul D recognizes what he has done and seeks to redress the wrong. The community never does so and doesn't come to Sethe's aid until her daughter Denver makes the proper gestures of abjection. Having submitted herself to the community's will in place of her mother, Denver allows the community in all its self-righteousness to help Sethe, even if they are coming to their own assistance as much as they are to Sethe's.

The community's shame has remained well hidden throughout the years even as it remains well concealed in the novel. It pops out only a little bit every now and then, as in Paul D's attempt to cover up his own bestial nature by accusing Sethe of being inhuman. It comes up more prominently in Ella's pride, the cover that hides her own shame: she is driven to think of Sethe as proud, as one who seeks to conceal her shame through arrogance in order to hide from the pride that conceals her own sullied past. And unlike Sethe, Ella never confronts her pride or accepts her shame. We see this most clearly near the end of the novel when we are told her reasons for intervening:

> It was Ella more than anyone who convinced the others that rescue was in order. She was a practical woman who believed there was a root either to chew or avoid for every ailment. Cogitation, as she called it, clouded things and prevented action. Nobody loved her and she wouldn't have liked it if they had, for she considered love a serious disability. Her puberty was spent in a house where she was shared by father and son, whom she called "the lowest yet." It was "the lowest yet" who gave her a disgust for sex and against whom she measured all atrocities. A killing, a kidnap, a rape—whatever, she listened and nodded. Nothing compared to "the lowest yet." She understood Sethe's rage in the shed twenty years ago, but not her reaction to it, which Ella thought was prideful, misdirected, and Sethe herself too complicated. When she got out of jail and made no gesture toward anybody, and lived as though she were alone, Ella junked her and wouldn't give her the time of day. (256)

Ella is a simple woman who thinks that all problems have straightforward answers, that "there was a root either to chew or avoid for every ailment." Reflection on the nature of things was not desirable in her view, and her own sense of appropriateness is strong and definitive, so much so that she is willing to be unloved by others who don't appreciate her attitude toward what they do. Like many pious people, Ella demands that everyone live up to her standard even as her sense of propriety derives from the sexual abuse she suffered at the hands of a father and son when she was young. "The lowest yet," the great indignity she suffers, becomes the mark of evil for her, and she measures every other human activity in terms of this "lowest yet" that marks her own sense of what is too much.

Inasmuch as Ella is a woman who is incapable of love and who finds it "a serious disability," and inasmuch as she has suffered mightily herself, it stands to reason that she would be sympathetic to Sethe's situation after she leaves prison. And she is to a certain extent, for she understands "Sethe's rage in the shed" but "not her reaction to it." The act itself is not something with which Ella has a problem. It is rather that Sethe seems to be "prideful, misdirected, and . . . too complicated." This woman who could just listen and nod to accounts about killings, kidnappings and rapes could not find a place for Sethe in her scheme of things because "When she got out of jail" she "made no gesture toward anybody, and lived as though she were alone." For this Ella cannot forgive her, and so she "junks" her. She doesn't ask why Sethe keeps to herself, doesn't question her about her situation; she doesn't consider what Sethe might be feeling as a member of a community from which she has been separated through her act. In Ella's mind, abjection is required of Sethe, a plea for assistance from the good community in a time of isolation and trouble, help that Ella herself would have unquestionably given and urged others to provide as well.

We are thus prompted to ask why Ella would insist that Sethe should make a gesture toward somebody? Does she want to know whether Sethe suspects that the community had an indirect role in the slaying? Does she want to figure out whether in such a situation Sethe herself refuses to have anything to do with those whose lack of action led to her shameful act? Does she take Sethe's silence as a rebuke of the community that condemns them for what they have done? Or is it simply that Ella will not countenance a prideful person? Certainly humans do have problems with those who are proud, but we have already seen that people tend to define pride in terms of the envy they feel toward another: Baby Suggs got her comeuppance because the community thought she was too proud, but in fact she was done in by the people's resentment of her, which they translated into pride so that it could be something they could blame her for. Is the same thing going on here with Sethe?

Ella may have difficulties with proud people, and she may be distressed by the fact that Sethe didn't lay herself at the feet of the community when she came out of jail, but she seems more interested finally in having someone pay for something than she is in performing any acts of charity. This fact becomes most clear when Denver comes looking for assistance, for then Ella can begin to think approving thoughts about the people at 124 once again. We are told that, unlike Sethe, "The daughter . . . appeared to have some sense after all. At least she had stepped out the door, asked for the help she needed and wanted work. When Ella heard 124 was occupied by something-or-other beating up on Sethe, it infuriated her and gave her another opportunity to measure what could very well be the devil himself against 'the lowest yet'" (256). What Ella thinks of as sense is little more than the required gesture of humility for which she has been waiting two decades. Like God, she is more than willing to take up "another opportunity to measure what could very well be the devil himself against 'the lowest yet,'" but only in circumstances that she finds appropriate. She will give charity, but only when the proper fealty has been proffered, and she construes Denver's act as sufficient to allow her to intervene in the life of 124. It may not be surprising that Ella is so proud that she will give only when the proper gestures of abjection are forthcoming, but it is striking that she waits quietly for twenty years for the opportunity to "help out" at 124. It is also striking that she appears less interested in giving assistance than in measuring the devil in the house against her own worst moments in life. It seems to be a test of her sense of evil more than a good deed designed to help out someone in need. Sethe the human, the person with a problem, isn't even mentioned here, an act of inhumanity that is far more a reflection of pride than anything Sethe ever did.

Whatever specific complaints Ella might have about Sethe's behavior, then, are clearly subordinate matters. They cover up the real problem, which is Ella's shame over what she has done, or rather failed to do. After the horrible scene at 124, the house itself becomes occupied by ghosts, and the rest of the town seems to get on with its life, but when we see the people returning to the house twenty years later to purge the place of the fleshly presence of Beloved, we also discover that the town too more or less died when Sethe killed her child and Baby Suggs turned away from them all:

> When they caught up with each other, all thirty, and arrived at 124, the first thing they saw was not Denver sitting on the steps, but themselves. Younger, stronger, even as little girls lying in the grass asleep. Catfish was popping grease in the pan and they saw themselves scoop German potato salad onto the plate. Cobbler oozing purple syrup colored their teeth. They sat on the porch, ran down to the creek, teased the men, hoisted children on their hips or, if they were the children, straddled the ankles of old men who held their little hands while giving them a horsey ride. Baby Suggs laughed and skipped among them, urging more. Mothers, dead now, moved their shoulders to mouth harps. The fence they had leaned on and climbed over was gone. The stump of the butternut had split like a fan. But there they were, young and happy, playing in Baby Suggs' yard, not feeling the envy that surfaced the next day. (258)

They had left their own lives behind on the day of the crime, or rather, they left them behind the day before during the great feast. At that time, they had not yet felt "the envy that surfaced the next day," but once they did, their lives were changed forever, and the ghosts of 124 were as much a part of their existence as they were of Sethe and Denver's. The quiet little word *envy* here makes the loss and the reason for it clear. It is the silent admission of guilt, the private acknowledgment of complicity in the event that has prevented Ella and the others from having anything to do with Sethe and her child Denver.

Ella demands abjection from someone in 124 because somebody must pay for the crime, but the question is, whose crime must the person pay for? It is not the murder itself that is in question but rather the community's unacknowledged guilt that must be atoned for, and until that debt is recompensed, until someone finds a way to relieve the community of that burden, Sethe and Denver will have to pay for it by being ostracized. As if by magic, then, as though it were all prechoreographed, the scenario comes together: Denver makes a move that can be construed as abjection, as a plea for forgiveness for that which the community has no business dispensing forgiveness for in any case, and the town can turn its self-righteous furies away from Sethe and toward the ghost. This allows them to reclaim their own lives even as they can feel that their redemptive gesture heals Sethe's wounds and those of the community at large. And given the fact that they have to prevent Sethe from another act of carnage when she mistakes the present for the past and is ready to go after the Schoolteacher once again, they can feel even better about themselves. The twenty years disappear into a hole that is seamlessly covered over, and they can once again be themselves.

But there is one remaining element in the mixture that allows the community to shun Sethe for twenty years: if they feel shame over the envy that prompted their act of omission, they also feel bereft because Baby Suggs has turned on them too. Right in the center of the description of their return to 124 we find that "Baby Suggs laughed and skipped among them, urging more." But when Baby Suggs declared her idea of grace to be a lie, she also abandoned those whom she had been "urging more" on all those years. Her great heart had kept them alive, and when she fell into despair, she left the community without a person to urge them on to more life. They were as bereft as Sethe was to become, and they must have felt Baby Suggs' act as a rebuke of their own behavior, their own lack of heart, for it was surely that which prompted them to do nothing when powerful actions were required.

In returning to 124 and helping Sethe get rid of Beloved's ghost, the community also manages to move away from its lack of heart in the crucial moment of the town's life. The people can cover up that lack by the generosity of their late embrace of 124 and do what they can to forget the shame of the smallness of their hearts. For even if Baby Suggs never blamed them for what happened, and even if she lost heart because of the horrors of the white people rather than the smallness of heart of those around her, still Ella and the rest had to know that they broke Baby Suggs' heart, were more than just a contributing factor in the demise of their leader. They killed her off because they wanted to, because they envied her and her lot, and they would not be satisfied until she broke. They may not have planned on Sethe killing her child, but they must have assumed that Sethe and her children would be returned to slavery because they failed to act, and that was a choice designed to bring Baby Suggs low. When it succeeded beyond their expectations, they could do nothing with their smallness but bury it as deeply as possible and project it onto Sethe and her crime and her pride. Here too is a measure of what is enough; here too is a gauge, a pattern that measures out what is and is not appropriate. Here too we find an invisible scheme of reciprocity that works quietly by determining how the effects of one act shall be recompensed by another, and how that one in turn shall be dealt with, and so on down the line. Good is knowing what is enough, and even in the worst elements of human society, that good is in play, is quietly to be found in the assessments others make of what to do in response to this or that act of another.

❦

If good is knowing what is enough, we are forced to ponder the implications of *Beloved* a bit more, for the goods are so mixed together in the novel—as they are in life—that it is hard finally to mete out guilt and innocence as we have been taught to do. One of the primary reasons for bringing the three goods back together where they belong is to address the fact that in the beginning the good has nothing to do with right and wrong. It is nothing more than a measure of how appropriate an action is in the context in which it takes place. If it is a proper gauge of the flows of the field, it is good. It is not right or wrong, but good. In effect, this is the ethos that Sethe takes upon herself. She doesn't ask whether it is wrong to take a life, whether it is even worse for a mother to take the life of her child; she assesses what a fitting response would be to the Schoolteacher's efforts to reclaim her and her children as his property, and she determines that because a mother's priority is to keep her children safe, the only way she can properly do that is to kill them. At least they won't be dehumanized by the slave owner and stripped of their dignity. Sethe makes this judgment "beyond good and evil," as Nietzsche would have it, and remains convinced throughout her life that her response was an appropriate one.

But Sethe also lives by the moral codes of her community, and those strictures say that murder is wrong, that murder of one's child is even worse, and she cannot escape from the force of those imperatives any more than she could deny the appropriateness of her act in the first place. Like Antigone, she is faced with two kinds of good that seem to be incompatible, but in Sethe's case the distinction is not between a personal, private sense of the good and a public, communal sense, as the matter is often phrased in Antigone's case. Rather, Sethe must deal with a good that has nothing to do with right and wrong and another good that has everything to do with right and wrong. If she refused the imperatives of the one, she would lose her integrity and her "aesthetic" sense of what was fitting and proper; if she refused the demands of the other, she would truly be what Ella and the others want to make her out to be: someone who thinks she is above the codes of the community, someone whose pride has blinded her to the good upon which society depends. But Sethe takes up both goods, and she even embraces the good of resentment as well, for she never complains about her treatment by Beloved or the community. She finds their actions to be as appropriate for them as hers are for her. It is that godlike vision of these mutually exclusive senses of the appropriate which gives the novel its tragic dimensions, for there is no way to reconcile these goods and make them work together as they unfold in the book.

And if Sethe's position is hopelessly ambiguous, what are we to do with Baby Suggs, that great minister of the spirit and flesh who brings life to the community and who suffers the requisite sacrifice of herself as a result? Given the parallels to Christ that rub up against Baby Suggs throughout the novel, we are not likely to assume that she will lose heart. On the contrary, we would expect her great heart to bear up under even the most horrendous pain, as the decimation of her family surely was to her. Is her lack of faith in human grace a comment on her heresy? An argument for the necessity of Christian faith? Is her break with humanity testament to the abominable cruelties of the white man, an object lesson of the degree to which the human spirit was pushed to the edge and beyond by the most inhuman condition of slavery? Was it necessary for Baby Suggs to break so that we could see that she was not Jesus but rather a human whose strength extended only so far? All of these possibilities could be posited as explanations for the outcome of Baby Suggs' life, but all of them are the imperatives of the good that distinguishes between right and wrong and not the aesthetic good which assesses actions in terms of their appropriateness. As with Sethe, we are caught between mutually exclusive codes and cannot resolve their ambiguities. We want to place a *meaning* on Baby Suggs' renunciation of grace, yet to do so would be to diminish Baby Suggs. We are forced to say at least in part that her act of denial has no meaning, is simply the kind of decision to which she was driven by the circumstances of her life. It doesn't negate the quality of her great heart, nor does it suggest that heresy will always be paid back with a vicious blow from God. It doesn't justify the acts of the community—far from it, given their complicity in her loss of heart—but it also doesn't lead to the conclusion that the community could have or should have acted differently.

If the ghosts of the past could be put to rest, we might be in a position to judge the community's actions in a light that would condemn them for Baby Suggs' loss of heart, but since the virtue of the book is to be found in the very tangibility of its ghost, we can hardly assume that this is possible. So we cannot pass judgment on these acts or the characters through which they come about. We cannot praise Sethe for her courage and integrity without recognizing the perniciousness of her deed; we cannot celebrate Baby Suggs' great faith in the grace of the heart without conceding that this grace did not carry far enough in her case; and we cannot condemn the community for what it has done to Sethe and Baby Suggs because their actions too had the kind of inevitability to them that made them appropriate in their own way. We are stuck on the tragic ground of goods that don't always resolve themselves, of moral goods that at the same time don't parse in terms of right and wrong; of aesthetic goods that have little to do with beauty as we think of it but everything to do with the relational patterns that generate both the beauty and the horror of the world; and with the resentment that is the most pernicious force in the human world, the ghost that haunts every human action regardless of our awareness of its presence, and yet also the force that prompts us to contain energies that would otherwise overrun and destroy any human community.

Good is knowing what is enough, and wisdom is to be found in approaching that happy mean, that middle path, that straight and narrow road which allows us to see things as they are and to act in ways that are perfectly appropriate to what is, but human wisdom never extends far enough because of the ghosts of the past: Baby Suggs can approach a knowledge of what is enough, but like everyone else, she can do so only by learning what is too much as well. If she had known beforehand that it was possible to urge too much good upon a person, that each of us can only bear the quotient that our place in the scheme of things allows for us, she would have been able to calibrate her ministrations in ways that would have prevented the events that lead to her own demise. If she had been sufficiently wise, she would have known that the community's refusal to pray for her was a mark of its resentment of her, and that therefore her sense of what was good and sufficient had to extend to embrace that knowledge as well. But she could only know this by going beyond the border of what was enough, by pushing the people to resent her so much that they turned on her rather than face their own lack.

If Baby Suggs' wisdom about these matters doesn't extend far enough for her to embrace all the possibilities that will emanate from her great heart, how are we to imagine a world that is devoid of the consequences her own good acts lead to? The answer is that we cannot, for we too can only learn what is enough by extending ourselves occasionally beyond it, by placing ourselves so thoroughly in the midst of the three goods that we see how difficult it is for us always to get them to work together. This in turn means that knowing what is enough requires understanding how far the good of that which is fitting extends in a given context, how appropriate the good of right and wrong is in the same situation, and how much one should attend to the demands of *ressentiment* that determine a community's general sense of the way to deal with the exception that threatens the carefully circumscribed order of the norm. The great literature of the world always places us in the midst of these imperatives and forces us to deal with them in ways that make us more human by prompting us to overcome our desire to reduce the world to one of its goods, an act which always provides momentary comforts but which also invariably lessens our love of life and takes away from the greatness of heart upon which the future of the species always depends.

3

Man Wants to Live

If the distinguishing features of Baby Suggs in *Beloved* are her greatness of heart and her attempt to make others feel the grace of the world of which they are a part, her heart also links her to a long line of people whose desire for life was their most striking feature. Most of the memorable individuals in history and literature have possessed a similar kind of desire, from Gilgamesh to Odysseus to Stephen Daedalus. But greatness of heart seems to become more problematic as human history casts a longer and longer shadow. As *Beloved* demonstrates, the ghosts of the past can snuff out the life of those in the present, and there are many before Toni Morrison who have demonstrated this fact, perhaps William Faulkner most notably. These ghosts are the residues of past lives that haven't yet worked out the guilt and shame that were an inevitable part of those lives, presences whose food is the envy through which we gauge those whose ardor for life is most intense, but they are as much present in people with greatness of heart as they are in those who want to usurp the place of the individuals who most fiercely desire life. As with the three goods, the problem of a great desire for life is that it is not a pure good, at least not for us. It might have been sufficient for Odysseus that *he* desired life and deserved it, regardless of the costs of that desire in other people's lives, but we can no longer live with that ethic and have long abandoned it.

Nevertheless, the simple premise of existence always remains before us: one lives always only at the expense of other life, whether it be human, animal, or plant. We occupy our place on the planet to the extent that we deprive other locations of theirs. This is neither good nor bad. It is simply the case, and it is not so much beyond good and evil as before it. It is the insoluble dilemma at the center of human life that requires us to develop a sense of good and evil to begin with, for the sacrificial nature of human cultures makes it clear that we have always had trouble reconciling our desire for life with our need to kill other things in order to stay alive. For us this is no simple trade-off, even less a mere fact of life. It is a troubling notion etched deeply into our sense of who we are and what we should be doing with ourselves while we are here. It is good to want to be alive, and it is a good to want to improve the quality of life for oneself and for others. That is what greatness of heart is all about.

Regardless of how much one improves the quality of life for oneself and others, though, some others will lose their lives, a fact that can be ritualized and asserted in different ways, but also a sign of something deeply unsettling within us that we don't know how to articulate. If we weren't troubled by the need to consume other living tissue, we would have less use for the good of right and wrong. The good of that which is appropriate would be enough, and that could be gauged purely in terms of how a given act enhances our lives or takes away something from them. In one respect, this dilemma is reflected in our current concern for the environment and the demands to "Save the Earth." As one commentator pointed out with no little superciliousness, what we are really saying is that we want to save ourselves. The world existed before us and will exist after us, so it surely doesn't need our husbandry to survive. If we minister to it, that is because we want to preserve the kind of life we have on the planet, and in order to do that we must make sure that the forces that sustain us don't get overwhelmed by our extensions of their processes. True enough, in its own way, it is worth remembering that the earth doesn't really need us. There is a kind of arrogance there that is troubling even if the intention is good.

But there is also something a bit awry in the notion that we would save the earth only because we want to save ourselves. It is true that the planet existed before us and probably will long after we are gone, but that doesn't mean that we can't have an interest in preserving the rich mixture of species that exist on the planet right now. It is difficult to make this argument in purely moral terms because we do need to take other lives to survive, and there seems to be no easy way to do this. It could be said to be *right* to want to preserve the diversity of species in spite of our need for other lives, and we could assert that it is morally right to know what is enough: it is one thing to consume species in order to preserve one's own life, yet another to consume them frivolously, wantonly, without concern for whether or not our acts of consumption are excessive. But how would one gauge the frivolous consumption of species: is it morally wrong to cut down a tree to build a house? Is is wrong to kill trees with the gases we fill the air with in order to keep ourselves warm in those houses? Or are those things fitting enough? If they are, are we then justified in killing off species with those same gases as a result of the cars we drive to get from one place to another? Is that also fitting in its own way? How much is too much? Where does one draw the line? Obviously the line would be traced in many different ways as a result of radically different strategies of life on the planet, so it would finally be impossible to justify anything much beyond subsistence level existence in this way. It is certainly morally wrong to consume species to excess, but such a way of calibrating our actions will not be very helpful to us in the long run.

The good of right and wrong in this case must at least partially give way to the good of what is enough, to the aesthetic good. We should not say that we want to save the planet any more than we should assert that we want to save ourselves. Rather, we want to imagine a world in which every consideration is not focused through the narrow self-interest of our own species. It is both fitting and morally good that this should be so, for it would be the utmost of human arrogance to assume that our only imperative is how to preserve our own lives. One cannot really say that diversity is good for its own sake and mean very much by that, although we can assert that the diversity of species does contribute in many ways to our own preservation, but again, both statements miss the point. Our sense of what is fitting suggests that the world is a more aesthetically pleasing environment in which to live when much of its activity has nothing at all to do with human concerns. Given that imperative, we must work to make a world in which we continue to be only a peripheral concern. This entails actions that encourage the diversity of species, but it also requires an ongoing sense of what is necessary and appropriate for the billions of people on the planet.

Greatness of heart is a necessary factor in the best of lives, but in itself it remains insufficient once the history of the species grows to the point where it has. We can best get a sense of the context through which greatness of heart must be understood if we consider for a moment an earlier era when the desire for life was sufficient unto itself. An example can be found in the biblical Jacob, or at least in Harold Bloom's idea of Jacob, a man about whom Bloom has the following to say:

> Jacob's career vies with that of any other figure in Western narrative tradition, if our criteria are essentially aesthetic rather than moral or theological. He battles Esau in the womb over which of them is to have priority of birth, and though bested by his fierce twin, he still emerges combatively, holding on to his brother's heel. We can say that his drive defines the Blessing once and for all: it is for more life. In the name of more life, for himself and his

> progeny, Jacob dares everything, and is rarely far from danger, loss, and the constant work of mourning, induced by the loss of his beloved Rachel and the long apparent loss of his favorite son, Joseph. He also must know humiliation, since his progress and survival are marked by fraud and tricksterism, by heel-clutching. Yet he holds us fast even when we cannot approve of him. Partly it is his energy of being, partly his heroic persistence, but mostly it is because J persuades us that Jacob, Israel, has the Blessing.[1]

"Jacob dares everything" for more life, and thus the Blessing of our religious tradition comes to be defined in that way. From his struggle to get out of the womb first to his usurpation of Esau's birthright, Jacob strives to be most among the living, not first so much as most, or most fully. That goal costs him a great deal, and he manages to survive and thrive as a result of tricks and deceit, but in his eyes, we are made to think, more life is worth any price one must pay for it.

Jacob thus becomes the figure of our own desire, yet at the same time he occupies a space within the Bible and in the *Book of J* that allows him to connive without condemnation. Although he violates the moral codes of his time and his parent, he gets away with it, and even though he treats his brother roughly, he is allowed the good fortune of having a sibling who will absolve him. How many older sons would so willingly forgive after having their birthright stolen away by cunning? The desire for life is seen in Jacob as something that allows one more latitude than one might otherwise have: his special drive, his genius for making life go his way, his ability to enhance his life in spite of serious obstacles, seems to justify his behavior: not only does he get away with it, but he thrives and is seen as a person worthy of emulation. There is indeed mourning through which he must go; he agonizes at times over what he has done and what it will cost him, and this helps to round out our sense of him, giving him more reason to be heroically driven than we might otherwise assume. But part of the charm of Jacob's story, as Bloom's distinction between an aesthetic reading of his journey through life and a moral or theological one suggests, is that even in the Bible his behavior is construed more through an aesthetic good than through the grid of right and wrong. At the beginning of Israel, before the normative tradition overtook everything, the desire for life for oneself and one's progeny was a good in itself; these were events that occurred before the moral codes took effect, so a greater latitude of activity was allowed. This is understandable enough given the imperatives of what became the Jewish people, and given the greater difficulties of seeing one's own clan thrive in those days. In our own world, however, Jacob's combative pursuit of life for himself can no longer be seen in quite the same way.

But there is something more in Jacob than the grasping mentality we see so much of today, and we need to discern it, for his desire for the Blessing of life can too easily be assumed into our acquisitive traditions: Jacob as an early Donald Trump trying to build an empire to satisfy his egocentric wish for fame. We see no evidence in Jacob of this kind of crass conniving, even if he does steal Esau's birthright. In a way that ought to offend us, he comes off finally as more worthy and deserving of it, even if he had to take what was not his. And his measure truly is *life*, not goods or fame or a vision of himself in the eyes of others. That much is obvious because he is not troubled by doing those things he feels are necessary. More than that, Jacob manifests a desire both for life and for life at its most challenging. He wants to be tested, he wants to be pushed to the limit of what is humanly possible, not so he can claim to be the world's strongest human or the bravest but rather because the imperatives of life within him demand that he seek the boundaries of existence. In this respect, we need to see Jacob's encounter with the angel in a fresh light, for as Bloom reminds us:

> "Wrestling Jacob" is a powerful image, particularly in Protestantism, where the agon is essentially seen as a loving struggle between Jacob and God. But the nameless

> being who cannot overcome Jacob cannot be Yahweh, at least not Yaweh in all his power and will, and there is absolutely nothing loving about this sublime night encounter, which exalts Jacob to Israel yet leaves him permanently crippled, and which is fought between a mortal and a supernatural being who fears the break of day, almost as a vampire or a ghoul would. (216-17)

Jacob's struggle with the angel is not a loving encounter with God that tests his spiritual strength but rather a fierce battle with "a supernatural being who fears the break of day, almost as a vampire or a ghoul would." This contest between angel and mortal is the kind of test Odysseus was used to facing, though he was never crippled by his struggles with the elements that tested human capabilities. And if "all of Jacob's career has been a continual battle to attain the Blessing, from the contest in the womb to determine whether Esau or Jacob would be the firstborn to this crucial encounter at the ford of the Jabbok . . ." (217), we can see both his epic strength and also his desire for such tests. He remains worthy of the Blessing only because he has the need to be pushed to the limit in this way.

Jacob, then, is no more looking to prove something through his struggles than he is seeking to demonstrate something to himself. He is devoid of envy as far as we can tell and has no desire to be seen through the other's eyes. In this respect his desire is *unmediated*; he doesn't want what Esau has because Esau has it: he wants the Blessing because he is driven to push life to the limit, and the push comes from within rather than from a social contest that would determine his quality of character through the equivalent of a strong-man's contest of wills or brute strength. And unlike Esau or those whose desire is filtered through the mediations of others, Jacob is willing for the ultimate test, the one with the angel, the encounter in which everything is at stake, both figuratively and literally, for Jacob continues to want to life and also fears for his existence on the morrow when he must confront his brother Esau, a man who has every reason to want to take

Jacob's life from him. With slight hyperbole, Bloom puts the matter this way: "To win the new name of Israel is to win also a very different Blessing from the one stolen away from Esau, for this new Blessing, as I read it, is extracted from the angel of death, or if from Yahweh, then from that dark side of Yahweh that later nearly murders Moses before Zipporah heroically intervenes" (217). This angel of death is the equivalent of a journey into the underworld for Jacob, the final encounter with the forces of anti-life that is required of one who will carry the Blessing on with him into future generations. He must be tested not only by his abilities in the physical and secular worlds but also by his capacity to contend with the "dark side of Yahweh that later nearly murders Moses before Zipporah heroically intervenes." A struggle to the death with death that leaves Jacob lame, that leaves the mark of death on him, proves to be that which is necessary to assess the character of the one who will pass on the Blessing of life to future generations.

The difference between the one who receives the Blessing, Jacob, and the one who gives up her grace, Baby Suggs, can be seen in the forces with which they must contend. One might think that Jacob's battle is the more difficult because he struggles with the angel of death whereas nothing that dramatic takes place in Baby Suggs' life until after she gives up. Beloved can be seen as an angel of death in the house of 124, but by the time her spirit arrives to take things over, Baby Suggs no longer cares. Baby Suggs' angel of death is not so easily located, for although she might see it exclusively in the whites who come to take Sethe and her babies away, the reader knows that the envy of those in the community toward her because she has "too much" life and too much of the good is as much a part of what her struggle is finally all about. Jacob is miraculously spared this struggle because he has an even-tempered brother who is willing to forgive and forget: Esau is not driven by resentment, nor does he connive to get his birthright back, even though it is the most powerful of Blessings. He amazingly accepts his lot without anger and allows Jacob to be assumed back into his good graces. So Jacob faces the angel of death in an unmediated struggle for life, but he escapes from the struggle with Esau that would have been over the lesser blessing, the one Esau lost that had more to do with privilege and property and name than with life itself. Which is the more difficult struggle, Jacob's or Baby Suggs'? There is no answer to such a question, but it is nevertheless one that must be asked because Baby Suggs' quest for the Blessing echoes Jacob's, and her overabundance of life and heart exceeds Jacob's in that her natural exuberance faces the greater obstacle of slavery and does so without resort to tricks and deceits. Yet in the end her grace disappears and life at 124 is cursed rather than blessed.

Jacob's story is such a useful contrast to Baby Suggs' because they are both contending for the same Blessing, yet they are doing so under radically different circumstances. Jacob is presented to us with marvelous complexity; he is far from being a character with a simple orientation to life. As Bloom reminds us, he is as divided within himself as Yahweh is, as prone to be mutually exclusive things at the same time as the God who gives and takes life in seemingly arbitrary ways, and who is as willing to haggle with one of the humans he created as he is to destroy entire cultures or provide the gift of a rainbow. Jacob's story is no simple tale of a peasant who works hard to achieve his birthright but rather a vision of considerable psychological complexity. And yet, even though Jacob knows that his own risks make him vulnerable to the fires of resentment, even though he considers the possibility that Esau will do him in because of his theft, he is spared the complexity of social warfare—he is passed over and doesn't have to deal with someone who desires the life he has so much of and the grace that so obviously fell his way. The later tale of Baby Suggs measures our distance not only from that simplicity but also from a context in which the push for more life was sufficient unto itself. It is no longer an adequate justification for the acts, benign and otherwise, of a heroic individual like Jacob, nor is it enough to overcome the social force of resentment that prompts one ceaselessly to be calibrating the strength of those around one to determine how much grace they can bear.

❦

A useful analogue to Jacob's and Baby Suggs' stories is one that on the surface bears little resemblance to either: the comic tale of Saul Bellow's *Henderson the Rain King*. Although Henderson appears in the guise of a Christian in the story, quite clearly he is Jacob's ancestor, and his goal is the Blessing. He doesn't wrestle an angel, but he does steal a birthright, and he does wrestle a prince, Itelo, and easily bests him. More importantly, he wants life. Early in the story he is told by Queen Willatale of the Arnewi that he possesses "grun-tu-molani," which is loosely translated into English as "Man wants to live," and there could be no better expression of Henderson's quest than that statement, even if he himself doesn't wholly know what it means when he first hears it.[2] He gets the gist, yet his egocentricity keeps him from completely comprehending the nature of the Blessing. He is too quickly smitten by the notion that he has just been paid a great compliment to realize that not everything in him cries out for life, as he thinks it does.

Henderson's exuberant response to Willatale's assessment of him reveals his decidedly mixed orientation to the world:

> Yes, yes, yes! Molani. Me molani. She sees that? God will reward her, tell her, for saying it to me. I'll reward her myself. I'll annihilate and blast those frogs clear out of that cistern, sky-high, they'll wish they had never come down from the mountains to bother you. Not only I molani for myself, but for everybody. I Grun-tu-molani, old lady—old queen. Grun-tu-molani, everybody! (85)

Henderson is flattered that anyone would say such a thing about him, and he believes that Willatale is right, though he has come to Africa precisely to figure out what drives him and why he is so dissatisfied. He *does* want to live, and equally important, he wants *others* to live as well. He may be a brash, foolhardy, egocentric American, but he truly wants "molani" for everybody. He is not seeking the Blessing for himself alone but for others and wants to redeem the whole world. He too has a great heart of sorts, twisted though it be by his own past, and he looks for that which will best give shape to the Blessing of life as he finds it. Henderson also clearly articulates the situation of the gift of life in the modern world by explaining that he "could not bear how sad things have become in the world and so [he] set out because of this molani" (85). The world has become a sad place. We have already seen that in *Beloved*, where the only joy in life came on Saturday afternoons in the Clearing and where life came tumbling down when grace spread back within the community to 124 and everyday life. The people could not deal with such grace and had to put an end to it. The world has become a *sad* place, a perfect choice of words to express why Henderson had to undertake his quest. His life is not in danger, nor does he lack anything he wants. He is a wealthy man, has had wives and children and everything a human could ask for, yet he feels that the world has become sad, that somehow the gift of life is not perceived as the Blessing it is. He sees in his own habits how he fails to appreciate life, and so he must find out what went wrong. He must discover some way of bringing life back to life "because of this molani."

At the same time, we find Henderson's idea of life bound up with the power to annihilate, another expression of what has gone wrong with his existence. He is so grateful to the Queen for the compliment she has paid him that he exults in the possibility of blowing up her frogs and freeing the water in the cistern from its curse. Yet he doesn't understand in the least that there is something awry (and funny) about a man who is thrilled to be told that he wants to live even as he expresses that will through a desire for violence against others, even if they are only frogs. If "There is a curse on this land" (38), as Henderson so eloquently phrases it, he is a perfect manifestation of it: a man who wants to live but who can find a fitting expression of that will to live only in the violence that brings death to others. Man may want to live, but he no more understands the nature of the Blessing he desires than Jacob does before his encounter with Yahweh. Henderson must wrestle with his own angel, the demons of his past, before he can properly appreciate what it means to want to live and what that Blessing constitutes.

What have we done with the desire to live? Why must Baby Suggs' grace turn into something that unintentionally destroys the community? Why must Henderson express his own fierce desires through repeated acts of violence? Certainly a good part of the problem is taken on quite early by Henderson, although again, he doesn't fully understand the ramifications of his own utterance. He tells us that "Society is what beats me. Alone I can be pretty good, but let me go among people and there's the devil to pay" (49). Henderson doesn't explain precisely what he means here, but we get the message when we see his acts. He is cruel to his wife, his temper is directly responsible for the death of his neighbor, Miss Lenox, he screams and shouts and chops wood to ease the tension a bit, and above all he runs from who he is. But he claims that society is what gets him. If he can do alright by himself, we see no real evidence of this. We have to take his word for it. But we do know that once he enters society, once he comes into the domain of mediated desire, he loses the Blessing and doesn't know how to recover it. If he leaves his own community and goes to a far-off land, he does so to escape from the mediations of society that have put him on the wrong track.

At the same time, Henderson doesn't fully admit to his own part in the botched nature of his life. He is honest enough to tell us more about himself than we might care to know, and he is straightforward enough to explain that he set out to raise pigs only because someone he met in the army said he was going to go home and raise minks. Henderson chose pigs only because the person who wanted the mink ranch was Jewish, and it seemed like a proper provocation of him to take up pigs. What differentiates Henderson from many in this respect is not that his choice of pigs was mediated through Goldstein's desire for a mink farm but that he actually followed through on his act of spite. Most people would say that they were going to raise pigs and then go on and do something else. But Henderson is driven enough to follow through on his weaker moments and enact them, in part because his desire for life is so thwarted that he deliberately degrades the gift and then loathes himself and resents society for pushing him to do so. That is why society gets him every time.

Put another way, Henderson exclaims repeatedly, as though it were something special, that he has a voice inside of himself that cries out *"I want, I want"*: "But this was all it would ever tell [him]. It never said a thing except *I want, I want, I want!*" (24). There was no expression of his desire that took on any particular form, so he was stuck on the one hand with a desire for life and on the other with countless mediations of that desire as expressed in other people's lives, but no true sense of how life's urge should manifest itself within him. When he would go out into society, his "I want" would be filtered through the desires of others, frustrating him and further contributing to his sense of having sullied the great urge to live that he felt every day. The result was violence, whether he was smashing coffee cups or pounding on a counter or screaming an obscenity. Man wants to live, but he doesn't know how to, and so he reacts with violence, the blessing of life inverted into a nihilism that exults in the destruction of life.

If the Blessing of life that Jacob struggles for has somehow been transformed into a nihilistic kind of energy that exults in destruction rather than creative outlets that contribute to life on the planet, we might think that the angel of death has found no one worthy to contend with in our time. Henderson is no Jacob, and yet he wants more than anything to be able to find a fitting expression for his will to live. He may be clumsy, and he may have a life that has been defined too much by other people's desires, but he continues to look for that clear expression of value that would transform his life into something worth living, that would strip the sadness from things both for himself and for others. He wants molani for everybody, and his savior impulse is not exclusively a function of ego: he genuinely wants life to have a say in the face of all the death around him. If he would like to lift the plague of frogs that bedevils his Arnewi friends, he also wants to lift the curse on the land that prompts him to leave his own country in the first place.

We can easily establish many of the elements of Henderson's situation that thwart a useful expression of his life energies and get some sense of his difficulty simply by asserting that everything in Henderson's world is filtered through his self. Baby Suggs' didn't ask herself what was to be gained by ministering to the people. She felt the need to contribute, and her ruined body told her that the best way for her to give something was through the exuberance of her great heart. She was no more inclined to ask what was in it for her than she was the kind to measure out her gifts in small quantities. She gave everything she had because that was what she thought one was supposed to do with the energies that were available to her. But Henderson has the luxury and the curse of a self that always thinks about its own interests. He too has what he characterizes as a "service impulse" and genuinely wants to help others, but he can't escape from his desire for self-aggrandizement at the same time.

When Henderson discovers that the Arnewi have a problem with frogs in their cistern that they cannot deal with, he more than willingly takes up the challenge. He exclaims: "I realized that I would never rest until I had dealt with these creatures and lifted the plague" (61). His great heart prompts him to want to help the Arnewi simply because he thinks he can, and his strong desire to do so—expressed here in his assertion that he knew he wouldn't be able to rest until he solved their problem—shows that his first impulse is a genuine one from the heart. When Henderson explains that "it was natural for me to want to relieve them" of their burden (87), we believe him. He doesn't tell us that his *ego* would not be satisfied until he took care of the frogs but rather shows us that the problem itself prompts him to want to address it.

But Henderson cannot keep things that simple, first because his actions in the world are always perversely filtered through his violent streak and second because he can't keep his ego out of play. First the violence: "'Poor little bastards' was what I said [to the frogs], but in actual fact I was gloating—yuck-yuck-yuck! My heart was already fattening in anticipation of their death. We hate death, we fear death, but when you get right down to cases, there's nothing like it. I was sorry for the cows, yes, and on the humane side I was fine. I checked out one hundred per cent. But still I hungered to let fall the ultimate violence on these creatures in the cistern" (89). Henderson is honest enough to admit that the thought of blowing the frogs up excites him greatly, and if the first impulse he works from derives from his desire to help the Arnewi, the second one comes from the wish to play god to the frogs, to decimate them the way a deity of awesome powers would destroy that which kept his people from sustaining themselves. We may hate death, as Henderson says, but still we revel in our ability to inflict it on others. If Henderson has not found a way of dealing with this inevitable aspect of his humanity, neither have we. And if he is more violent than we are, that is only because his desire for life is fiercer than ours.

Then there is the self-interest, and again, Henderson is straightforward in his account of his motivations: "I lay grinning at the surprise those frogs had coming, and also somewhat at myself, because I was anticipating the gratitude of Willatale and Mtalba and Itelo and all the people; and I went so far as to imagine that the queen would elevate me to a position equal to her own. But I would say, 'No, no. I didn't leave home to achieve power or glory, and any little favor I do you is free'" (94). Again arrogating to himself the role of god, he sees himself as one who dispenses favors to others out of the goodness of his heart, the freely given gestures of a man who can fully afford to give things away. And he did begin with such freely given gestures. The problem is that it is not long before he is imagining the gratitude of others and construing his generosity through the smallness of his own ego. He dreams of being made an equal to Mtalba and of the dramatic gesture of refusing such an honor, and he wakes up in the morning thinking "'This is going to be one of my greatest days'" (100). Children's dreams are the stuff that contaminate Henderson's vision, and he is the first to admit it.

So Henderson's desire for life and the expression of the Blessing remain thwarted, and he doesn't understand why this repeatedly happens to him, regardless of whether he is in the United States or in Africa. He ends up blowing up the cistern and is forced to leave the Arnewi in shame: he has gained nothing in travelling all this way only to duplicate the kind of acts for which he is already very well known at home. As Henderson explains: "The confusing thing is that I always have some real basic motivation, and how I go so wrong, I can never understand" (93). If ever there were an expression of the fact that wanting to live is not enough, that a zealous quest for the Blessing of life is no longer what it once was, this is it. Henderson cries out for a fitting expression of the greatness of his own heart, desperately wants to make use of his capabilities in ways that are both beautiful and helpful, but his basic motivation, his quest for the Blessing, goes wrong, leaving him more mystified than ever about what he is doing wrong.

In our own day we might be inclined to say that Henderson suffers from problems of the self. On the one hand he fetishizes the self and filters all his experience through its arbitrary grid, and on the other he greatly desires to abandon it. He tells us: "I have a positive ability to lose myself in practical tasks" (103), and his desire to lose himself for good is as much a part of his problem as is his desire to construe everything in the universe through that same self. He oscillates between feelings of grandeur and self-loathing and doesn't know how to stop the back-and-forth of his life. His self always comes between him and the life he so ardently desires to express, and he seeks a way to get out from under the burdens that prompt him to see the world as a tourist rather than a participant. This is one way of talking about the conditions that contribute to the sad display of the gift of life in our world, and it is sufficient as long as one doesn't take the rhetoric of self too seriously. But these explanations also have a way of missing the point, chiefly because we too share Henderson's obsessions with the self, however much we live in an era in which the self has been declared dead.

❦

If Henderson needs to see the world in a new light, outside of the constraints of the self that thwart his desire to express life purely, then King Dahfu of the Wariri seems to be the guide he needs, for Dahfu both senses the greatness of spirit that Henderson possesses and also understands the way his equally profound desire for suffering moves that spirit in the wrong direction. Dahfu has his own theories to explain what goes wrong with humans when their desire is mediated in false ways through the perversions of the self. In his view, the problem is that "'Fear is a ruler of mankind. It has the biggest dominion of all. It makes you white as candles. It splits each eye in half. More of fear than of any other thing has been created. . . . As a molding force it comes second only to Nature itself'" (258-59). Although Henderson seems to be one of the last people to admit it, Dahfu's theory applies to him as well: fear rules him as much as everyone else, perhaps even more so, yet he runs from this knowledge because it would force him to face too many things he doesn't want to deal with.

Henderson claims throughout the novel that he embraces life as exuberantly as anyone possibly could, and he prides himself on his relations to the real. Time and again we hear him say things like this: "I have always argued that Lily neither knows nor likes reality. Me? I love the old bitch just the way she is and I like to think I am always prepared for even the very worst she has to show me. I am a true adorer of life, and if I can't reach as high as the face of it, I plant my kiss somewhere lower down" (150). Henderson is right in a way, for he is a man who wants life, and he does adore it in some respects, but the notion that he is "always prepared for even the very worst she has to show [him]" is ludicrous, and by the end of the novel he is forced to swallow his pride and admit that he too is driven by fear of reality: "And I thought how I had boasted to my dear Lily how I loved reality. 'I love it more than you do,' I had said. But oh, unreality! Unreality, unreality! That has been my scheme for a troubled but eternal life" (307). The virtue of unreality, after all, is that it lets one hide from one's fear.

Dahfu's assertion, however, is very carefully calibrated, for if he says that fear is a ruler of the human world, he also states that "as a molding force it comes second only to Nature itself." Because the dominion of fear is not quite as extensive as that of nature, it does not totally dominate our lives. Nature molds us to want to embrace her, to cry out that we love her as Henderson repeatedly does, but these affirmations always take place in the midst of the fear that prompts us away from the real into unreality. Henderson's egocentric attitude and his violent tendencies are manifestations of his flight from the real, are the ways in which he hides from the private parts of existence in order to convince himself that he loves things as they are much more than he actually does. He tells us in the beginning that his basic problem has to do with society and that is what he is trying to resolve. This is true enough in its way, but his problems with society are really a function of his flight from the real he purports to embrace. If wanting to live is no longer sufficient unto itself, that is because fear has become such a ruler of humans that the molding force of nature no longer has the space it requires to provide for our thwarted needs.

Fear rules the human world, according to Dahfu, and this means that it rules him as well. Yet Henderson finds no mark of fear on Dahfu and wants to emulate him precisely because he seems at home in the world. If on the one hand Henderson's ego comes between him and the world, on the other envy is at the center of much of what he does. As a measure of their difference from one another, Dahfu even goes so far as to ask Henderson whether he envies him, and Henderson explains why he does: "'Why do I envy you? You are in the bosom of your people. They need you. Look how they stick around and attend to your every need. It's obvious how much they value you'" (157). To Henderson Dahfu has the ideal master's life: he is loved and needed by his people, they attend to all of his needs, and he is warmly embraced by them and life as well—the ideal life, one in which one is truly at home in the world and therefore lacking in the fear that drives Henderson.

Dahfu points out to Henderson that his warm relations to his people and his life are temporary, that when his "faculties weaken" "'These same ladies, so inordinate of attention, will report me and then the Bunam who is chief priest here, with other priests of the association, will convey me out into the bush and there I will be strangled'" (157). He assumes that this scenario will have some effect on Henderson's envy of him, but it seems so incredible to Henderson that he cannot really assimilate it. Like the idea of his own death, it is inconceivable that anyone would kill a king the moment he got weak, and so it remains unthinkable. But it is precisely that unthinkable idea that keeps Henderson away from the reality he proclaims his desire to embrace and precisely that unthinkable that keeps him in his thwarted state. If Dahfu seems so at peace with the world, that is not because he isn't aware of his mortality and his fragile hold on power within his kingdom but rather because he is consummately aware of the thin thread that keeps him connected to everything Henderson desires. Indeed, when Henderson asks him whether or not fear is a part of his life, Dahfu exclaims: "'Oh, certainly. . . . Though nothing may be visible, still it is heard, like radio. It is on almost all the frequencies. And all tremble, and all are wincing, in greater or lesser degree'" (259). Dahfu also wants to live, but he manages to make his way in the world with a different attitude toward his fear than Henderson, and he refuses to let it dominate him the way it does his newfound friend. Nevertheless, fear is also Dahfu's daily companion.

If Henderson's fear needs to be dealt with for him to be on friendly terms with the life he so desperately wants to live, he needs a way of focusing on it, and Dahfu provides that vehicle in Atti the Lion, the creature that will reveal the strategies Henderson employs in order to escape from the necessities of his own life. In urging Henderson to establish a relationship with her, Dahfu explains the virtue of doing so:

> First, she is unavoidable. Test it, and you will find she is unavoidable. And this is what you need, as you are an avoider. Oh, you have accomplished momentous avoidances. But she will change that. She will make consciousness to shine. She will burnish you. She will force the present moment upon you. Second, lions are experiencers. But not in haste. They experience with deliberate luxury. . . . Moreover, observe Atti. Contemplate her. How does she stride, how does she saunter, how does she lie or gaze or rest or breathe? I stress the respiratory part. . . . She do not breathe shallow. This freedom of the intercostal muscles and her abdominal flexibility . . . gives vital continuity between her parts. It brings those brown jewel eyes their hotness. Then there are more subtle things, as how she leaves hints, or elicits caresses. (260)

If Henderson's fear is to be dealt with, he must first confront the fact that he has accomplished momentous avoidances in an effort to escape from it, for only by realizing how much he tries to avoid reality will he be able to appreciate the beauty around him.

This by itself, however, would not account for Dahfu's different mien, even if it is clear that he has mastered his own fear by dealing with Atti as well. In moving past the desire to avoid life and the fear it involves, Dahfu has made "consciousness to shine" within himself. If Dahfu explains that Atti "will force the present moment upon you," he demonstrates how she has done that for him by being so much in touch with his own fate and his own present moment. Like Atti, he has learned how to "experience with deliberate luxury" because there is no other way worthy of expressing the life that he has. Those who are always ready to move on to the next experience with great haste, like Henderson, aren't really so much eager to find out what the next event will be as they are in a hurry to escape from whatever fear they find themselves in the midst of at the moment. Ruled by their fear, they deliberately reduce the effects of their experiences to a shallow flow in order to escape from their linkage to the events on the planet.

For Dahfu, the point is to experience life with the deliberate luxury of the lion, even if this is more difficult for a species that has self-consciousness and thereby knows fear in a way that the lion does not. And that deliberate luxury of experience involves not only the deep and rhythmical breathing to be found in Atti but an acute sense of the rhythms of the world in general, from the respiration to the way the lion "leaves hints, or elicits caresses." Atti's existence is nothing more than a manifestation of an animal's intent understanding of its relations with that which surrounds it, and that is precisely what Dahfu has had to learn through his dealings with Atti, and what Henderson must learn as well if he is to put an end to the madness that drives his life. If he cannot do that, the fact that he wants to live will no longer suffice, for when its effects are filtered through his fear and the protective mechanisms he has in place, they are finally pernicious and destructive to him and to other forms of life as well.

Dahfu is even more precise about what he has learned from Atti, though, and he is careful to link his experience of her to beauty. He has already explained that "'What a Christian might feel in Saint Sophia's church . . . I absorb from lion. When she gives her tail a flex, it strikes against my heart'" (260). In order to deal more specifically with Henderson's fear of her, Dahfu makes his point more insistently: "'Now watch the way she walks. Beautiful? You said it! Furthermore this is uninstructed, specie-beauty. I believe when the fear has subsided you will be capable of admiring her beauty. I think that part of the beauty emotion does result from an overcoming of fear. When the fear yields, a beauty is disclosed in its place. This is also said of perfect love if I recollect, and it means that ego-emphasis is removed. Oh, Henderson, watch how she is rhythmical in behavior'" (262). The purpose of a relationship with Atti, for Henderson or Dahfu, is not specifically to learn how to overcome fear; that is a result of dealing with what Atti presents to them. Nor is Dahfu suggesting a kind of economy in which the payoff for dealing with one's fear is an awareness of beauty. Rather, beauty is that which is available to us as long as we are capable of fully contemplating the way things are. We can see Atti's uninstructed specie-beauty only as long as we do not fear for our lives in her midst, just as we can see the uninstructed beauty of reality all around us only as long as the fear that makes us white as candles doesn't dominate our lives and make us constantly want to flee. The rhythmical flow of things, the beauty that drives the novel, is that which we most desire, the Blessing of Jacob or the grace of Baby Suggs, but in order to perceive it we must first be willing to forego the "ego-emphasis" that separates us from the rhythms of life around us. Atti's rich presence forces this rhythm upon Dahfu and finally Henderson as well, and it is a rhythm that is always available to humans when they observe the world from an aesthetic perspective.

Dahfu's sense of beauty, though, is hardly an aestheticized vision of an ideal world. First, he has already conceded that even for him fear is heard on almost all of the frequencies. Beauty does not cover over the fear of the world any more than it eliminates those frequencies from one who has faced the real. Rather, the lion urges a simple imperative that places fear and beauty next to each other: "'by means of the lion try to distinguish the states that are given and the states that are made. Observe that Atti is all lion. Does not take issue with the inherent. Is one hundred per cent within the given'" (263). Dahfu's lesson is as simple as that. In a world driven by fear, the beautiful becomes an anodyne for our pain, and even then it is more an accident than anything else, for it cannot be found within the natural world without giving up the ego-emphasis that makes fear the dominant factor in our lives. The lion, of course, doesn't have a problem distinguishing the states that are given from those that are made, whereas humans do, but that is precisely the point: Atti forces Henderson to look at what is inherent in order to distinguish it from the states that he has created out of his own fear, the fictions of a self so driven by terror of the real that he has lost the ability to appreciate the value of his own experience.

It is worth emphasizing that the need for a deliberate and luxurious experience of life is precisely what Henderson lacks and what most differentiates him from those figures in our past who also were moved by a desire for the Blessing of life. Whether we think of Jacob or of someone like Odysseus, we find characters whose lives are different in tone from ours in that most fundamental way: they seem so real to us because there is a palpable sense of their reality that is conveyed along with their stories. One cannot read Odysseus's tale without having an acute awareness of how fully in the midst of life he was. This is available to us not only in the quality of sensuous detail the work depicts but also in the little side notes that are accidentally a part of the narrative. Odysseus, for example, has to be reminded by his men after a year of life with Circe that it is time for them to move on, suggesting that if Odysseus has a problem, it is not with his ability to experience things fully but rather in getting lost in the luxury of the moment. We don't see such lapses in Jacob, but we do get a strong sense of his need to wrestle with life, to extract every last bit of its tangibility through a rhythmical tussle with the given.

Henderson lacks the grace to be able to experience things in this way, and so do we. Dahfu is such a startling presence for him because of the deliberate luxury that surrounds his life. When Henderson first sees him, he is lounging around being attended to by his wives, echoing our clichéd images of Greek and Roman sybarites who lay on their sides mashing grapes between their teeth while they contemplate their next sexual adventure. This scene is so important for the novel because of what it reveals about the nature of Dahfu's experience. It is a complex, overdetermined moment: Dahfu lounges as he does because he has learned how to experience life with deliberate luxury. At the same time, he can do so only because of his position. Even more, he is *required* to lounge and to exude the luxuriance of the kingly life. That this is also a role Dahfu must play for his people, taking up a spot they all desire, doesn't negate its other value but simply reinforces the luxury and the fragility of the position: Dahfu is in effect *commanded* to luxuriate because that is what his people expect him to do, and failure to do so could bring the gravest consequences. The luxury the Wariri provide for their king is in turn linked to Dahfu's very real fears: he knows that when he becomes the least bit weak, the envy the people feel for the position he occupies will allow them with impunity to take him out to the bush and strangle him. As a result, Dahfu experiences his life with luxury because he realizes how tenuous his hold on it is, but equally important, he luxuriates as he does in order to avoid wasting energy, for he lives under a dual imperative: to live as fully as he can, and to forestall the moment when the life he has already lived will lead to the diminution of his powers, thereby prompting his strangulation and the end of his life. He must husband his energies in order to extend the richness of his life as far into the future as possible.

These intersecting elements place great demands on Dahfu and demonstrate the difficulties of being one who fully takes up the Blessing of life, for they by no means go together seamlessly. The imperative that suggests Dahfu should conserve his energy in order to extend his life easily enough works against luxuriating in one's experience, for such luxury invariably involves intensity, and intensity expends more energy than a superficial kind of experience. Thus, out of fear for his life Dahfu could easily restrict his engagement with reality so much that he would lose the complete contact with it that is essential for the beauty that he finds in the world. Likewise, the imperatives of his role, the demand to perform as one who has a life of luxury, could easily lead to an existence in which the role overtakes all: Dahfu learns how to create the *appearance* of rich experience but loses his ability to embrace life fully. For him to be able to combine the demands of his role with a real immersion into experience is no small achievement, and it is even greater when we consider his acute knowledge of the limited span of his energy and the consequences that will come from his ultimate weakening.

Like the lion, then, Dahfu learns when not to and when to expend energy. He doesn't diminish the quality of his experience and fully revels in those states he embraces, but he also learns when not to engage himself, when to save his energy for an experience more worthy of his attention. In this respect too Dahfu resembles Atti, for he doesn't contest the givens of his life but rather learns how to deal with them in such a way that they don't deprive his life of the fullness he wants to give to it. This is what Henderson has failed to learn in his 55 years, and his envy of Dahfu springs from his awareness that Dahfu does indeed know how to experience the richness of life in a way that he does not. What Henderson fails to appreciate until the end of Dahfu's life is how much contact with the radio frequencies of fear was also involved in the deliberate luxury of his life and how strenuous a middle path Dahfu had to tread in order to achieve the fullness of his existence.

❦

If Dahfu has a thoroughgoing sense of the need to experience life luxuriously, and if he urges that luxury upon Henderson in an attempt to move him away from the momentous avoidances he has built his life around, he also has an ethic to go along with it, a code that is presented to the reader through Henderson's contrary view that the good and the true are inherently linked to violence. In contrast to Henderson's belief that truth comes in blows or that the true pleasures of life come from acts of violence like blowing the Arnewi's frogs to bits, Dahfu asserts another vision:

> They say . . . that bad can easily be spectacular, has dash or bravado and impresses the mind quicker than good. Oh, that is a mistake in my opinion. Perhaps of common good it is true. Many, many nice people. Oh yes. Their will tells them to perform good, and they do. How ordinary! Mere arithmetic. "I have left undone the etceteras I should have done, and done the etceteras I ought not to have." This does not even amount to a life. Oh, how sordid it is to bookkeep. My whole view is opposite or contrary, that good cannot be labor or conflict. When it is high and great, it is too superior. Oh, Mr. Henderson, it is far more spectacular. It is associated with inspiration, and not conflict, for where a man conflicts there he will fall, and if taking the sword also perishes by the sword. A dull will produces a very dull good, of no interest. Where a fellow draws a battle line there he is apt to be found, dead, a testimonial of the great strength of effort, and only effort. (168-69)

Henderson's life has been full of conflict, of course, so Dahfu's definition of the good calls his entire existence into question. Even more, Dahfu's belief that good cannot be labor or conflict goes against the grain of our entire century, for we have learned from Nietzsche that the Dionysian energies that create are also those that destroy. We have committed ourselves to a Janus-like vision of the good even before we begin to deal with the social conflicts that seem to pit one person's heartfelt sense of the good against another equally heartfelt sense of things that is deeply at odds with the first person's vision. We may not be quite as willing as Henderson to link good and violence, but we have nevertheless done so in all sorts of ways, from our philosophy and literary theory to our popular movies and sports, and as a result, however much Dahfu's ideas conform to conventional morality, we have in fact moved away from the idea that conflict and the good have nothing to do with one another.

Dahfu associates the good with inspiration and contrasts it with any scheme that links it to overcoming something else, which by definition would be predicated on a conflict that needed to be dealt with in order for the good to win out. Like Confucius's belief in the need to investigate the nature of things, Dahfu's discipline of life is not devoted to overcoming obstacles but rather to stripping away the lies we tell ourselves in order to avoid the real. Instead of seeing the good as a result of a life of avoidance, he imagines it as a reflection of the creative joy of living, of the force of the Blessing of life manifesting itself in all its exuberance. He doesn't deny the value of the "many, many nice people" who are good in conventional ways but rather focuses on the aesthetic good as the origin of the most profound vision of the ethical. In contrast to the bookkeeping vision of good and bad, the tallying of individual deeds, of things done and not done, Dahfu envisions an ethic that is predicated on distinguishing the real states from the imagined ones and acting in accordance with that which is.

Still, Dahfu's vision of the good sounds like the Nietzschean Dionysian stripped of its violent and inherently destructive tendencies, and we wonder how he can pull off such a feat. If Dahfu wants to establish an ethical regime that is predicated on the good of creative expression, how can he escape from the destructive potential inherent in our models of the aesthetic when it is stripped of any links to a good outside its own exuberant energies? Any aesthetically grounded vision of the good must address this problem, and it may be that Dahfu doesn't really have an answer for it. We could hypothesize that his creative evolution of the good doesn't preclude destructive effects but only denies their presence at the origin of the act, but that too begs the question. Either the creative act, the one that establishes new values, is inevitably destructive as much as creative—destructive precisely because it is creative—or the theory doesn't correspond adequately enough to the complexity our ideas have placed before us.

One could look at the problem another way and suggest that like Henderson, Dahfu's vision works fine as long as he doesn't enter the social world. Maybe creative acts and the good that comes from them aren't inherently destructive as long as they don't have to deal with the history of social structures and the need to overturn forms and codes as a result of creative acts that undermine them. The problem here is that even outside of social forms we all develop our own histories with codes that would also need to be violated by a creative act that called them into question. Nevertheless, we might hypothesize that Dahfu's own untimely end is a result of his failure adequately to consider what any ethical theory must address: *ressentiment*. His theory of inspirational good fails to account for the fact that the Bunam and his men are not interested in the good but only in power, and in the face of their determination, creative good by itself is not enough, will not carry the day. Thus, Dahfu dies because he fails to heed properly the effects of resentment in life. Not that he isn't fully aware of the conspiracy that threatens his life and regime, for he is. Rather, he is too confident that his own goodness and wisdom will prevail. Perhaps Bellow means for us to see this as a limit to Dahfu's wisdom, or perhaps his vision of Dahfu's goodness is not complete enough.

The same problem applies to Dahfu's sense of the truth, upon which his idea of the good is predicated. Again in contrast to Henderson's theory that truth comes in blows, Dahfu finds the entire regime of blows to be pernicious and is quick to discount Henderson's idea. It is also worth emphasizing that Dahfu's explanation of the regime of blows comes right after he tells Henderson that "'They are against me here . . .'" (212), something Henderson fails adequately to pick up on. He launches instead into his truth in blows argument, which leads to an abstraction of Dahfu's very concrete problem. Dahfu responds in kind rather than going back to his own difficulties:

> As things are, . . . such may be related to the case [that truth comes in blows]. I do not believe actually it is so. But I feel there is a law of human nature in which force is concerned. Man is a creature who cannot stand still under blows. Now take the horse—he never needs a revenge. Nor the ox. But man is a creature of revenges. If he is punished he will contrive to get rid of the punishment. When he cannot get rid of punishment, his heart is

> apt to rot from it. This may be—don't you think so, Mr. Henderson-Sungo? Brother raises a hand against brother and son against father (how terrible!) and the father also against son. And moreover it is a continuity-matter, for if the father did not strike the son, they would not be alike. It is done to perpetuate similarity. Oh, Henderson, man cannot keep still under the blows. If he must, for the time, he will cast down his eyes and think in silence of the ways to clear himself of them. Those prime-eval blows everybody still feels. The first was supposed to be struck by Cain, but how could that be? In the beginning of time there was a hand raised which struck. So the people are flinching yet. All wish to rid themselves and free themselves and cast the blow upon the others. (213)

However much we might be convinced that Dahfu's vision is predicated on an omission of human frailty, his assertions here suggest otherwise. If there is a flaw in his theory of the good, it is not found in his ignorance of resentment, for there are few clearer expressions of what Dahfu characterizes as the "earthly dominion" than this one. As with his theory of the good, Dahfu's vision of the true is that it cannot be predicated on blows, that the blows are a function of our fear in the face of our mortality that thwart rather than reveal the truth.

More pertinently, Dahfu assumes that our lives are dominated by an endless round of blows, violence against others that derives from our need to pass on blows that have been meted out to us. It is, as he says, "a continuity-matter, for if the father did not strike the son, they would not be alike. It is done to perpetuate similarity." The reciprocal gestures of parent and child, the one striking out at the other, the other responding in kind, reflect the psychology at the center of human labor. Each of us believes that we have been unfairly struck, and each of us therefore feels the need to strike out in turn to get rid of the pressure of the blow upon us. Dahfu earlier complained about a vision of the good that was based upon bookkeeping, and the ethic of blows is one such form of bookkeeping: we must keep track of the degree to which the blows we have received have been merited. To the extent that they have been unfairly inflicted upon us, we feel the need to even the score. And inasmuch as each of us is the sole person who sees the world through our own eyes, it stands to reason that we are likely to find the blows that come our way unmerited in ways that no other site within the world will. Thus, it is inevitable that *all* of us will feel unfairly burdened by blows, and all of us will strive to relieve ourselves of their pressure.

Dahfu's theory of blows is an updated version of Nietzsche's assertions about the nature of revenge and *ressentiment*, that it is a mark of our revulsion against time and its "It was," and he is as adept at locating the problem as Nietzsche was: when we are struck, we want to know the origin of the blow and cannot rest satisfied until we find out. We want to reciprocate with a blow upon the origin of our own pain, though if we cannot find the origin we will settle for striking someone below us. These are questions of priority, of who came first: father hits son, stronger hits weaker, someone hit us first. Something happened to us within time that prompted a violent reaction on our part, and we seek to put off the force of history that blights our lives: we will not be satisfied until we can get our life back to where it was *before* the blow was struck and life took a bad turn for us. So we strike out in turn, only exacerbating the problem of blows, for every blow reciprocally implies another, leading to an endless realm of violence. This is why Dahfu is so careful to deny an origin to the blows. Instead of claiming that they began with Cain or God or someone else, he says simply that "In the beginning of time there was a hand raised which struck. So the people are flinching yet." Humans are incapable of discovering an origin for the blows that come at them, and so it is better to put that question out of play. The only thing of which we can be sure is that in the beginning of time there were blows, and there always will be.

Part of the problem with Dahfu's theory—though like Nietzsche's it is also its strength—is that the blows aren't finally a personal matter. In some respects that changes nothing at all, but most of us are doubly wounded by the blows meted out to us: on the one hand, they simply hurt, and we react with cries of pain. But on the other, the pain is psychological: we are devastated that someone thinks so ill of us that they would strike out at us when we don't really deserve it. We can't believe that another person would negate us that way. That these blows are often nothing personal, that what is being passed on to us is less someone's resentment of us and more their resentment against things that have happened to them with which we might have had nothing to do, at least relieves some of the psychic burden even as it prompts us to withdraw our own blow in the knowledge that the person we shall be striking is probably unrelated to the pressures we feel. If the blows perpetuate continuity within the human community, if they are a manifestation of an imitative rhythm that we all manage to express, yet that rhythm most often has nothing to do with the victim of the blows, for better and worse. The rhythm prompts us to strike out, and we find a victim. We should prefer to hit the origin of our difficulties—son striking father—but we will settle for any victim rather than suffer the effects of the blow in silence.

The incredible and awful fact at the center of Dahfu's view is that when a person "cannot get rid of punishment, his heart is apt to rot from it." If we are endlessly creatures of revenge who strike out in order to address our own fears, there is something within our psychology that demands that we do so, that tells us that we will rot from within if we don't find expression for our resentment against the blows we have received. This makes no literal sense, for we should be able to realize when a blow is nothing personal and move on, but we seem incapable of doing so. Henderson himself expresses astonishment at this idea, exclaiming "'You say the soul will die if it can't make somebody else suffer what it suffers'"? (213). Dahfu explains: "'For a while, I am sorry to say, it then feels peace and joy.'" This is one way of expressing the great enigma at the heart of the species, of accounting for the endless round of blows that is second in dominion only to the realm of nature itself. As Henderson demonstrated when he expressed joy over the prospect of blowing the frogs to oblivion, humans have discovered that one path to peace and joy is to strike out at others: the act of violence is in some perverse way a purgative that relieves us of the feeling of having been put upon by another's blow. For a while, we do indeed feel peace and joy, although our blow will also engender guilt over the fact that we struck out at someone or something that didn't deserve to be struck, which will in turn contribute to our need to relieve ourselves of this burden somewhere down the road, prompting yet another round of blows. Once one falls within the regime of blows, there is no way out, for one's own acts become blows to one's psyche through the guilt that they accrete: we become our own accusers who feel the need to strike out, then feel guilty about having done so, and thereby feel the need to strike out yet again. There is no reason why humans should be constituted in this way, but as Dahfu sadly states, it seems to be the case that they are. There is nothing to be done about the fact that this regime of blows exists, for it is there. The only question is how we deal with our knowledge of its centrality in our own lives and those of others.

Dahfu's vision of the good and noble individual is thus predicated on renouncing one's place within the regime of blows. Henderson suggests that some people are capable of returning good for evil, and Dahfu agrees:

> Every brave man will think so. . . . He will not want to live by passing on the wrath. A hit B? B hit C?—we have not enough alphabet to cover the condition. A brave man will try to make the evil stop with him. He shall keep the blow. No man shall get it from him, and that is a sublime ambition. So, a fellow throws himself in the sea of blows saying he do not believe it is infinite. In this way many courageous people have died. But an even larger number who had more of impatience than bravery. Who have said, "Enough of the burden of wrath. I cannot bear my neck should be unfree. I cannot eat more of this mess of fear-pottage." (214)

If we are stuck within the regime of blows, we encounter at least two kinds of slavery: bondage to the need to pass on blows, and the enslavement that forces us to eat "this mess of fear-pottage" without striking out. Both condemn us to deal with *ressentiment* on a daily basis, but the one strives to overcome its effects within human lives whereas the other does not. Great discipline is required to restrain the effects within us of the blows we receive, for they compel redress, and we must work hard to avoid the necessity they impose upon us. But Dahfu at least posits the possibility that humans are capable of putting off the regime of blows that circumscribes our lives in narrow ways.

Lest we think of Dahfu as some benign figure whose utopian vision of a human future is inconceivable, Bellow lets us know that Dahfu is fully aware of the obstacles in the way of such a future. He tells Henderson that he believes that "good exchanged for evil truly is the answer," but he also admits that "it appears a long way off, for the human specie as a whole." Nevertheless, he declares: "Perhaps I am not the one to make a prediction, Sungo, but I think the noble will have its turn in the world" (214-15). Dahfu may be right, and his ethic of creativity may indeed be a way of escaping the fundamental violence of the blows of life in the end, but he is also correct in assuming that even if the noble will one day have its turn, that day "appears a long way off." Baby Suggs was destroyed by the realm of blows as it was inflicted upon her, and she was as strong a manifestation of Dahfu's vision of nobility as one can find. Dahfu himself loses his life in the end to the powers of resentment, so his theory has to be qualified by our knowledge of what happens to him. He tried to keep the blows, he refused to strike out at the Bunam and his conspiracy, but the result is his own death. Made vulnerable by his unwillingness to play the game of blows, he was struck down in the prime of life.

In one respect, then, we must conclude that Dahfu has not completely addressed the problems that result from his own theory. In a way Bellow makes it easy on him by allowing him to die at the hands of his vengeful brothers, those who seek to usurp his power. True, Bellow also makes it clear that Dahfu passed on a blow to Henderson when he failed to tell him that the Rain King becomes successor to the King if he dies without an heir, thereby demonstrating that Dahfu was human too. But we are told quite accurately that the "heart is apt to rot" from blows that are not addressed in some way, and Dahfu himself never deals with the force of his own statement. Of course we should all try to keep the blows to ourselves, and of course we should also do what we can to keep the blows from coming at us in the first place. But they will come regardless, and our hearts will rot from their effects upon us if we don't strike out. Is knowledge of the process sufficient to keep our hearts from rotting? Is the attempt to be noble adequate in a case where the word "rot" is not the least bit excessive? If there is an almost organic process that takes place within us when we confront and attempt to deal with the dominion of blows, how will personal resolve alter the biological changes that come from blows that aren't redressed? Dahfu doesn't answer, and this difficulty is even more compelling than the one posited by Dahfu's own end, for if we need to be concerned about being beaten to death by those who continue to believe wholeheartedly in the value of blows—as Nietzsche said repeatedly, the strong always need to be protected from the weak—we need to be more concerned with how we can keep our hearts from rotting when we refuse to pass on the blows. Dahfu never faces this head on, and whereas this might not diminish the ethical force of his remarks, it may qualify them in ways that Bellow hadn't anticipated.

Henderson's will to live, his desire for the Blessing of life, is regularly thwarted by his willingness to jump into the reign of blows and strike out with the most active members of the regime. He loves violence and experiences joy in its midst, failing to realize that such force is a negation of the life he so incessantly seeks for himself. He is stuck within a long history with dual imperatives: seek the Blessing of life, and strike out when you are struck; it has taken him most of his life to realize that he has been a tourist rather than one who has truly lived because he has construed the realm of blows—an arena in which he performs quite well—as the domain of life rather than the nihilistic attempt to strike back at existence because it comes to us under circumstances with which we fundamentally disagree. Henderson sees the Blessing of life as something that is only worth having if he can escape from the regime of the blows, hence his desire so regularly to pass them on to others. But inasmuch as passing the blow on only reinforces the regime rather than eliminating it, he needs all the more to try to escape from the effects of his own actions. So he may want to live, but he hasn't learned how to. He has only discerned that he doesn't want to live as he currently is.

Dahfu puts the problem of the blows as an ethical imperative most succinctly near the end of the novel when he talks about the shallowness of graves and their impact on our lives:

> No, graves are not deep but insignificant, a mere few feet from the surface and not far from fearing and desiring. More or less the same fear, more or less the same desire for thousands of generations. Child, father, father, child doing the same. Fear the same. Desire the same. Upon the crust, beneath the crust, again and again and again. Well, Henderson, what are the generations for, please explain to me? Only to repeat fear and desire without a change? This cannot be what the thing is for, over and over and over. Any good man will try to break the cycle. There is no issue from that cycle for a man who do not take things into his hands. (297)

True to his vision of origins, Dahfu has no specific sense of ends. If he deliberately refuses to account for the origin of blows in the human world, he also cannot articulate what life should be about. There is no otherworldly explanation or imperative to which humans must respond in Dahfu's mind, nor is one necessary. Any attempt to deal constructively with our own history would be more than sufficient to begin to establish an ethic that was truly committed to the Blessing of life. Recognizing as we do that for millennia humans have repeated the same cycle of fear and desire over and over, fearing the blows of life, desiring to put them upon another, striking out, fearing further blows in the knowledge of one's own arbitrary violence and so on, we realize that we can either comfortably continue to fit ourselves into this model of behavior, or we can begin to imagine another one. Dahfu cannot explain specifically what this other model might be other than to say that it is predicated on our willingness to accept the blows of life rather than pass them on. But he can assert that our own history repeatedly brings us to the necessity of trying to break the cycle of fear and desire, of blow and counter-blow, that keeps us from doing anything more than that which generations and generations before us have done. Dahfu cannot chart the consequences any more than he can know precisely where to go himself, but he does understand that "There is no issue from that cycle for a man who do not take things into his hands," and he knows that the cycle of violence dissatisfies us all, even if like Henderson we also take delight in destroying the lives of others.

❦

The novel itself details in a fittingly complex way the difficulties Dahfu's ethical vision faces. First, we come to understand how deep the conspiracy against him is, second we see that it finally succeeds. We also discover that his own good intentions put Henderson at stake in ways of which he remains oblivious, though he does figure out that he "was caught between the king and the Bunam's faction" (254). In becoming the king's friend, he had made an enemy of the Bunam, and in agreeing to take on Atti, he allowed everyone in the kingdom to hear his roars with the lion who was bad for the kingdom. Thus, he demonstrates complicity with a man who is trying to escape from conspiracy and dissolve the realm of blows in his own kingdom, yet his act of friendship is a blow on its own, even without the collateral problem of letting Henderson become Rain King without telling him precisely what the stakes were. The king needs someone to share his views with, yet the very act of conversation with Henderson places him at risk.

Henderson comes to understand this and quite properly doesn't blame Dahfu for it. There is, after all, nothing Dahfu can do about the relations that surround him. He has explained that the Bunam is against him and has tacitly brought Henderson into his confidence for support, and that is as it should be. This is part of Dahfu's attempt to write a new chapter to the history of his kingdom. If the Bunam wants to employ Henderson as a king in ignorance over whom he has complete control, Dahfu wants to use him to help further his noble ideas. Relations have effects, effects have unintended consequences, and Dahfu can no more escape these thickets than anyone else can. Indeed, he is the last person to be able to escape from them because he wants to find a way around these networks of constraint, of history, from which we seek to remove ourselves through the blows we pass on to others. We strike out for freedom *from* history yet increase our complicity by doing so, and Dahfu cannot overcome this pattern any more than the rest of us. He can only try to sway the rhythm of history in a different direction through the new relations he establishes with Henderson and others of like mind.

In the larger scheme of things, the problem of moving relations in new directions is confronted when Henderson talks with Dahfu about Dahfu's relations with the codes of his kingdom. When the Bunam displays a white mask in order to give the king's quest a bad omen with which to begin, Henderson gets upset and wants to do something about this deliberate attempt to foil Dahfu. The king explains that this is part of his agreement with the universe of which the Bunam is a part, to which Henderson responds: "'But you told me that the Bunam and the other fellow in the white pigment were from the old universe and I assumed you were out of it'" (296). Dahfu explains: "'No, no. Do you know how to replace the whole thing? It cannot be done. Even if, in supreme moments, there is no old and is no new, but only an essence which can smile at our arrangement—smile even at being human. That is so full of itself. . . . Nevertheless a play of life has to be allowed. Arrangements must be made'" (296). Like any good revolutionary, Henderson simply wants to abandon the old universe and start a new one. After all, if one could begin anew with an ethic that avoids passing on blows, one would stand a much greater chance of succeeding than one would if one had to accept the blows that always already surround one. But Dahfu realizes that one can no more abandon the old universe of human history than one can become God. That is precisely the problem. There may be supremely powerful aesthetic moments when old and new cease to exist, when there is "only an essence which can smile at our arrangement—smile even at being human," but for the most part the only possible way of moving the world in a new direction is to allow a play of life, to make arrangements with the old universe in order to sway it ever so slightly in the right direction.

The danger, of course, is that one might be swallowed alive by the old universe, either because it deliberately devours one, as the Bunam kills Dahfu, or because it forces one to compromise so much with it that one fails to escape from the realm of blows one is seeking to deal with in the first place. If Dahfu states that at best it will be a long time before the species is thoroughly informed by the nobility he imagines for it, that is because he knows how much history there is to move in another direction and how hard it is to shape it in ways that go against its own powerfully vengeful tendency. Dahfu's death is in this respect necessary, if tragic, for otherwise his regime would be too easily instituted and the novel would be purveying a kind of utopian goods that ironically expressed resentments of its own through its assumption that history could so easily be passed over. Instead we are led to think that Dahfu must die, but his effects live on in Henderson, and that is enough to suggest that his death does not destroy the value of his conception of nobility.

It is fitting, then, that the man who wants to live should become the embodiment of Dahfu's ideals, if not the best expression of them. And it is equally appropriate that Henderson should have his own tangled history with which to deal. Buried deep within him are the manifold inscriptions of revenge, and he must first allow himself to address these wounds of the past. The process begins when he finally agrees to submit himself to Dahfu's regime, when he allows himself to become like the lion:

> And so I was the beast. I gave myself to it, and all my sorrow came out in the roaring. My lungs supplied the air but the note came from my soul. The roaring scalded my throat and hurt the corners of my mouth and presently I filled the den like a bass organ pipe. This was where my heart had sent me, with its clamor. This is where I ended up. Oh, Nebuchadnezzar! How well I understand that prophecy of Daniel. For I had claws, and hair, and some teeth, and I was bursting with hot noise, but when all this had come forth, there was still a remainder. That last thing of all was my human longing. (267)

Fifty-five years of sorrow and blows come out in the roars that scald Henderson's throat, and he gives up this misery in order to go where his heart has sent him, to a place that suggests the Blessing of life has been violated by his violent existence. Henderson comes to dwell with the beasts of the field and is forced to humble himself as a result of his arrogant assumption that he could rise above his own human state. As he realizes while he is writing a letter to his wife Lily, "*I wanted to raise myself into another world. My life and deeds were a prison*" (284). The endless acts of violence and revenge have only become the prison from which he cannot escape, the cycle of blows he desperately wants to rise above yet cannot hope to do so until he accepts his life and deeds as *his* life and deeds. They were not something added on or thrust upon him but rather the direct result of his own actions within the cycle of blows. In becoming Atti, in stripping himself of his pretensions, Henderson gradually becomes capable of accepting his life and deeds as genuinely his, as much a part of the given with which he must deal as any social or political problem outside of his own control.

The last thing to go, Henderson informs us, is his human longing, his "*I want, I want,*" and even that doesn't go so much as become transformed into a more comprehensive knowledge: "'I had a voice that said, I want! *I* want? I? It should have told me *she* wants, *he* wants, *they* want. And moreover, it's love that makes reality reality. The opposite makes the opposite'" (286). Longing, desire, can express itself in a narrow way, as an "I want" that filters the entire universe through a wish for something one doesn't have, or it can express itself as love, and the generosity of spirit of Dahfu, or the greatness of heart of Baby Suggs, and as such it is not longing for something that isn't so much as it is a manifestation of the Blessing of life, the desire to share with others the beauty of the universe. This is the direction Henderson's emulation of Atti takes him, and it is the equivalent mode of Atti's specie-beauty: just as Atti's beauty most fully reveals itself in her being wholly who she is, so too humans reveal their own specie-beauty when they allow their desire to express itself as an exuberant affirmation of the value of life.

As with those times when the struggle between the old universe and the new one cease to matter and become a smile that celebrates everything as it is, though, Henderson must do more than simply arrive at a moment when he understands that love makes reality reality, a statement which in its abstraction is rather useless, even silly. He must find a way of accommodating the old universe even as he strives to move into the new one, and for that to happen he must find a way to make peace with his past. In one respect he manages to do this even before he heads back into the 55 years that made him what he was, for he is able to return to the formative moment of his life only after he refuses to act on his desire to kill the Bunam and those who put his friend Dahfu to death. Rather than going through with his plan for murder, he comes to understand that "Revenge is a luxury" (317), and one that he can ill afford given his long indulgence of it. Killing the Bunam would only celebrate his act of revenge on Dahfu and thus confirm the realm of blows, so Henderson must resist that tendency, however hard it is for him to do so. Tested in this way, he will then be able to retrace his steps through the thicket of his own past to encounter the ghosts that have haunted him throughout his adult life.

Knowing as he now does the power and course of *ressentiment*, Henderson can return to the moment when the heaviest blow in life hit him. He has twice mentioned the death of his brother Dick in the course of the narrative, but after a short account, he immediately swerves onto something else. His new understanding of resentment, however, allows him a perspective on that death and his father's reaction to it that provides him with some comfort:

> after my brother Dick's death I went away from home, being already a big boy of about sixteen, with a mustache, a college freshman. The reason why I left was that I couldn't bear to see the old man mourn . . . the old man, gushing white beard from all his face, he made me feel our family line had ended with Dick up in the Adirondacks, when he shot at the pen and plugged the Greek's coffee urn. Dick also was a curly-headed man with broad shoulders, like the rest of us. He was drowned in the wild mountains, and now my dad looked at me and despaired.
>
> An old man, disappointed, of failing strength, may try to reinvigorate himself by means of anger. Now I understand it. But I couldn't see it at sixteen, when we had a falling out. . . . On the day of Dick's funeral, I went to work, too. And in the evening, when I washed myself in the back of the house under the garden hose, I was gasping as the chill water rushed over my head, and the old man came out on the back porch. . . . The water blurted over me. It was cold as outer space. Fiercely, the old man started to yell at me. The hose bubbled on my head while inside I was hotter than the cutting torch that I took to all those old death cars from the highway. My father in his grief swore at me. I knew he meant it because he put aside his customary elegance of words. He cursed, I guess, because I didn't comfort him. (336-37)

For almost forty years Henderson has been carrying the weight of his father's blow around with him, desperately trying to put it off on others through his various acts of violence, but until this moment he has insufficiently realized that even if his father had made him feel as though the family line had ended when his older brother died, this was more a reflection of his grief over the death of his son than a deliberate attempt to wound Henderson.

Henderson had failed to comfort his father, had failed to ease his pain, and his father struck out and cursed him. Even worse, the blow was harder because he was not used to seeing his father curse, so when it came out in the midst of his own grief it stung all the more. Henderson had been trying to work off his woe by putting the torch to old cars, through a physical labor that would take him away from his sense of bereftness, but his father brought him back to his own terrible problem: he too felt as though the line had ended. Indeed, he feels responsible for Dick's death: "Now listen, I loved my older brother, Dick. He was the sanest of us, with a splendid record in the First World War, a regular lion. But for one moment he resembled me, his kid brother, and that was the end of him" (34). Survivor guilt has plagued Henderson throughout his life, for if he was stung by his father's blow, that was because he felt that, like Jacob, he had usurped his older brother's place. Unlike Jacob, he did not seek to be first, but his own feelings of inadequacy kept him wrestling throughout his life with the fact that he should have been the one to die, not his brother. He was the one who had failed to do something useful with his life. He was the one who couldn't live up to the house they owned, the family line in general, or his father's sense of things, and when that guilt was compounded by being left behind with a father whom he couldn't comfort, he was struck so hard he was reeling from the blow forty years later.

Not that Henderson hadn't tried to redress the blow many times over the years. He tells us, for example, that he specifically took up the violin to try to get in touch with his dead father. He just happened to find his father's old instrument one day, and:

> Then I began to recall my old man. Maybe he would deny it with anger, but we are much alike. He could not settle into a quiet life either. Sometimes he was very hard on Mama; once he made her lie prostrate in her nightgown at the door of his room for two weeks before he would forgive her some silly words, perhaps like Lily's on the telephone when she said I was unkillable. He was a very strong man, too, but as he declined in strength, especially after the death of my brother Dick (which made me the heir), he shut himself away and fiddled more and more. So I began to recall his bent back and the flatness or lameness of his hips, and his beard like a protest that gushed from his very soul—washed white by the trembling weak blood of old age. Powerful once, his whiskers lost their curl and were pushed back on his collarbone by the instrument while he sighted with the left eye along the fingerboard and his big hollow elbow came and went and the fiddle trembled and cried. (25)

The image of his father and the violin he took up for comfort are permanently etched in Henderson's mind, so, thinking that maybe his father had found a way to deal with his grief through the music, and hoping that he can communicate with his father's ghost by working with his instrument, he takes lessons and learns how to play it.

Quite properly realizing that the ghosts of the past inhabit the present, he tries "to reach his father by playing on his violin": "Down in the basement of the house, I worked very hard as I do at everything. I had felt I was pursuing my father's spirit, whispering, 'Oh, Father, Pa. Do you recognize the sounds? This is me, Gene, on your violin, trying to reach you'" (30). Henderson feels the need to be forgiven by his father for being the one with whom he was left instead of his more proper brother, and long after his father dies he is still trying to pay him back for what he feels was his fault: his brother's death. That he was not to blame and that his father cannot forgive him because there is nothing to forgive have nothing to do with the woes that consume Henderson. Only when he gets old enough to have experienced the blow of Dahfu's death does he come to realize how the blow of Dick's death was nothing personal either, didn't signify a sin for which he should pay his entire life. Nevertheless, that is more or less what he has done, for he has run from this blow all the way to Africa and has in the intervening years struck many another out of his own sense of grief and madness.

Henderson's understanding of the nature of *ressentiment* thus allows him to return to his life, the one he lost when his brother Dick died, and it allows him to gather together his own grief and woe and see them for what they are, his deep sense of loss and his guilt over being the one who survived. His Oedipal problems have been the result of receiving his father's curse rather than his blessing, but he now knows that the curse was an accident of history rather than an intentional denunciation of his own kin. He suffered and had nowhere else to turn, so Henderson became his victim. From father to son, from son to father, so the people are still flinching to this day. Having kept one blow to himself, however—the death of Dahfu—Henderson is prepared to integrate his history with his will to live, bringing them together for the first time.

❦

The Blessing of life is not enough by itself, for it can be transformed into violent acts that work against it and that bring harm to others. Henderson's career is a fitting example of this, for he has always had a burning desire for the Blessing, yet he has never been able to understand just what it involved and what it demanded of him. The result was a life devoted to torture of himself and others, a will to life that was transformed into a nihilism that struck out at things both animate and inanimate. Even in the midst of his nihilism, however, Henderson has always had the ability to appreciate the value of the world; he has simply not known how to make it fit with the rest of the life. Like Paul D in *Beloved* who suffered mightily and who deliberately restricted the flow of his life but "could not help being astonished by the beauty of this land that was not his,"[3]

Henderson has always had a keen sensitivity to the wonders of the world. It has been clouded by his need for violence, and it has been out of place in a life that has moved in a more destructive direction, but he has always intensely appreciated the beauty of the world, as he tells us on and off throughout the novel.

Henderson has felt beauty, but he has not known the specie-beauty that Dahfu tried to teach him through Atti. His own self-loathing kept him from seeing how he too was involved in the beauty of the world, just as Paul D's enslaved status kept him from being meaningfully related to the beauty that seemed a part of someone else's land rather than his own. The classic example of Henderson's relationship to beauty comes when he is with the Arnewi. Mtalba comes to dance in front of him to show that she wants to be his bride, and he is overwhelmed by the event: "Thus I realized as the night and the dancing wore on that this was enchantment. This was poetry, which I should allow to reach me, to penetrate the practical task of demolishing the frogs in the cistern. And what I had felt when I first laid eyes on the thatched roofs while descending the bed of the river, that they were so ancient, amounted to this same thing—poetry, enchantment" (98). Henderson even goes so far as to explain that "Somehow I am a sucker for beauty and can trust only it, but I keep passing through and out of it again. It never has enough duration" (98). On the one hand, he has a true appreciation for the poetry of life, is transformed by the enchantment of Mtalba's dancing and everything that is involved in it, but on the other he wants to find a way of allowing this beauty to "reach him" so that it can "penetrate the practical task of demolishing the frogs in the cistern." He has no sense that the act of demolishing the frogs is unrelated to the beauty he is experiencing on this enchanted evening in Africa. If he is regularly distressed by the fact that beauty comes and goes so quickly without any rhyme or reason, he also fails to understand what the powers and limits of beauty are.

Henderson claims that he is a sucker for beauty and explains that it is the only thing in the world he can trust, and he also understands that its enchanting force provides him with a knowledge he doesn't want to be without, but he immediately seeks to pervert the knowledge of beauty with the violence of blowing the frogs up. He senses that there must be a relation between the wisdom to be found in beauty and the pragmatic disposition of everyday life, but he cannot bridge the gap between the two because of his problems with himself, because of his self-loathing, because of his inability to appreciate his own specie-beauty, that manifestation of the beautiful that would allow the moments of wonder in his life to be integrated into his daily disposition of the events in his life. Hence, the beauty comes and goes while the violence remains, a violence that intensifies in part out of frustration over his inability to sustain enchantment in his life.

It would be safe to say that Henderson has a glorified vision of beauty and links it to his own salvation, as he tells us when he explains that "chaos doesn't run the whole show. That this is not a sick and hasty ride, helpless, through a dream into oblivion. No, sir! It can be arrested by a thing or two. By art, for instance. The speed is checked, the time is redivided. Measure! That great thought. Mystery! The voices of angels! Why the hell else did I play the fiddle?" (175-76). Beauty is no anodyne for Henderson but rather that which arrests the chaos all around one, that which brings measure to life and allows us to hear the voices of the angels. The Blessing of life is to see and feel precisely the measure and the mystery to which Henderson here adverts, and the goal is not to feel good about life but to redivide the time, to measure the value of things anew and celebrate their relations. Henderson even goes so far as to write to Lily that "Humankind has to sway itself more intentionally toward beauty" (282), and that is one way of expressing the gist of his new understanding of things, that which comes from his appreciation of his own specie-beauty and that which is felt when the furies of resentment are held in abeyance rather than allowed to express themselves with every new moment.

Henderson has always had a sense of the relationship between the good and the beautiful, but he has never been able to put it into play in his own life because he was driven by *ressentiment*, by the hope that somehow he could overcome the blow his father inflicted upon him, as though that were the first or the only blow he had ever received. But he also suggests indirectly the way our own culture reinforces our misunderstanding about the relationship between the beautiful and the good when he addresses the nature of his quest for a noble life:

> "We're supposed to think that nobility is unreal. But that's just it. The illusion is on the other foot. They make us think we crave more and more illusions. Why, I don't crave illusions at all. They say, Think big. Well, that's baloney of course, another business slogan. But greatness! That's another thing altogether. Oh, greatness! Oh, God! Romilayu, I don't mean inflated, swollen, false greatness. I don't mean pride or throwing your weight around. But the universe itself being put into us, it calls out for scope. The eternal is bonded onto us. It calls out for its share. That is why guys can't bear to be so cheap. And I had to do something about it. Maybe I should have stayed at home. Maybe I should have learned to kiss the earth." (318)

Greatness, nobility of spirit, a full expression of the Blessing of life, is all that Henderson has sought throughout his life, but it has been hard to find because of his resentment and because of the way the business slogans of society try to sell us illusions instead of nobility of character. In contrast to the Henderson we have seen earlier who confesses that "Sometimes I think that pleasure comes only from having your own way" (295), the Henderson who craves reality (even in the midst of the woe of Dahfu's death), demands nobility of himself and seeks for ways to express the manner in which "the universe itself [is] being put into us," argues against "pride or throwing your weight around." He is not looking for a position of power. On the contrary, he is being humble here, asserting his ability to recognize the way the universe "calls out for its share." Ordinarily the blurt of Henderson's self has been so loud that the call of the universe has been muffled, almost snuffed out, but he has always managed to hear it and to keep it in mind, even as it was a recessive part of his life. But he now realizes that true greatness in a human being has nothing to do with the will to power and everything to do with the humble assumption that we have to give the universe its share, have to express fully the way the eternal is bonded onto us. The need to do so was the origin of Henderson's quest, and he has found that for which he was looking.

Henderson's spirit does burst its sleep. He learns to accept the Blessing of life with the nobility of spirit that is demanded of one who seeks it, and he best expresses his sense of the Blessing in the midst of his fever when he returns to the mystery of measure, the gift that allows us to hear the song of the angels:

> Oh, you can't get away from rhythm. . . . You just can't get away from it. The left hand shakes with the right hand, the inhale follows the exhale, the systole talks back to the diastole, the hands play patty-cake, and the feet dance with each other. And the seasons. And the stars, and all of that. And the tides, and all that junk. You've got to live at peace with it, because if it's going to worry you, you'll lose. You can't win against it. It keeps on and on and on. Hell, we'll never get away from rhythm, Romilayu. I wish my dead days would quit bothering me and leave me alone. The bad stuff keeps coming back, and it's the worst rhythm there is. The repetition of a man's bad self, that's the worst suffering that's ever been known. But you can't get away from regularity. (329)

Dahfu has led Henderson to see that there are two rhythms in life, the rhythm of the universe and the rhythm of *ressentiment*, the inhale and the exhale and the endless reciprocity of blow followed by blow followed by another. One can live ignobly, passing on the blows in an attempt to get rid of the rhythm "of a man's bad self" out of a desperate feeling that "The bad stuff keeps coming back, and it's the worst rhythm there is"; or one can accept one's place within the rhythms of the universe, discern the ways in which one's own patterns are a part of the inhale and exhale, the systole and the diastole, the patty-cake of hands and the seasons and tides "and all that junk."

The problem, Henderson realizes, is that we all arrive at the point when we "wish [our] dead days would quit bothering [us] and leave [us] alone," and we think we can fend off our history by striking out, by trying to lift ourselves into another world where our deeds are no longer a part of us. But in attempting to raise ourselves into another world through the blows we pass on, we only end up contributing to the repetition of our bad self from which we are trying to escape. We are in flight from the temporal nature of existence, that which the rhythms of the universe make unalterably clear to us, and we seek to rise above those rhythms to exist outside of time and beyond the effects of our past actions. We seek to escape our ghosts because they remind us that we too shall be ghosts before long. But Henderson asserts that "'You've got to live at peace with it, because if it's going to worry you, you'll lose. You can't win against it.'" The rhythm of life is the essence of its Blessing, yet it is also that against which we most strenuously rebel, for it means accepting our full complicity in the patterns of the universe, and we have at best only given part of our commitment to this life out of a sense of dissatisfaction of what the rhythms of the universe demand of us: our lives. And the burden of our past grows and grows as we age, making it harder and harder to accept the rhythms from which we came and into which we are always moving. As Henderson concedes even as he celebrates the noble rhythms of life: "'But my back is breaking. I'm loaded down. It isn't fair—what about the grun-tu-molani?'" (329). Having only one life, one chance to celebrate the rhythms of the universe, we find it unfair that we should have to haul around with us all the dead days that keep bothering us. We should be able to embrace life outside of the repetitions of our bad selves, yet it is precisely that kind of thinking that leads us to renounce the rhythms of life in the first place.

So it is perfectly human for Henderson both to accept the Blessing and to lament that he will have to carry around the repetitions of his bad self for the rest of his life as well, for that doesn't seem to be part of the bookkeeping that we have come to expect. Once we are assumed into the mysteries of the universe and accept the beauty of its rhythms, we think we should have moved beyond that other rhythm. But that is the mistake that dooms us every time and that keeps Henderson desperately seeking to quell the noisy voice of his desire for so many decades. The bad self is part of the rhythm too, cannot be avoided or overcome; the ghosts are as much us as the living tissue, and we have to live with them as well. We must play our violins to embrace the voices of the past as much as we kiss the earth and celebrate the Blessing that was given to us in the first place.

For Henderson, these rhythms come together at the end of the novel in his memory of Smolak the bear, the creature with whom he did time at the amusement park in Canada he ran to in order to escape his father's curse and his own sense of unworthiness. He tells us

> As Smolak (mossy like a forest elm) and I rode together [on the roller coaster], and as he cried out at the top, beginning the bottomless rush over those skimpy yellow supports, and up once more against eternity's blue (oh, the stuff that has been done within this envelope of color, this subtle bag of life-giving gases!) while the Canadian hicks were rejoicing underneath with red faces, all the nubble-fingered rubes, we hugged each other, the bear and I, with something greater than terror and flew in those gilded cars. I shut my eyes in his wretched, time-abused fur. He held me in his arms and gave me comfort. And the great thing is that he didn't blame me. He had seen too much of life and somewhere in his huge head he had worked it out that for creatures there is nothing that ever runs unmingled. (339)

The wild rides with Smolak reflect the pattern of Henderson's life as a whole, a trip he has taken "with something greater than terror" that also reflected (albeit too dimly) his joy at almost touching the top of eternity's blue in his gilded car. The terror and the joy, the rhythm of the elements that reflect everything we most value about life and all the elements of our bad selves that we should prefer to leave behind, commingle to create life as we know it. Henderson learns to deal with the fact that "for creatures there is nothing that ever runs unmingled," which means that he accepts himself as a creature—he identifies with rather than differentiates himself from Smolak—and that he is willing to live with the inevitable negativity that is an inherent part of life.

Henderson also embraces the comfort that others give us, whether they be bears or humans. Ironically for one who has been so abusive to those he has known and loved, he asserts "Once more. Whatever gains I ever made were always due to love and nothing else" (339), hardly the sentiment we would expect from a man more accustomed to striking out than hugging others for comfort and support. But the beauty of the world involves him in the warmth and comfort of Smolak's "time-abused fur" even as Smolak's own stoicism prompts Henderson to see that blame is not something that can be applied to the fundamental situation of life itself. We may spend our lives looking for someone who is responsible for the nature of our own seemingly wretched lives, and we may often blame ourselves for what we have done—a gesture Henderson habitually makes as he assumes that his body shape and everything else about him are due to things he has done to himself—but as Dahfu has explained to Henderson earlier: "'if you are inclined to blame—no! No blame redounds. We are far from so free as to be masters'" (237-38). Intent upon finding the origin of his woes, Henderson is more than willing to blame himself, particularly because he feels guilty for having survived his older brother, but in committing himself to the rhythms of life, he has accepted that he is incapable of being a master of those rhythms. His choice is only to accept or reject the effects they have in his life, to work within them or rebel against them. He has spent a lifetime working against them even as he has desired the Blessing that accrues to one who learns to make use of them, and by the end of the novel Henderson has presumably found a way to live with the woe of life, to celebrate that life nonetheless, and to accept the Blessing without complaint about the manner in which it is given to him.

Henderson the Rain King, shows us that the Blessing of life in itself is not sufficient, nor is the simple desire for it. Henderson is a destructive and impulsive person who is incapable of properly measuring out his life because he is unwilling to submit to the rhythms that govern it. Even though he is susceptible to the aesthetic effects of beauty, he can find no way to integrate those effects into his life so that they have the ethical implications that are part of them, again because the ethos of the aesthetic is linked to an acceptance of the rhythms through which our behavior and understanding of the world is modulated, and without a proper appreciation of our participation in those rhythms, we cannot begin to develop an ethos that is consonant with the other activities around us. Just as important in the present world, acceptance of these rhythms also necessitates the embrace of the past in all of its positive and negative respects, and Henderson is quite right to think that it will nearly break his back to take up this imperative. The largest burden of life in the modern era is the acceptance of the past that brought us to where we are. Jacob must accept his history and his usurpation of the Blessing in order to be renamed and to obtain the life he so ardently desires, but for the most part his past involves only his own deeds: the measure of his bad self is simply what he has done to Esau and Jacob. But Henderson has to accept a two-thousand year history, one that involves not only his own bad deeds but also the ones that brought his culture to the developed yet troubled state in which he finds it. This is enough of a burden to kill anyone, and it requires courage to be willing to embrace it, yet that is finally what Henderson does because his desire for life is so great, because he has grown wearier of running from the mess of fear-pottage that is his daily lot than he has of trying to accept that which has already been done and can never be undone.

If a desire for life is no longer enough, if it is not in itself a sufficient context through which to develop an ethical orientation to the world, it probably never was. But the desire for life can seem almost enough in an era with low population and little history whereas in our own time we cannot begin to imagine a site that embraces the three goods without also assuming the full burden of what has brought us to where we are. We must bring out our violin and play to our ghosts even as Henderson does in order to keep them from consuming us, as Beloved almost devours Sethe in *Beloved.* This additional burden and our growing awareness of it have been that which has dominated our actions for the past century, and they seem almost too much for us to bear. Even in simple ways today, we seem unwilling to accept the portion of the past that has made us who we are. The most pertinent example is the way in which middle-class whites in the United States seem to think that twenty years of social programs—*regardless* of their worth or effectiveness—more than compensates for the slavery and racism that took centuries to develop and that extend themselves even to our own time. We think we have more than paid our debt, as though accepting the past were merely a bookkeeping matter. But as Dahfu pointed out, true nobility of spirit has nothing to do with bookkeeping, with measuring how much one has put out and how much one gets in return. Rather, nobility is based on a full acceptance of the reality we have been given, including all of the history that led to our greater or lesser advantage in the social world. We can no more escape the advantages of our position than the disadvantages, for both are part of the rhythm that has brought us to where we are. And only a willingness to take it all as that which has been given to us will allow the nobility that is required of us when we embrace the Blessing of life.

4

The Fair Play of the World

As the events of both *Henderson the Rain King* and *Beloved* make clear, human beings have a hard time dealing with the history of which they are a part. In the case of the characters in *Beloved*, this is easy to understand, for they had been slaves, and most of the things that affected the disposition of their daily lives had in one way or another been determined by others. Most of the blight that smeared their sense of the Blessing of life came from the white people who oppressed them. Henderson, however, was a wealthy man, a necessary distinction in the novel inasmuch as we have to recognize that his problem has nothing to do with the financial constraints that limit desire in most people's lives. Henderson can buy himself anything he wants, yet his desire still cries out *"I want, I want."* Positively put, Henderson wants the Blessing of life; negatively put, in his mind this means being free from the burden of the past which weighs so heavily upon him. In some respects we all bear the weight of survivor's guilt, regardless of our wealth, class, skin color or gender: at the moment we possess life and others do not, and when we are old enough to realize this, part of us must suffer under the feeling that somehow we have usurped the place of another: we live at the expense of other life, and there is no good reason why we should exist and they shouldn't, outside of the kind of species-arrogance which would assert that humans should have priority in all matters on the planet.

Whatever guilt we might feel for being alive at the expense of other life, though, most of us spend more of our time dealing with a history whose effects we do not choose to embrace. In a country like the United States, most people are willing to argue that everyone should have a fair shake, that they should be able to develop their skills and capabilities and make use of them in fitting ways. We have been less willing to consider the ways in which our common history has made this outcome more or less likely in individual cases. The social programs of the sixties were an honorable attempt to try to address the wrongs of the past that discriminated against positive outcomes in lives for no good reason, and there have been other efforts to redress the inequities that our history has led to, but we have yet to arrive at a level of historical thinking that allows us a proper sense of how deeply implicated our fates are in the history that allows us to establish a position in the world.

It is often difficult for white people in a racist society like ours to see how much privilege accrues to them as a result of their skin color, how much the blessing of life has been predisposed toward those who share that racial marker, for like many gifts, it is something they live with every day and have never thought to question. When it is pointed out to them that their color is not a marker in every utterance that has to do with them—white achievement, white attitude, white socioeconomic problems—they fail to appreciate what a difference that little adjective makes. After all, *they* don't discriminate in their lives, so why should they pay a penalty for those who do. As Captain Delano says at the end of Melville's story "Benito Cereno," and as leaders such as Ronald Reagan would surely agree: "'the past is past; why moralize upon it?'"[1] When one points out to such individuals that we need to moralize on it precisely because it has done much to determine the outcomes of all of our lives, good and bad, those whose lives have gone well tend not to see this as much as those who have suffered discrimination.

The point is not to try to induce white guilt over the benefits that have come to individuals because they are white in a racist society any more than it is to induce a sense of victimization in those who have been discriminated against because of their skin color. The question we need to address is the one that links us to our history in all of its many effects, the question that places us next to the resentment that is an inevitable part of history even as it is an essential aspect of every human life. We might wish for a different world in which resentment no longer had its effects and in which individuals had moved beyond their desire to overcome the past events that generated the resentment within them, but this seems not to be an option for the species, even if it is a quasi-utopian goal worth striving for. Resentment permeates history and the Blessing of life, and it drives people to thwart their own best characteristics and to wreak havoc in their lives and others. It poisons the relations between people even as it convinces individuals that life owes them something. If we are taught that virtue is its own reward, few of us really believe that, and most of us cry out for proper recompense for what we do. As Nietzsche says through Zarathustra in his speech to the virtuous: "'You want to be paid as well, you virtuous! Do you want reward for virtue and heaven for earth and eternity for your today? And are you now angry with me because I teach that there is no reward-giver nor paymaster? And truly, I do not even teach that virtue is its own reward.'"[2]

Zarathustra is not interested in bookkeeping, indeed laments the fact that "reward and punishment have been lyingly introduced into the foundation of things—and now even into the foundation of your souls, you virtuous!" (117). Somewhere in the course of our history, in the transformation from the polytheism of the Greeks to the monotheism of the Judeo-Christian tradition, the "paymaster" was introduced and the notion that life could be measured out by double-entry bookkeeping became a part of the way we think about our lives. So even the virtuous want recompense and are at least convinced that virtue is its own reward. We have translated the measure of the world—the rhythms that Henderson comes to understand—into profit and loss, reward and punishment, and once we introduced bookkeeping "into the foundation of things—and now even into the foundation of [our] souls," we were unable to extricate ourselves from this mistake. We habitually order the world in terms of reward and punishment and develop our resentments accordingly. Nietzsche considers this a great mistake, the fundamental error of our civilization in some respects, and tries to imagine a world without a paymaster at the center. He is also clear about the linkage of reward and punishment to our modern sense of economics, reducing God to a paymaster rather than a dispenser of good and bad in life. Our first reduction was to decide that everything in life had to do with the reciprocities of reward and punishment; our second was to determine that all reward and punishment was fundamentally economic in nature, could be measured by the double-entry bookkeeping method and thereby kept under our control. It was a simple matter of the distribution of money and how to direct its flows. How do we escape from this history?

But we were the ones who introduced this concept into the center of our ethos, so how could we possibly escape from it? Nietzsche's answer is that we cannot, however much we should like to. It has become an element of our cultural landscape that cannot be erased by the stroke of a pen, even if it is part of our history from which we should hope to extricate ourselves. In some respects that is precisely what Nietzsche sought to do. His tragic vision of human existence is an attempt to move away from the paymaster toward an acceptance of the uneven fates that have been distributed to the billions of people on the planet. Nietzsche was an elitist, so it was easier for him to imagine a world in which one simply embraced one's fate and ignored the unpleasantness of others', but we who are more egalitarian in nature have a harder time reconciling a tragic sense of the accidents of life with the unfavorable outcomes of so many lives that are blighted by things that should never have affected them. The ethos to be found in the tragic vision may work well as a means to construe one's own behavior, but when it is used to ignore the fates of others, to hide from the ways in which history has disposed itself in our direction and not in others, it can become callous at best and pernicious at worst. One needs to be concerned about the fates of others, just as one must do what one can to address the good and the bad of one's own history, for the two are inseparable, as Henderson learned.

At the same time, one must wonder along with Nietzsche why the paymaster was introduced in the first place. Although the early Greeks had some sense of the economy of fates, as demonstrated in their attempts to placate the gods through sacrifice, still they did not expect Zeus to even things out or even to explain why the rough forces of the gods were tossing the people about as they were. There is an economy of sorts—we know that Odysseus is paying a price for offending Poseidon by poking out Polyphemus's eye—but it does not extend itself into every nook and cranny of life and has little effect on the disposition of ordinary people's lives. Even in the Old Testament there is much less of the paymaster than we find in the Christian era. Yet we have introduced reward and punishment into the very foundations of things and now don't know how to extricate ourselves from this erroneous characterization of the play of forces in the world. Even more, many—doubtless most—people aren't the least bit interested in firing the paymaster and reorganizing the way we think about the outcomes of individual lives. We have come to depend on the economy of profit and loss so much that we think we cannot do without it anymore. And we may be right.

What *are* the origins of our profit-and-loss, reward-and-punishment view of the economy of the world, and why do we continue to give it so much credence? Most simply, we think at once of *ressentiment*. At least within our own cultures children learn early on to assess the outcomes of things and to determine what should and should not have happened. My eight-year-old daughter long ago became adept at determining whether the results of a game were fair or not, and even if in most cases her assessments have turned out not to be self-serving but accurate, still I wonder why she insists so much that the proper outcome be determined. As a parent, one tells one's child that regardless of the outcome, the important thing is that one knows the way things went and the way things should have been determined, but this is akin to asserting that virtue is its own reward, and Nietzsche is right to maintain that this statement is also tinged by the poisons of reward and punishment. On the other hand, a parent is given to saying that life isn't always fair, a statement that seems more accurately to reflect the uneven outcomes of events, but one that no more satisfies the parent than it does the child. The parent may think it so, and the child may rebel against it, but so does the parent, who, after all, would like the best for his or her child and therefore doesn't want to have the larger outcomes of life work unfairly against the child. It is one thing for a parent to watch his or her child settle for third in a race the individual has really won, but no parent wants to think of these things when it comes to how the child's entire life turns out.

For children the sense of fairness begins on the social playing fields. My daughter has complained bitterly about this or that social unfairness, but she has yet seriously to complain about some of the givens of her life: her parents, her physical features, her native abilities. The unfairness of the world as it relates to these more crucial features of a life comes later and is far more troubling, again because anyone who has lived much past youth knows that the most horrifying unfairnesses in life have to do with early death and dismemberment, the stripping away of the richness of life's grace from those who so marvelously displayed it. These are the thoughts we run from even as our children complain about the fact that their seat in the classroom doesn't properly reflect their contribution to the class. We may try to underplay the seriousness of that "slight" in the overall economy of things, but we can hardly dismiss the complaint itself because it stems from our own deepest fears. In the world of privilege in which many of us in the West live, the fairness of life in both social and accidental ways is a consuming presence in everyday life, a dominating force that never goes away as long as one lives.

Our preoccupation with fate and the outcomes of lives is nothing new, we know, just as we can appreciate how one of the greatest accomplishments of the West, tragic drama, drew its strength from precisely this concern. If Greek tragedy imposes on us the injunction to say nothing about a person's life until after he or she is dead, we know that the imperative comes from the Greeks' acute sense of the twists of fate, of the way the accidents of life can turn the most wonderful existence into the most horrifying: Oedipus is the most revered person in Thebes one day and the most reviled the next. And in spite of our tendency to moralize, to want to blame Oedipus's fall on his pride, it seems more accurate to assume that the best Greek tragedies were based less on this simple-minded sense of responsibility—Oedipus was so taken with his own great skills that he lost sight of his human stature and therefore was condemned by the gods to suffer the awful fate that came his way—than on the accidents of fate: life shook itself out in such a way that Oedipus ended up with the life he did. He had accidental encounters with his father and mother that destroyed his life and that of his progeny, but they were accidents of fate more than payoffs for Oedipus's hubris.

We cannot bear the accidents of our fate, even if we sense the value in Nietzsche's repeated assertions that we must love our fates and turn the "It was" into a "Thus I willed it." This is a powerful site for our endless consideration of the fairness of life, and it is one to which we shall return because the question of fate is the most profound link we have to that which makes us human. First, though, we need to entertain some of the points of entry into our developing sense of fate, one of the most profound of which is Hegel's master/slave relationship, particularly as mediated by Alexandre Kojeve's commentary on it. Through Hegel's eyes we see the question of fairness disposed through the desire for recognition: our sense of autonomy depends on the recognition of another, and we strive to achieve that recognition through a metaphorical "fight to the death" with the other that results in one of the two combatants capitulating to the other:

> Man's humanity "comes to light" only in risking his life to satisfy his human Desire—that is, his Desire directed toward another Desire. Now, to desire a Desire is to want to substitute oneself for the value desired by this Desire. For without this substitution, one would desire the value, the desired object, and not the Desire itself. Therefore, to desire the Desire of another is in the final analysis to desire that the value that I am or that I "represent" be the value desired by the other: I want him to "recognize" my value as his value. I want him to "recognize" me as an autonomous value. In other words, all human, anthropogenetic Desire—the Desire that generates Self-Consciousness, the human reality—is, finally, a function of the desire for "recognition." And the risk of life by which the human reality "comes to light" is a risk for the sake of such a Desire. Therefore, to speak of the "origin" of Self-Consciousness is necessarily to speak of a fight to the death for "recognition."[3]

In wanting the other "to 'recognize' my value as his value," I seek to find ways of achieving a state in which I am taken at my word, am seen as an autonomous individual worthy of specific recognition. According to Kojeve, this is the desire "that generates Self-Consciousness" in the first place and thus establishes "the human reality." Without the recognition of the other, we feel as though we don't exist. Therefore, we will risk our lives in order to fulfill the desire of Desire and achieve an autonomous status in the eye of the other.

As Kojeve demonstrates, Hegel doesn't believe that this process works out that simply, for one would suppose that the person who won the struggle would achieve recognition, become the master, while the loser—who conceded before he had to give up life altogether—would be reduced to a subordinate position. This lowered status of the slave eventually degrades the master's sense of recognition inasmuch as it is "one-sided, for he does not recognize in turn the Slave's human reality and dignity. Hence, he is recognized by someone whom he does not recognize . . . he can be recognized as such only by making the Other his Slave. But the Slave is for him an animal or a thing. He is, therefore, 'recognized' by a thing" (19). The recognition the master achieves turns out not to be much of a recognition at all. It is inevitably a mediated desire to begin with, and if it is filtered through one who is seen to be less than human, it fails properly to recognize that which that master sought to establish in the first place.

Ironically, then, the master who won the fight to the death ends up being subordinated to the slave and fails to achieve the proper recognition because he devalues the worth of the slave, whereas the slave, who became less than human by agreeing to subordinate himself to the master, achieves autonomy through the labor he performs for the master: "In becoming master of Nature by work, then, the Slave frees himself from his own nature, from his own instinct that tied him to Nature and made him the Master's slave. . . . The Slave, in transforming the given World by his work, transcends the given and what is given by that given in himself; hence, he goes beyond himself, and also goes beyond the Master who is tied to the given which, not working, he leaves intact" (23). Far from being in control of the situation, the master in his dependence on the slave is deprived of the labor that would allow him to rise above his instinctive nature and achieve an objective reality. In the end, "Man achieves his true autonomy, his authentic freedom, only after passing through Slavery, after surmounting fear of death by work performed in the service of another (who, for him, is the incarnation of that fear)" (27).

If the mediated desire that establishes the rhythms of the master/slave relationship is that which prompts us to assess the outcomes in the world according to our own sense of what is proper and thereby leads us to create a context where we achieve a recognition that is not based on our own subjectivity—either by establishing mastery over another or through the labor that allows us to objectify ourselves within the natural world—then inevitably all assessments of what is fitting depend on that which is outside of our own domain, whether it be the fruits of our labor or the recognition of another. Our sense of fairness is dependent on the recognition of another who establishes the value of our labor by declaring it good and worthy, which is to say worthy of appropriation, worthy of his desire as well. In this way, Hegel may be right that humans achieve freedom only by passing through slavery, by producing something objectively other that marks out their value in the field of nature and the other. At the same time, though, one wonders how well that freedom can be achieved, how thoroughly it can be rooted in a world of endless dialectic, where the productions of labor are consumed by another and generate still further desire.

In this respect it may be that René Girard's sense of this world of desire is more accurate, at least when it comes to the value that is established by the oscillation of production and desire among individuals. In Girard's appropriative mimesis, desire cannot work itself out in quite the same way: "If one individual imitates another when the latter appropriates some object, the result cannot fail to be rivalry or conflict. Such conflict is observable in animals; beyond a certain intensity of rivalry the antagonists tend to lose sight of their common object and focus on each other, engaging in so-called prestige rivalry. In human beings, the process rapidly tends toward interminable revenge, which should be defined in mimetic or imitative terms."[4] The so-called "prestige rivalry" to which Girard refers here is very much like the fight to the death between master and slave. Hegel left out the initial interest in the object of desire that the other possessed, but otherwise the rivalry, and the desire for recognition, remains the same. In Girard's scenario, no vision of freedom evolves, no moment when the recognition is fitting and the rivalry ends. The conflict "rapidly tends toward interminable revenge," and the only way it can be properly resolved is through victimage of one sort or another. For Girard, the victim inevitably becomes a scapegoat, and it is through this means rather than any autonomizing recognition that the conflict comes to an end. But inasmuch as the one who victimizes must repress his awareness of his act of victimization, leading to guilt and dependence on the one who is victimized, we are back in a world in which no autonomy is achieved and individuals fail to arrive at a fitting sense of what is proper for their particular place in the scheme of things.

Both Girard's and Hegel's assessments of the patterns of human desire reveal the elements that are involved in our determination of what is proper even as they demonstrate the futility—even the impossibility—of doing so. In the world of mediated desire, nothing can be known for sure, nothing can be definitively established. Every object of appropriation can be appropriated and consumed, but the object itself is only a fig leaf to cover up the desire that desires the desire of the other. Bound tightly to the desire of Desire, as Hegel puts it, we cannot hope to establish a system of weights and measures beyond it, nor can we therefore assume that a proper sense of our own value can ever be established, in our own eyes or in the eyes of others. Both visions require a transcendental mode beyond the play of mimetic desire in order to ground the assessments upon which humans base their sense of autonomy and freedom, yet no transcendental mode has been forthcoming that would sufficiently determine any such thing. These mimetic modes strive for a place outside of the play of desires but cannot finally establish one, thereby leaving us within the swamp of mimetic desire, of endless desire of the desire of the other.

❦

Hegelian and Girardian desire may thus be useful in a description of how we seek to establish our autonomy yet are never able wholly to do so, but they fail to account for the need for recognition or for fair play. In this respect they are in the position of the story of Cain and Abel in the Bible: they articulate the desire for recognition and its consequences, but they don't tell us what we need to know. The Bible informs us that God found Abel's sacrifice fitting and spurned Cain's gift, but it doesn't explain either to Cain or to us why Cain's sacrifice wasn't as good as Abel's. One could argue that Cain's murder of Abel was a function of mimetic desire—he wanted to appropriate the recognition that Abel had achieved through the production of his gift—but one could just as easily assume that Cain's problem was as much related to God's unwillingness to explain what the standard of achievement and autonomy was. We can fill in the blanks and suggest that Cain's heart wasn't really in his sacrifice, that it was all form and no meaning, but there is nothing in the Bible that tells us so. No, the problem is precisely that Cain both lacks recognition *and* a sense of what he can do to achieve it. As far as the account goes, Cain did what he thought was necessary for recognition, produced the objective fruits of his labor in such a way that he should have been acknowledged, but he was not, and from his perspective that can only mean that recognition is dispensed *arbitrarily*.

Again, we are stuck with the sense that the fates of both the natural and the social world are distributed arbitrarily, that there is no rhythm of reciprocity that ties production to recognition, that trades labor of one sort for time of another. No matter what one does, no matter how much labor one performs, one is no more guaranteed additional time than one is allowed an objective sense of recognition. These values are determined within the social flows of mimetic appropriation, and those flows do not work according to the standard that humans desire any more than the natural rhythms guarantee one a long and healthy life if one is a good person and maintains a strict discipline that is based on sincerity of heart. Economy does not work here, at least not as we imagine it, and yet we insist that it does. We demand that the paymaster, whoever that may be in whatever context, even the scales so that we get proper recognition for a day's work. In the end, we trade our labor for recognition and for time, for more time to be recognized, yet we all realize that there is no necessary correlation between what we do and what we get.

As Henderson's survivor guilt suggests, the process works both ways, for if we are constantly assessing what the fruits of our labor should be, and if we determine in a regular way whether what we have accomplished is achieving the recognition it deserves, there are also measures for those who are better off which reveal their good fortune to be no more the fruit of their labor than their misfortune. Not only is Henderson alive whereas his brother is dead, but he has inherited a fortune that bears no relationship to what or who he is. It is passed on to him because he is the one who is left standing when his father dies, and if he feels unworthy, unfitting for the fortune that comes his way, he has every reason to feel so. In this respect, many of us who are better off have multiple standards of assessment, one of which applies to the givens of our lives, one of which pertains to our achievements, and others which address additional aspects of our multifarious situation. Any typically middle-class individual in a Western country is given something unmerited in an intrinsic way: one is born into a life in which nutrition, education, and comfort are available or one is not, and there is nothing in one's character that makes such providence fitting or otherwise. One may seek to live up to what one has been given without reason, thereby attempting to achieve recognition from the paymaster by using one's talents fully. Or one may take such dispensations for granted and start measuring the value of recognition from where one is at the moment rather than where one began relative to the rest of the human population. Either way, the standards invariably conflict and cannot be reconciled, however much we seek to even out the scales and make ourselves feel fitting to the station in life we occupy.

No one had to teach us about fairness, even if we all have to be taught how to be fair. All of us have built into our natures a carefully calibrated sense of the patterns of the world and have determined that inasmuch as inhale leads to exhale, systole to diastole, good should beget good and bad should engender bad. We conclude that our actions can indeed be assessed by a paymaster who will determine how much we should have coming on the basis of what we have done. Nietzsche may wonder how this idea of good and bad and the system of recompense was introduced to the world, but it is to be found in one way or another in all religious systems and cultures, so it is not a function of any particular Western bias. Rather, it seems to be related to the way humans extract a sense of rhythm in the world and seek to establish the same kind of reciprocity within domains where it doesn't apply.

Henderson tells us that we can't get away from rhythm, and he also shows how we have tried to avoid the consequences of measure in some contexts and yet have depended on them in others. We deny the effects of the rhythms of the natural world upon us even as we ground our sense of fair play in the kind of reciprocity that is most easily discerned in our respiration, our walk, and our passage through the seasons. At the same time, we have no trouble relating to Dahfu's remarks about blows and can readily link them to Girard's mimetic desire:

> Man is a creature who cannot stand still under blows. Now take the horse—he never needs a revenge. Nor the ox. But man is a creature of revenges. If he is punished he will contrive to get rid of the punishment. When he cannot get rid of punishment, he heart is apt to rot from it. . . . Brother raises a hand against brother and son against father (how terrible!) and the father also against the son. And moreover it is a continuity-matter, for if the father did not strike the son they would not be alike. It is done to perpetuate similarity. Oh, Henderson, man cannot keep still under the blows. If he must, for the time, he will cast down his eyes and think in silence of the ways to clear himself of them. Those prime-eval blows everybody still feels. The first was supposed to be struck by Cain, but how could that be? In the beginning of time there was a

> hand raised which struck. So the people are flinching yet. All wish to rid themselves and free themselves and cast the blow upon others.[5]

I have taught *Henderson* and discussed this passage enough times over the years to recognize that if there is one thing my students will be able to relate to in the entire course it will be this. We all know what it feels like to be hit by blows that we believe to be unmerited, and we know what it is like to strike out at others even when the blow isn't really meant for them. Everyone understands that there is indeed a rhythm here, one that is as symmetrical and predictable as Hegel's and Girard's accounts suggest: it is one of the modulations of the natural rhythms within the human community.

Dahfu is no doubt right that neither horse nor ox needs revenge. *Ressentiment* is one of the uniquely human expressions of the rhythms of the world that is not to be found elsewhere, at least once we broaden our conception of it beyond Girard's, for he is content to see in mimetic desire only prestige rivalry, whereas resentment goes far deeper than that, as best expressed by the one who established its priority most powerfully in modern life, Nietzsche, who informs us that revenge is "man's revulsion against time and its 'It Was.'"[6] Girard is correct in observing that in many respects there is little to distinguish the mimetic rivalry one finds between two humans and two monkeys who have an interest in the same banana, but he loses the temporal dimension of the problem by focusing on the rivalry for its own sake. He is doubtless right that at a certain point the rivalry overtakes anything else, thereby burying the temporal problem in the background, but at the deepest level resentment is always a temporal concern.

If the origin of *ressentiment* is to be found in our revulsion against time and its "It Was," that is because we deeply resent having to pay for that which we had no hand in establishing, or that which we contributed to in ignorance of the effects it would have upon us. The "It was" in this respect embraces a multitude of human problems: having to suffer unfairly as a result of some social policy that discriminates against one on the basis of something that has nothing to do with that which one is deprived of; having to bear an accident of fate that has nothing to do with the social world—genetic forms of blindness, irreparable damage done through disease or even terminal illness; having to spend the rest of one's life at an economic disadvantage because when one was young and ignorant one thought it was smarter to leave high school than get one's diploma. The permutations are endless, and to some degree we all suffer under such burdens. If we don't all die "unfairly" as a result of something beyond our control, most of us know someone to whom we are devoted who has. If we have not been deprived of social prestige as a result of other people's resentment, we know someone who has, and everyone has felt unfairly penalized in the social world at one time or another. It is finally only a question of degree, of how blighted one's life has become as a result of discriminations that derive from *ressentiment* of one sort or another. All of us past the age of five have done things that have forever altered the course of our lives in ways that might not always be what we should have preferred, even if it takes us decades to discern this. We are in the midst of such blows and can never escape from them.

If resentment is finally a temporal problem, that is because in one way or another—excepting questions of an afterlife—each of us knows at some fundamental level that we have only this life at the moment to live, and when it is blighted, we know it cannot become unblighted again. Even if we believe in an afterlife, such a vision cannot specifically address the fact that our life on this planet will never be the same again. And as Nietzsche pointed out, in many respects the vision of another world is specifically designed as an instrument of revenge: we know our life is blighted here and now, but we assume that we shall therefore have a better life in the future than those whose lives are seemingly blissful on earth. The blot cannot be erased, the life is irrevocable, and the effects of our choices always come too late for us to be able to avoid their negative implications. We know that Henderson is right about rhythm because we have spent too much of our lives rhythmically responding to something we hoped wouldn't happen. The event occurs and undercuts our sense of what should be going on in our lives, so we undertake an action, rhythmically respond to the situation, in a way that we hope will cancel out the ill effects on our life.

One of the best metaphors for the rhythm of blows in this respect is the relatively recent innovation that will soon be appearing on cars and other noisy instruments that manages to induce silence by cancelling out the sound waves of the engine. Instead of trying to eliminate the noise of the engine itself, engineers design a counterwave to cancel out the wave of the engine. The result is silence, blessed silence. The rhythm of one wave blends into the other and there is peace. This is the same effect we constantly work for in our lives as we strive to eliminate the negative aspects of the "It Was" that continue to make noise in our lives. If we dropped out of school, we go back to school, thinking that one wave will cancel out the other. The difference, of course, is that things don't work in the human domain as they do at the level of sound waves: one act never cancels another out because they cannot occur at the same time. One can indeed go back to school and get one's degree, and one may indeed thereby achieve a better position and standard of living than one would if one hadn't done so, but the act still doesn't cancel the earlier one out. At the very least, time was lost suffering under the weight of unaccredited work, and the psychological effects of being caught in a regime not to one's liking with no future to it will never disappear, however much the degree can compensate in other ways. One loses the time one spent doing something one didn't want to do, and one loses the time that one invests in psychic worry about one's socioeconomic lot, something that will not go away once a better position is obtained.

If one wonders like Nietzsche how and why this sense of good and bad was introduced into the scheme of things, one can easily lose track of how fundamental resentment is to the species. It is intrinsically related to our self-conscious, temporal natures. That is precisely why the horse never needs a revenge: it doesn't have the kind of memory to link events to specific effects in the way that humans do. The horse doubtless has a memory that will help it avoid certain negative things, but it doesn't take on the specificity of human memory and lacks the density that prompts one to realize that the effects of events can never be undone. We respond to them in one way or another, and having done so, we have further written them into the scheme of our lives and into the unfolding of the universe. We know this, even if we bury the knowledge, and the horse does not, nor does the ox. Resentment is a function of our ongoing inevitable awareness that for all practical purposes this life occurs once and once only.

When my eight-year-old daughter complains about the lack of fairness in some sporting event at school whose outcome should have worked in her favor, she may not be protesting against the temporal loss involved in the situation. She may be more specifically responding to prestige rivalry. She should have won if things were judged fairly, and she was not; therefore, she has not achieved the recognition she deserves. In construing her woe in this way, she perhaps remains unaware of the fact that she has also been responding to the resentment that makes apparent to her that she will never have that opportunity again, but this is as much true of the situation as is the problem of rivalry. For even if she wins the same event on another occasion, it will be *on another occasion*, it will be a belated win, one that loses priority to the occasion on which she should have been able to achieve the recognition she thought she deserved. Even more, she may not realize that these resentful events accumulate in a life, may not know as Dahfu does that once the ring of blows is entered it becomes endless, and the wounds accumulate over time. Thus, she will not comprehend fully how after a certain number of blows she will better accommodate herself to the unfairness of things—she will learn how to express her resentment more appropriately in social situations, she will have mediated her desire through the clichés of good sportsmanship—nor will she properly understand that in some respects she will *never* sufficiently accommodate herself to the "slings and arrows of outrageous fortune" no matter how long she lives, that the wounds leave scars that add up to massive amounts of dulled tissue. She will have to be older before she arrives at a fuller understanding of the ways in which the discrete events that engender resentment become linked together over time: to call up one "unfair" blow is to conjure up all the others.

By the time a person achieves middle age, however, these things become clearer, even as the power of resentment grows with each year. For if there is a temporal loss with each perceived act of unfairness, there is an even more obvious temporal loss involved in having lived more than half of one's life. There can be no getting around the fact that much of the good will never come back as well. In youth one resents the bad that negatively affected particular outcomes in one's life; by middle age one resents the passage of many of the best moments of one's life: one's resentment grows more abstract because it finally becomes apparent that one's basic complaint is against life itself, where there are no second chances and no ways for us to escape from the rhythms that were established before we were born and into which we were assumed with all the other children who came into life at the same time. That is to say, one usually knows by middle age the rhythms that define the patterns of one's life, and although the measure is also that which provides the articulation of one's best moments, the very fact that it is for the most part unalterable is often more than individuals are willing to contemplate.

Even worse, one comes to realize that in the best of cases the rhythms that make up one's bad self will be carried on into the next generation. When one contemplates having children, one doesn't ask oneself which of one's bad features are going to be found in one's child. This is something that comes up only gradually as one notices that, yes, there's that feature appearing, and sure enough, she's got that one too. When one includes the intentional and unintentional blows that one inflicts upon the child as it develops, one begins to get a sense of the ways the rhythms of life play themselves out over and over again in a slightly different fashion. It *is* a continuity matter, as Dahfu says, and it is often done to promote similarity, but it is also true that much of the continuity and many of the similarities are not intentionally passed on at all. Life's rhythms, as manifested in the mixing of genes and the interactions of people, accomplish the task regardless of one's desires in this matter.

Dahfu explained that as a molding force, fear was second only to nature in its powers, and that is true because the rhythms of human interchange are so intertwined with the blows that appear regularly in everyone's life. "In the beginning of time there was a hand raised which struck. And so the people are flinching yet": this is the earthly dominion, to use Dahfu's language, and it is an integral part of things, however much we should wish it to be otherwise. One of the reasons we try to imagine an origin for the reign of blows, in our own lives or in general, is so that we can also imagine a way back before they began to fall upon us, but Dahfu has taken both origin and end out of the equation. The blows have always been with us because they are a product of the beginning of time, of self-consciousness, of history, of memory, and only an individual without these most fundamental human constituents would be able to live in a different kind of regime. Nietzsche provides a regulative measure of our commitment to revenge in his conception of the overman, that post-human who would be delivered from the effects of *ressentiment*, but this is for us no more than an ethical ideal, something to strive for in everyday life.

If we have a commitment at some basic level to notions of fair play that we can't seem to get beyond, and if that belief prompts us to imagine a paymaster who provides an exchange where everything finds its compensatory gesture, it is worth emphasizing once more that our contemplation of the accidents of life that modulate the rhythms of our existence must also include the good things that are unmerited. Henderson doesn't deserve his wealth and stature any more than he is responsible for all the woe in his life. He can no more take credit for his fortune than he can take the blame for his brother Dick's death. Yet he is committed to an economy in which he must wrestle with both as offshoots of his own choices, not because they were but because good and evil have been introduced into the origin of things, and we have yet to be able to establish a regime that would more carefully calibrate those things over which humans actually have some control and responsibility. We noted that Henderson's advantages caused him as many problems as the effects of his blows, that indeed many of the blows he passed on were a result of the fact that he couldn't accept the good fortune that he felt, justifiably, was unmerited. The psychic trauma his unmerited fortune caused him was also a result of a false economy, one that involved an artificial implementation of good and evil into a regime where it didn't belong.

Beyond the false imposition of values upon the inevitable flows in the rhythms of life, though, we must come to an understanding of the effects of unmerited good and bad fortune, and we have yet to do that. Nietzsche's conception of the overman, the human who can accept the notion of the eternal return, who would deliberately will everything in his or her life to return again and again forever exactly the way it has already happened, provides us with a vantage point on one hypothetical future, for it reminds us of the ways in which both the good and the bad accidents of fate are a function of the same rhythms and cannot be separated into different patterns. If it is good that one cannot get away from rhythm because it manifests the beauty of the world in our lives every day, it is bad that one cannot get away from it because it also produces the rhythms of our "bad self," of that product of the unmerited bad fortune that we accumulate over the years and harbor resentment over. They are part of the same pattern, and in order to embrace the powerful beauty of our lives, and of the rhythms themselves, we must embrace all the things we most want to escape from as well. The repetition of a person's bad self may be the worst rhythm there is, but it is one we have to live with and embrace as our own.

This is the ethical ideal that is implicit in all great religions, yet somehow it ends up being transformed into its opposite. One can assume without difficulty that the purpose of the Jesus who appears in the Bible is to provide the equivalent of Nietzsche's belated interpretation of him, an overman who through his actions manifests an attitude toward the rhythms of life that modulates the negative effects of *ressentiment* without becoming resentful himself. Jesus is precisely this kind of ideal, one who will absorb the blows of resentment around him without passing them on to others, one who will pass judgment on people on the basis of their resentment or lack thereof, one who compels others to focus on that which is worth attending to, the wonder of life, rather than on that which most humans are consumed by, the resentments that drive the social machines of which they are a part. He also demonstrates the great difficulty of doing so and the perilous possibilities: he receives the ultimate blow, death, because the resentment of the people is too much, because, driven by Girardian mimetic appropriation as they are, the people cannot bear that Jesus should live and allow his non-resentful ways to shame them so much they cannot look at themselves. Jesus must go so that they can live through their *ressentiment* without being publicly shamed by it.

Yet this same Jesus becomes the paymaster's son, the one who comes down to instruct the people in a different economy that fosters individual resentment rather than attempts to put it out of play. He becomes the balancer of books, the one who will establish another kingdom to rectify the unmerited blows we have received in this world. His lectures on the virtues of the poor and the children are translated into documents of revenge, examples of how those whose lives fall out in unfortunate ways will receive the Kingdom of God as their reward. The ethic that embodies a nonresentful approach to life ends up involving itself in a more elaborate scheme of resentment than the one that was in place before Jesus arrived on the scene. Now it may be that the regime of blows and resentment was not intrinsic to the ethic that Jesus sought to establish; it may be that this is the way the ethic was translated into practice by his followers because they were incapable of moving beyond their own deep resentments and thus could find no other way to apply his words about that which is good and that which is bad and about another Kingdom beyond the blows of resentment. And it may be that the rationalization of any charismatic leader's words inevitably becomes a manifestation of *ressentiment* regardless of whether it is intended to be so or not because the groups that support such figures invariably demand recompense for their woes, insist that whoever they give fealty to must also address their resentments, not by urging them to put them out of play but by assuring that the outcome of their lives will eventually be fair according to their own sense of what they deserve.

It is worth emphasizing that those who are most driven by *ressentiment* are often those who also have a high proportion of unmerited good fortune as well. The totally abject, those whose lives are overwhelmed by the misfortune of poverty and the blight of disease, don't have the energy for resentment. R*essentiment* tends to be more a function of the degree to which one also has had more than one's share of good fortune. It is not an accident, for example, that many of the fiercest resentments are to be found in those who have achieved the most. The classic examples would be artists and writers of one stripe or another who have achieved enough to establish some kind of reputation. After ten, twenty, or thirty years, however, they are not as famous as they think they should be, so they become consumed by *ressentiment.* Of course their resentment fails to take into account their gifts, doesn't question where the abilities to write or paint came from, or the opportunities to develop those gifts to their highest powers. It seldom occurs to those whose lives are filled with the poisons of resentment that much unmerited good fortune must have happened to them for them to have made it far enough in the social world to be resentful of their reputation in the first place—the scales of value come into play only *after* their gifts are in place. Only then do they measure what they have coming; only then do they begin to calibrate the world in terms of the economy of the paymaster and the fair play they think should rule the world.

Resentment can also be found in places where the gifts of life haven't been so liberally dispensed, the ghetto, for example, but it is hard to imagine entire ghettos being driven by seething resentment every day. On the contrary, here too it is usually those who are more gifted than others who are most resentful, those whose sharp mind has not found a fitting use or whose canny sense of human relations has only found an outlet in scams and crime. If everyone in the ghetto has cause for resentment, and if many feel resentment on a regular basis, still few lives are directly driven by the forces of *ressentiment*. The others may express their buried sense of the unfairness of their lives through collective violence like a riot, but otherwise they will simply try to get on with their lives as best as possible. There is no law of nature that declares that those with the greatest gifts are also the most resentful, for one's sense of resentment is based not only on a notion of fair play but also on one's willingness to see things clearly, to be able to calibrate with accuracy the gifts and misfortunes that have come one's way, and many people are not sincere enough in their evaluations—or clear enough in their considerations of their relations to the world—to be able to measure such things with accuracy. Often those who pity themselves have little reason for either their pity or the consequent self-righteousness. But resentment does tend to find its most powerful expressions in those whose gifts are also beyond the ordinary.

The human desire for fair play is deep-seated. Indeed, we could say that it is a function of being human. Whether that means that good and evil should be introduced into the scheme of things from the very beginning is another matter. But it is clear that human beings measure the flows of the world from their locations within them, and they are aware at some level of the temporal nature of their lives—and hence their brevity—and thus they gauge the degree to which they have the life they deserve or instead are forced to live through more woe than they feel should accrue to them. The standards we apply to our lives in such cases may be sincere, or they may be developed out of self-pity, but either way they have no useful value in the end even if we cannot wholly escape from them. Confucius in his wisdom may be able to calibrate precisely that which he should achieve as a result of his gifts and that which has come his way through unmerited misfortune and establish a formula that determines whether he has been treated fairly or not, but he does not do that. Thus, the answer to resentment is not to be honest in one's examination of the gifts and misfortunes in one's life, for that standard itself is the problem. No amount of honesty in such assessments can get away from the fact that the standard of fair play is inevitably an ethical system based on *ressentiment.* Even if one concludes that on the whole one's gifts have outweighed one's misfortunes, one is still gauging life by a standard that has no applicability and that can only be pernicious in the long run. The problem is that all the greatest human figures have invariably told us in one way or another that the standard of fair play is an insufficient mark of the rhythms of the universe and the appropriateness of human action within them, yet humans cannot get away from their commitment to a notion of fairness regardless of the values that are established by those who know the fundamentally flawed nature of systems based on the poisons of resentment.

❦

The imperatives of fair play and the need to go beyond them as a measure of the value of human life can be found in all the sacrificial scenes of literature. Jesus, we could say, provided us with an ethic that sought to move beyond resentment, and the result was that he became the magnet for other people's resentment: he who seeks to put an end to the regime of *ressentiment* is put to an end himself. If Girard is right to note that there is a mimetic "mechanism" at the heart of human existence that demands sacrificial victims in order to dissipate the poisons of resentment that build up in everyday social life, he fails adequately to note how many times the victim is precisely the one who is calling for an end to the powers of resentment. He makes a distinction between the non-resentful regime of Jesus and other sacrificial figures, but he too easily lumps all the other victims into two categories: the anonymous victims that can bear the collective guilt and resentment of the people precisely because they have no name and status that would make them stand out, and the figures at the top of the hierarchy, the kings and queens whose sacred status seems to exempt them from the laws of resentment until the poisons within their social regimes build to a point that they all coalesce on the victimage of the sacred king or queen. But there are many kings and queens who are deserving of their fates, many who abused power and failed to note that the whole point of their sacred status was to be above the reign of blows down below them. Like the robes we dispense to Supreme Court Justices to cover their *ressentiment* in impartiality, the sacred figures are supposed to be beyond the resentments of the people either because they are wise or because their status presumably allows them to have everything they want and thus provides a context in which they can distribute gifts to themselves and save the misfortunes for other people's lives.

The sacred individual is supposed to be beyond good and evil because he or she is not involved in the social resentments that drive those below the person, and some sacred figures are indeed capable of taking up that role. These individuals end up suffering the same fate as those who cannot escape from their resentments even when they are given sacred status, but we need to note that they pay the sacrificial price for a different reason: they must die because they remind the people that they too must move beyond good and evil, and when the people fail miserably to do so, they must kill the one who exemplifies their failures. The other kind of sacred figure must die because he or she failed to live up to the necessity of being beyond good and evil: the figure's regime is driven by resentment and by the unfair distribution of good and bad fortune, so the people must kill the person because he or she has failed to put an end to the reign of blows from which we all want to escape even as we cannot because we are unwilling to abrogate the standard of fair play.

Two figures who manifest the sacred and pay the price for it are Baby Suggs and Dahfu. Baby Suggs had a great heart and a concomitant desire to do something for others, and she had the stature in the community she achieved because she quite literally brought people back to life. She possessed grace because she was able to demonstrate to people that resentment was not a sufficient organizing principle in life, because it destroyed the life to which it purported to bring order. If Baby Suggs exhorts her flock to love their flesh, that is because they have "Flesh that needs to be loved" and because "Yonder they do not love your flesh."[7] These two statements are essentially linked for the people, but not just because they are blacks who have known slavery, although that is certainly reason enough. Those statements take their force not because whites would sooner see blacks dead than to love them in any way, but rather because in the social world no one is loved as he or she should be. No matter how deserving of love one is, one will not find fitting recompense in the social world, for that is not what it provides. It is easy enough to focus on the fact that Baby Suggs refuses to exclude the evil other here, that she rhythmically emphasizes the need for the people to love their flesh even as she asserts that their flesh will not be loved by the whites. One could construe this as an argument for resentment: you should love your flesh *because* the whites will not. One could even be more honest and go beyond racial barriers and say: you should love your flesh because virtually no one, white *or* black, will love it. One can read Baby Suggs' remarks this way, in which case resentment becomes the focal point rather than the need to love one's own gifts and one's own precious body.

One can also construe Baby Suggs' appeal as a simple statement of fact, one that doesn't depend on feeding the resentment that the worst demagogues always make use of. Instead of saying that they should love their flesh because the whites will not, Baby Suggs could be telling the community that they should love their flesh because that is their obligation. The whites don't owe them that love any more than the people in their own community do. We may all feel as though we deserve everyone's love, at least until we demonstrate our incapacity for it, but there is nothing in the scheme of things that makes this a law of the universe. It is function of our sense of fair play that if we love others they should in turn love us. Baby Suggs is in effect taking issue with that ethic here. She is asserting that the people should love themselves because there is no point in depending on someone else to do so. So one could accuse her of fostering resentment by telling people to love their flesh out of resentment over the fact that white people will never do so; or one can argue that the point is not to love one's flesh out of resentment but out of a more profound necessity: one must learn to cherish the gifts one has even in the face of the unmerited misfortunes that have also come one's way.

Nevertheless, it is important that those "Out yonder" in Baby Suggs' speech are the whites, not simply other humans. There is resentment to be found in the sermon even if it is not necessarily the point of it, and if Baby Suggs is finally crushed under the weight of the events of the novel, that is in part because of her resentment of the whites. When she turns on life, she does so because there is nothing of value that the whites cannot ruin. And while this may be true, it ignores the fact that it applies equally to the blacks in the novel, who do not seek to do Baby Suggs in because they are tired of her sermons that foster resentment of the whites. They cut her as they do because they are resentful of her grace, of her life, of her love of her body and this world. They cannot bear to see such grace because they cannot find sufficient place for it in their own lives.

And Baby Suggs has told them that it is their responsibility to do so. She doesn't tell them that *she* will love their flesh. That is not her affair. It is *their* business to love what they have, and when they fail to live up to that ethic, the only thing they can do is eliminate the one who manifests their failures to them merely by living and being who she is. If they don't have the strength and the courage to find the grace in their own lives, they must get rid of the grace in Baby Suggs that shows them what they don't have and demonstrates their lack of courage to them. Jesus may have exhorted the people not to hide their light under a basket, but Baby Suggs comes to learn that one should shine only as brightly as those in one's midst are capable of bearing. Otherwise one becomes an image of the sacred and runs the risk of being sacrificed to the other's resentment and sense of inadequacy.

Dahfu likewise demonstrates what happens to the sacred when the individual seeks to implement a non-resentful regime in the midst of a universe that is driven by the forces of *ressentiment*. He regularly attempts to make accommodations between the old universe of resentment and the new one that is dedicated to the beauty of the species rather than its poisons, but he doesn't find a way of successfully bridging the gap between the two universes. His goodness could only compete with the will to power of the Bunam if the people were on his side, but the Bunam has managed to play on the superstitious fears of the community by emphasizing that Dahfu's new regime is based on the evil presence of Atti the lion in the basement of the palace. In demonizing the lion, and thereby Dahfu as well, the Bunam succeeds in unsettling the people, in making them concerned about the disposition of their own lives. They become worried about whether the bad fates will visit themselves on the kingdom as a result of Dahfu's insistence on keeping the evil lion in the palace.

In the novel we don't in fact see much of "the people" at all, so not much more can be said about how they contribute to Dahfu's death. But we do know that the old universe is driven by superstitions that exist precisely to guarantee the kind of fair play that the people so assiduously seek in their lives. And we also know that like every other kingdom on the planet, the Wariri one is driven by the powers of revenge. This is most apparent in the ceremony through which Henderson becomes the rain king, the collective efforts of the people to sway the natural world in the right direction by ritual gestures to the forces of nature. They have placed their images of the gods out on the playing field, and the central event of the ritual is predicated on their movement of the statues:

> Several men in black plumes, like beggarly bird men . . . began to lift the covers from the gods. Disrespectfully, they pulled them away. This irreverence was no accident, if you get what I mean. It was done to raise a laugh, and it did exactly that. These bird or plume characters, encouraged by the laughter, started to perform burlesque antics; they stepped on the feet of the statues, and bowled some of the smaller ones over and made passes at them, mockeries, and so on. The dwarf was set on the knees of one goddess and he rocked the crowd with laughter by pulling his lower lids down and sticking out his tongue, making like a wrinkled lunatic. The family of gods, all quite short in the legs and long in the trunk, was very tolerant about these abuses. . . . [T]hey had dignity—mystery; they were after all the gods, and they made the awards of fate. They ruled the air, the mountains, fire, plants, cattle, luck, sickness, clouds, birth, death. Damn it, even the squattest, kicked over onto his belly, ruled over something. The attitude of the tribe seemed to be that it was necessary to come to the gods with their vices on display, as nothing could be concealed from them anyway by ephemeral men. I grasped the idea, but basically I thought it was a big mistake. (180-81)

Henderson may have been told that the tribe felt it necessary to come to the gods with its vices on display, but more is involved in this ceremony than such a frank admission. The situation defies Western logic, for the people clearly perform the acts of the ceremony to get the favor of the gods, yet at the same time the deliberate attempt to move each god in accord with their own needs manifests a direct effort to manipulate the same gods. They figuratively move the clouds over the mountain so that water will come from the skies.

Even more, the people beat up on and abuse the gods, expressing the blows of *ressentiment* in a blatant fashion that astonishes Henderson, who expects these figures to be treated with respect. The Wariri, however, are understandably angry with the gods for having so much control over their lives and are resentful of the fact that rain has not been forthcoming. The fertility of the tribe and the surrounding region depends on the rain that the gods are capriciously withholding, and the arbitrariness of fate so rankles the people that they have violence against their gods built into the same ceremony through which they are supposed to demonstrate their fealty toward them. Obeisance, manipulation, and fierce resentment permeate the ceremony to reveal the core emotions that drive Dahfu's people, and as highest representative of the gods in the land, he too stands ready to absorb the same blows should the lives of the Wariri go in a direction to which they are opposed. Bellow's masterful job with the rain ceremony, in all of its comic splendor, places before the reader the same emotional brew that drives all social systems, the blend of reverence, fear, hatred, desire for control and overpowering resentment that coalesces when a crisis appears and the life of the community is threatened. How can Dahfu presume to think that he will be able to overcome the forces of this old universe?

Henderson is a comic novel, but still it depends on facing this question, much as *Beloved* requires a similar confrontation with resentment, for even if Sethe and Denver are taken back into the community at the end of the novel and the ghost of Beloved has been purged, still we know that the community would only take them back on its own terms, when it had found the proper condition of abjection in 124 to merit an act of kindness on its part. Whatever lip service Ella and the others pay to the need to do a good deed for the people of 124, one cannot escape the fact that they have had many years to do such a good deed, and the transformation of the ghost into bodily form is not a sufficient explanation for their reluctance to move until the climax of the novel. At the center of the community is a core of cruelty that is finally covered over by the good act of rescuing Sethe and Denver, but it cannot be totally disguised.

Likewise, Henderson heads back home with all sorts of symbolic gestures in tow. He has the baby lion as a symbolic Dahfu to convince himself that the spirit of Dahfu lives. He meets up with a young Persian boy with whom he dances around the ice in a celebration of life. And the novel itself ends in Newfoundland, suggesting that a noble transformation has indeed occurred. Henderson will defy the temporal resentment that declared him too old to go to medical school and will become a doctor and bring life and health to others. Well and good, and just what we'd expect from a comic novel. Dahfu's spirit must live on, for there are always those who will declare the essential need for humans to put off their resentment and embrace life fully in spite of the woes that are attached to it. But if some find Dahfu's own inability to keep from passing on a blow to Henderson to be a problem—something that seems to me only a manifestation of the fact that he is a human and not a god—the resentment that drives his kingdom is far more troubling. For the most ironic fact of the novel is that Henderson goes to Africa to escape the poisons of his own society, yet he ends up being dealt a serious blow by the same poisons as they manifest themselves in the lives of the Wariri. True, by changing his context he can observe the full effects of *ressentiment* in a way that he cannot when he is in the midst of his own biases: the rain ceremony reveals things to him precisely because it is not a ceremony he gives any weight to. He can thus see the creaky machinery of resentment at the center of it in a way he would be unable to in related events within his own culture.

But if society is what gets Henderson every time, and if his fundamental problem in life is his incapacity to deal sufficiently with his resentment when it comes into contact with the equivalent pool of resentment in his society, he no more moved away from these problems by going to Africa than he did in taking on the role of Sungo, the Rain King who dispenses fertility throughout the land. For that which gives life also brings death, and that which brings rain also withholds it, building up fires of resentment in those whose lives are blighted by their lack of fertility. If Henderson learns about the crucial necessity of keeping the blows to himself, he also comes to understand their omnipresence throughout the human community. He faces formidable odds in his new life not only because the repetitions of his bad self have grown so numerous that they will be most difficult to root out but also because he will continue to find himself in the midst of a sea of blows regardless of his attitude toward resentment, and as Dahfu pointed out, that is a dangerous position to be in. Any regime of social fair play into which humans can imagine themselves must come to grips with this very formidable—perhaps insuperable—problem.

From another angle the problem of the reciprocities of *ressentiment* manifests itself in an individual way in the figure who has done most to make us aware of the furies of resentment, Nietzsche, for however much he understood the need to move beyond the *ressentiment* that drives human social systems, and however much he was capable at his best of embracing the world fully without resentment, he was not always at his best any more than we are, and he was therefore also a man of seething resentments. How else would he understand so well its power over us if it didn't have power over him as well? So we find that Nietzsche cannot keep the dogs of resentment at bay. They hound him incessantly, and he doesn't know how to stop their barking. Thus, in *Ecce Homo* we find repeated remarks like the following:

> Then there is the gruesome silence one hears all around one. Solitude has seven skins; nothing penetrates them anymore. One comes to men, one greets friends—more desolation, no eye offers a greeting. At best, a kind of revolt. Such revolts I experienced, very different in degree

> but from almost everybody who was close to me. It seems nothing offends more deeply than suddenly letting others feel a distance; those *noble* natures who do not know how to live without reverence are rare.
>
> Thirdly, there is the absurd sensitivity of the skin to small stings, a kind of helplessness against everything small. This seems to me to be due to the tremendous squandering of all defensive energies which is a presupposition of every *creative* deed, every deed that issues from one's most authentic, inmost, nethermost regions. Our *small* defensive capacities are thus, as it were, suspended; no energy is left for them.[8]

In Nietzsche's psychic economy, the great expenditures of energy that creative work requires leave one with no energy left over to fend off the small stings of resentment that bite one every day. Thus one finds oneself susceptible to this "absurd sensitivity of the skin": it cannot bear the stings, is driven nearly crazy with the little nibbles that everyone wants to take. Regardless of whether this sensitivity comes from having exhausted one's energy or from some other phenomenon, Nietzsche has not been able to rise above the stings of resentment he feels every day. Indeed, his distress at his inability to rise above the pettiness of humans in the face of greatness rankles at least as much as the stings themselves. Logically speaking we should think that the master of the forces of resentment would himself be able to rise above them, but he is perhaps even more susceptible to the bite of *ressentiment* than we are because he has no energy left to defend himself from the blows that others mete out. He finds himself helpless in the face of the stings and doesn't know what to do about it.

It is worth emphasizing that this passage on the stings of resentment comes in the middle of a discussion of what Nietzsche calls the "*rancune* of what is great."[9] This rancor is established in the passage as though it is an inevitable force in human life, a necessary part of the rhythms of life. It may be that every great deed extracts something from the person who performs it. It may be that all great creative acts turn on their creator in some fashion, if only because they exhaust the person and thus make the individual susceptible to forces he or she ordinarily would be able to deal with without a thought. In Nietzsche's own economy the contrast is usually between *strong* and *weak*: when he is strong, Nietzsche is capable of shrugging off the stings of resentment with ease—they mean nothing to him. But when he has been weakened by the great energy required in his creative enterprises, he becomes consumed by these stings and exacerbates the problem by turning on himself because he finds himself incapable of dealing with them. There is an echo of the Hegelian dialectic here, for the strong are made weak in this way, at least as far as Nietzsche is concerned, and their energies are dispersed by the weak whose millions of tiny small stings can sap the energy of even the greatest human being.

The stings that bedevil Nietzsche are related to Hegel in another way because the fundamental problem he faces is that his works are ignored. He has the need for recognition, he wants to achieve a position of mastery, yet no one acknowledges his existence. He faces nothing but gruesome silence in his personal and his creative life. No one reads his books, and those who do are resentful because of the distance they find in them, because of the chilliness of the view that is demanded of them. Without the recognition that Nietzsche feels he deserves, he becomes consumed by the countless tiny, thoughtless acts that define everyday life. These stings are beneath his dignity to acknowledge, yet acknowledge them he must. He cannot escape their force precisely because he knows he *deserves* recognition: he has made the journey into the underworld and come back alive with the wisdom to distinguish the essential need joyously to affirm life in the midst of its horrors and to put off resentment, and yet he is greeted by the silence of resentment everywhere he goes. This is not fair, it is not fitting, and even though Nietzsche himself knows better than to assume that life should be fair—or that good and evil should be introduced into the subject in any way—still he cannot keep himself from doing just that. At his best he can be contemptuous of the error humans make when they moralize about everything and demand that the paymaster come to the window and dispense favors in accord with the rules of fair play; at his worst, tired out by the acts of a great writer, he can no more escape from the desire for the paymaster than anybody else. Fair play matters even to those who realize the absurdity of assuming that the world is constituted in a way that would have anything to do with such a sentimental notion.

So Nietzsche, surrounded by the chilly Alps, taken over by the distance of greatness that his own work imposes on him, having to suffer the silence that comes to one who contemplates the nature of things from the heights of the world, full of confidence that his work is the most significant since Plato's, is consumed with *ressentiment* even as he lectures us against it. As a molding force, the rhythms of resentment are powerful indeed. None can escape them, and few have found ways of absorbing the blows that accrue to one regardless of one's status or good fortune, and that may in some respects accrue more to those who have achieved major status and have had the best fortune one can imagine. If humans have a deep-seated desire for fair play, as each of us defines that term from our own necessarily self-interested perspective, then each of us necessarily is driven by resentment, for the one is an expression of the other. Our desire for fair play doesn't come first and lead to resentment. No, resentment leads to our desire for fair play, which in turn leads to the establishment of a regime of personal and social structures that are designed to go at least some way toward instituting the possibility of fair play. But always only the possibility, for even the most benign of social systems and the most fortunate of lives are forced to deal with accidents of fate that can overwhelm the fragile tissue of rules that any system of fair play must work through. The desire for fair play, driven by a rancor for what is great that will not acknowledge its own name, is that which introduces the paymaster into the equation and that which continues to insist that he must exist.

For me, Nietzsche's great inability to escape from the stings of resentment is a cautionary tale that is as important on one side as his declaration to love one's fate is on the other. If we are to embrace our lives so thoroughly that we would gladly live them over and over again an infinite number of times, if we are fully capable of imagining a human who can turn the "It Was" into a "Thus I Willed It," we must also see that human in the light of a man with absurdly thin skin who cannot escape the small stings of life. Not that the two go together, but rather that the regulative impulse of the one must be qualified by the regulative impulse of the other. To be human is to be stung, to be hit, to suffer within the regime of blows, and this is an inescapable fact that is by no means exclusively located within the social world. If resentment most powerfully expresses itself in the endless dialectic between master and slave as each seeks the recognition of the other or in the endless prestige rivalry that creates a fundamental mimetic pattern through which we all live too much of our lives, still resentment itself is a function of processes that are wholly natural. The only thing humans bring to them is their sense of time, their awareness of the "It Was" that invariably limits and yet also makes possible everything a human can do in a short, all too short lifetime.

Ressentiment is not an addition to human nature, not a supplement, but a fundamental condition of life as humans know it, and there is no dialectic we know of at the moment that will help us escape from this fact. Fair play is an idea that has value when it comes to imagining social structures into which we should like to move, but it can only be destructive as a measure of an individual human life as conceived by the occupant of that life. There is no particular human measure that can adequately establish a regime of fair play that would properly account for each individual's own complex sense of his or her location on the planet because only the individual knows what is fitting and proper for the specific circumstances of his or her life. If our lives are not solipsistically contained by the hoops of ego, still they are constrained by the fact that their individidual specificity is such that no other person who ever lived could have a sense of the dense fabric of experience, memory and capability that each of us is. More crudely put, one could say that it is absurd to imagine fair play within the world because each of the billions of human inhabitants imagines that fair play according to the specifics of his or her own life whereas the universe as a whole cares not a bit for the specifics of any of those lives, and there is no way to bridge the gap between those two views. Still, we seem unable to move away from an unceasing engagement with the world on the basis of how well or poorly it has dispensed its gifts to us.

Perhaps the best way of looking at the burdens that resentment and fair play place upon us is to forget the Hegelian imperatives of recognition and ignore the Girardian mechanism of mimetic rivalry and return to Dahfu's simpler statement that when a human cannot find a way of getting rid of punishment that seems undeserved, "his heart is apt to rot from it." This is not a scientific formulation, but what it expresses is in some respects more important precisely because it deals with the psychological burdens humans feel in the midst of their resentments. It makes no sense that one's heart should rot if the blows of resentment are not passed on, no sense at all. Why should our heart, our great heart that is capable of manifesting the grace of Baby Suggs and the wisdom of Dahfu, *rot* if we cannot find an outlet for the blows that have been passed on to us? Why can't we simply concede that life involves blows that are meted out without regard for who is deserving and who is not? *Rot* is such an appropriate word for the condition because it is as though a disease overtakes us when we can find no way of dealing with that which has unfairly come our way, because when we can't successfully deal with these blows they do indeed consume our energy and destroy our motivation for living. At best they turn us into nihilists and at worse they make us turn our head to the wall and refuse entry to life altogether.

We consume ourselves when we can't deal with the blows, and yet there is no satisfactory way of handling them either. Henderson's fictional career is fitting testimony to the human dilemma because he has tried out all the possibilities and found each of them problematic. Most obviously, he has discovered that passing on the blows to others only leads to death and destruction, whether it be the unintentional death of Miss Lenox, the spiteful cruelty he shows to his wives, or the deliberate degradations he takes up in his life to demean the unmerited fortune he has come into or the even more deliberate degradations of his human gifts and of life itself. These blows do not work. They do not satisfy his craving for a world that addresses his "I want," and they fail to make him feel better about himself. On the contrary, they make him feel worse, so they only add to the burden of the bad self from which he is so desperately trying to escape.

Henderson has also tried to use up the energies of resentment on inanimate objects, but that hasn't worked either. He dispenses with this possibility early on in the novel:

> What do you do with yourself if you have a temperament like mine? A student of the mind once explained to me that if you inflict your anger on inanimate things, you not only spare the living, as a civilized man ought to do, but you get rid of the bad stuff in you. This seemed to make good sense, and I tried it out. I tried with all my heart, chopping wood, lifting, plowing, laying cement blocks, pouring concrete, and cooking mash for the pigs. On my own place, stripped to the waist like a convict, I broke stones with a sledgehammer. It helped, but not enough. Rude begets rude, and blows, blows; at least in my case; it not only begot but it increased. Wrath increased with wrath. So what do you do with yourself? (23)

What indeed does one do with oneself? Henderson establishes that hitting inanimate things, passing on the blows to non-living tissue, is no more a solution than striking out at humans. Wrath increases with the expression of wrath. Blows lead to more blows. The repetition of a man's bad self repeats itself ever more insistently every time it comes back. Any attempt to displace these resentful energies onto things that will not feel the pain of them seems as doomed to fail as any other possible solution.

So we are left with the need to keep them to ourselves, but we know that what Dahfu said seems to be the case: if we cannot find a way of passing on the blow, our hearts are apt to rot from the effects of keeping it to ourselves. We *must* find a way of keeping the blows, yet human nature loses its grace, its greatness of heart, when it can find no way to express the negative energies that build up within it. These human imperatives account for the great struggles in life even as they explain the smallest ones as well. They embrace our great fear of death and our distress at the rapidity of life even as they account for the many little acts of resentment through which we seek to contain or get rid of the "bad self" that always threatens to rot away our good self. Whatever dynamic is in play here, it cannot be wholly accounted for by anything other than literature because no philosophical or theological system can adequately capture the nature of the word *rot* as it relates to the self-destruction we always fear any more than it can properly account for the word *beauty* as it manifests itself in the midst of the rot we always remain concerned with.

❦

The rhythm of blows, the dynamic of resentment, is in the end not simply an unfortunate part of the human condition, nor is it an element of social life that can be rooted out with the proper system of government, although some governments are better than others at mitigating the forces of *ressentiment* as they express themselves in the social world. Resentment is nothing more or less than a regulative force within the human world and an inevitable part of the good, even if most often its manifestations are contrary to our sense of what is fitting. Just as the fissures along the tectonic plates build up pressures that must eventually give way to shocks and earthquakes, so too do the patterns of humans create tensions that accumulate and create their own kind of shocks, whether they be the peaceful overthrow of a government, a riot that causes great damage, or a falling out between friends that comes about as a result of a small thing that finally leads the manifold and increasing differences between the two to make an ongoing relationship impossible. In each case resentment inevitably plays a part, and one thus comes to learn about one's powers by experiencing such tectonic shifts in small and large ways.

If the regulative force of *ressentiment* is the third good, that doesn't mean that we should choose to allow our sense of good to be determined by it. Rather, it is a regulative force precisely to the extent that it addresses the effects of human lives in which the first two goods are not adequately pursued, though even in cases where they are, the accidents of life can bring on the furies of resentment at any time. Those who live by the gauge of the first two goods, who assess their lives in terms of the aesthetic imperatives to be found in a sincere investigation of things and who attend to the normative good as it applies to their practice, also suffer the inevitable strains of being self-conscious creatures in a world with more than its share of woe, and so there is always a residue of resentment in them. It is impossible to live free of resentment, inconceivable to do so in the human domain, and the small stings of life thus remain present even if unthematized. As a result, a trauma or unexpected event that reverses the flow of one's life in unpleasant ways can bring those resentments to the fore much as a single incident can spark many people to riot. The practice of the first two goods is never a guarantee that the force of the third will not come into play, for it is always in the wings.

To be more precise, we could say that resentment is more than in the wings: it is attached to everything we do like the spores of a mold that always threaten to get out of hand and cover the entire fruit. Every event of our lives takes place in time, each one is unrecoverable and nonrepeatable, and the stamp of time has built into it the fury of resentment. It may be silly for us to develop a grudge against "life" because it won't allow us to repeat things and because it goes by too quickly and doesn't give us the opportunity to do everything we want to do, but many people do indeed hold such a grudge while many others are always close to such a threshold and go over it at times. Regardless of how appropriate one finds the unfolding of life to be, no matter how much one sees that things could not be otherwise and that the richness of life is a function of its nonrepeatability and even its woes, one can never get past the fact that it can't be done again, that youth doesn't return, that middle age will go as well, that finally one is bonded onto the universe in such dispersed ways that one cannot be readily located at all. There is a sadness to all this that cannot be wished away by benign sayings or stoic acceptance, and that sadness is a part of the economy of life. It is always capable of festering into something more, into resentment, into the force of an act that deliberately brings down the pillars of the temple out of a sense of outrage at the limits of life.

Individuals can face their sadness, they can live off of hatred of their temporal nature, or they can practice deliberate avoidance of the subject in ways large and small. It is easy to hide from things, easier still these days to cover up problems with cosmetics of various sorts, ranging from a deliberately superficial life to one that literally covers up the effects of time in a futile effort to run from them. We know that such effects will eventually come to the fore and have their day, just as we have come to think along with Freud that when the repressed returns, it returns with greater intensity. We assume that the more an individual hides from the sadness of life, the more likely it is that he or she will suffer greater backlash from the rhythm of resentment in the end. When the forces that are measured by time accumulate enough to shock one into an understanding of what it means to be living tissue, the reaction can only intensify to the degree that one has been holding off such an awareness. But regardless of one's approach to the sadness of life, resentment is as much a part of human flesh as is water.

Nietzsche's ethical imperative was to love one's fate, to will it all again and again exactly as it was, to be delivered from revenge and turn the "It Was" into "Thus I Willed It," and these are fitting tests of character that assess life in terms of the aesthetic good. Everything is indeed as it should be, and how could we do otherwise that celebrate it as it is? But Nietzsche also knew how formidable a task he had set for humans. He thought it was possible to move from man to the last man to the overman, but he held out no timetable for such an event, and as we saw with the small stings of his own life, he was hardly the overman himself. The ethical imperative is a regulative idea rather than a currently imaginable scenario, and in the end one might question whether it is imaginable in any kind of future we might conjure. Whether it is or not, though, is less important than the question of the degree to which it is a fitting measure of the ethos into which we as a species ought to move. With billions and billions of people on the planet and billions more ready to make their appearance, we need to have some sense of the relationship between resentment and *amor fati.* We need to know whether Nietzsche's pithy expressions of hope for the species will work for us a hundred years after he uttered them.

It would be hard to argue with the logic of *amor fati,* the need to love one's fate, for who would want thoroughly to dislike the life they have? Of course we should love our fate and embrace it with all the intensity we can muster. But we must also question the relationship between this assertion and the great numbers of humans whose lives are defined by abject squalor. Should they too love their fates? Should we be content to love our fate in the midst of a world that makes such love impossible for the vast majority of humans? Should we, like Nietzsche, embrace an elitism that effectively eliminates from our purview the billions who suffer so much that *amor fati* could be little more than a sick joke? There is nothing within Nietzsche's work to suggest that one's fate also means accepting the barbarities of one's social system. On the contrary, one has to imagine that Nietzsche was driven by the impulse to reform human behavior, and there are many things that are presently a part of our fate that we shouldn't assume as inevitable aspects of the way things are. Social systems can be changed, and we should seek to alter their activities to bring them more in accord with the good as we construe it.

Nietzsche doesn't disallow efforts at social change, but he does tend to assume, much as Confucius does, that all such efforts begin with the individual. If one loves one's fate, that in itself has effects upon the social world that will lead others to adopt the same practice, and in theory the chain of events that follows thus works for the improvement of society. As Confucius believes that everything depends on a sincere investigation into the nature of things, out of which comes personal order, domestic order, social order and world order, so too Nietzsche's *amor fati* can be a fitting ethical criterion through which social change is imagined. And there is likewise no reason that one's conception of one's fate couldn't involve more assiduous and deliberate work within society to bring about positive change. Even then, aside from any tendency toward sentimentality, the love of one's fate must be involved with the billions whose fates are not loved and not worth loving. And the billions without a lovable fate are inevitably part of the resentment that shadows life, the crushing weight of historical effects that has engendered a great many people but nowhere near enough lives that are worth living. In the abstract, we may think that even the starving person in a third-world slum should embrace his fate, but in practice this is an evasion of the very nature of the word *fate*. That which has been dispensed to the majority of the people in the world may not be sufficient to embrace, as even Nietzsche would perhaps agree. This doesn't eliminate the force of the idea of *amor fati*, but it does show that in the best of cases our lives cannot escape from the shadow of resentment, even as we embrace and celebrate that which we have.

More difficult problems present themselves when we think of the need to turn the "It Was" into "Thus I Willed It."

Most importantly, we need to face the question of the will, a notion that is in some respects fatally essential to Nietzsche's conception of things. It is worth recalling that Nietzsche's other fundamental expression of resentment was his hope that "Man be *delivered* from revenge,"[10] for the word *delivered* suggests that something other than will is involved. The statement that we should turn the "It Was" into "Thus I Willed It" assumes contrarily that we can indeed will it. Nietzsche's thought is caught in this bind, for on the one hand the *delivered* of the one statement suggests that any such change is outside of questions of will whereas the other statement reduces the imperative almost exclusively to a question of human capacity. Nietzsche himself oscillated between a vision that was grounded in will and one that saw will as a fiction along with the other self-conceptions through which we have created the delusions of autonomy and control upon which the Western scheme of things is based. But the will does not suffice. We cannot assume that we are capable of willing a transformation of the "It Was" into a "Thus I willed it" because the only act of will we can imagine that would cover this terrain is that which we call *repression*, and that human function has no more to do with the will than does embracing one's fate. We can repress the "It Was" and assert that we have willed it instead, but the deliberate imposition of human will into a context in which it obviously has no place can only be seen as self-deceit. The fact is that we *didn't* will the "It Was," and it therefore does no good even as a regulative principle to think of our relationship to it in that way. To do so is only to indulge in a fiction whose value is purely delusionary in nature. However much it sounds perfectly appropriate for us to turn the "It Was" into "Thus I willed it," that is not a fitting expression of how to achieve a love of our fate.

The will is a fiction we created to imagine a way out of the impasses of the past as they impinge upon our lives. It is a function we conjured to allow us the psychic space to think of a world that wasn't overrun by that which has already been done and can never be undone, and as such it is so thoroughly implicated in the resentment that Nietzsche wants to will away with it that it hopelessly contaminates any attempt to love one's fate. Part of this problem concerns the fact that it is inconceivable for us to imagine a non-resentful human, but the larger problem is the word *will* itself, for it covers a space that doesn't exist, fills up a gap that cannot be filled, overcomes an impediment in our way that cannot be surmounted. Strictly speaking, there is no such thing as the will. It no more helps us get through the difficulties of the day than it allows us to transform the past into something we want to embrace. It conjures acts of power over the elements of life that humans simply don't have and thereby contributes to the false notions of control that so many depend on to get through their everyday struggles.

We can say that the ethical ideal is predicated on accepting our fate *as though* we willed it ourselves, but that leaves the same objection: even as a fiction that dirty word *will* sticks out as hopelessly inappropriate to what is at stake. Certainly we have to think of our lives in a specific way in order to be able to love our fates. We have to be able to address the resentments of life and our relationship to our temporal natures in order to see that everything is as perfect as it can be and our lives are therefore exactly as they should be. But even assuming we can do so, this is not an act of will but rather a willingness to see things as they are. It depends on Confucian *sincerity* and not on will. We don't will ourselves to see the world aesthetically; we find ourselves convinced of the fittingness of such a view. At the same time, we can only find such a view appropriate if we are capable of getting past our resentment toward things, so the problem remains as it was: we need to find a way to bridge the gap between where we want to be and how we are to get there.

Perhaps there are only two ways of addressing that which Nietzsche wants to cover by the word *will*. There seem to be some humans who are disposed to see the world as it is. This doesn't mean that they aren't bedeviled by delusions or misinterpretations or repressions but only that their disposition is such that they prefer to see things as they are rather than distort them into a wished-for world. Physiologically speaking, for example, there are people who crave the effects of artificial intoxication, who love to get drunk, whose cells seem to cry out for that which will intoxicate. This doesn't mean that such people can't deal with their love of intoxication, for they can. But some individuals take pleasure in the effects of one kind of intoxication or another, and others do not like intoxicating effects at all. If one were to reduce the matter to brain chemistry, some people's brains do not generate feelings of intense pleasure out of intoxication whereas others do. Those whose chemistry prompts them to find more pleasure in what is the case than in intoxication are disposed to derive their love of fate from seeing what is the case, from probing ever more deeply into the network of relations that constitutes life as they live it. These people are no more choosing by an act of will to love their fate than those who enjoy intoxication will the effects of intoxication. They will love their fate because they are disposed to find the world an endlessly interesting place whose intrigue is worth the pain that comes along with it. Such individuals are fated to love their fate, although even for them this can be a trying task.

Others arrive at a love of their fate through different means, chiefly, one supposes, by coming to a place where their "Being-toward-death," to use a Heideggerian phrase, becomes obvious to them. The quickest path to a love of one's fate is a brush with death, a full awareness of the alternative to the fate one is living. People who face their death as best they can do not *will* a change in their behavior that makes them love their fates. Instead, they are placed in a situation which makes them realize the great value of what they have, and they proceed to find ways of establishing reminders in their daily life of the great value of their fate, of that which they have, including their woes and concerns. People can find a discipline to remind themselves of the value of their lives, but they cannot will themselves to value what they have. They first have to be placed in a context in which that value becomes apparent to them, again, either by disposition or else by an accident of fate from which they cannot run for one reason or another. From this vantage point, Nietzsche's emphasis on the will is seen as something that needs to be thrown out, as he himself made apparent in many other ways.

One can phrase the matter one more way to bring it back to resentment: if, as I have asserted, *ressentiment* is a regulative force in life, that is because it is that against which our fates are regularly rubbing up, and without that constant rubbing we wouldn't be induced to love that which we have. Anyone who has experienced the tone of life as lived through the poisons of resentment knows that whereas resentment may keep one's mind acutely focused, it does not provide either a pleasant or a pleasurable orientation toward one's activity. One may arrive at the exultant pleasure of destruction through an act of revenge, as Henderson noted when he contemplated killing the frogs, but the path to that moment of bliss is colored by a cankered disposition toward oneself and the life around one. Inasmuch as we have all felt resentment on many occasions, we know well enough that it pollutes our attitude toward life and undermines the simple pleasures of existing. We are thus fully aware that it is preferable to find ways of living that bring a warmer tone to things, that allow the glow of everyday life to warm us with its charm. Passing into and out of the pockets of resentment that all lives involve, we come to realize that the tone of life is far more pleasing when we are not consumed by *ressentiment*. As such, resentment is a constant marker within us of that disposition toward the world that we should prefer to avoid.

❦

When we consider resentment as a regulative force in life, we have little trouble in seeing the ways in which it works through its contrast with that which we prefer. It regulates precisely by telling us when we have gotten off of the straight and narrow that provides us with the love of our fate. We know we have moved away from the middle path when we find ourselves stuck once again in the thicket of resentment, and we then seek ways of getting back on the path to the golden mean. The problem is that it is too easy to see this regulative force in specifically negative terms: we know when we have veered off the track because we can taste the bile in our throats and therefore seek ways of eliminating the bitter taste. This is true enough in its own way, but in itself it wouldn't allow us to see *ressentiment* as a good. We could think of it as an agent of the good to the extent that its negative example of it prompted us back where we should be, but that is different than seeing it as an agent of good on its own. Indeed, it may be too difficult for us to see it as a good in itself, for that is truly to move beyond good and evil as we have come to think of them. Nevertheless, the rhythms of *ressentiment* are unequivocally *rhythms*, and they seem also to be unquestionably part of that which links us to the stars and the tides and all that junk, as Henderson put it, so it will not do to construe them exclusively in negative terms. We must find a way of thinking of them as good in and of themselves, even if their effects in individual lives and social contexts are invariably seen in a negative light.

As a point of entry into the good of *ressentiment*, we might think for a moment once again about the act of rioting, as exemplified by the events in Los Angeles in 1992 or in the many other contexts in which it appears throughout the world. Surely rioting is a violent activity that causes much harm, that leads to death and destruction, and that further poisons the relations between people. In a negative way, we can see how such actions can be part of the regulative force of resentment in that they prompt within those who experience them the need for change. Anyone who has seen rioting humans cannot help but realize that their actions tell us most powerfully that something is wrong, that we as a society must attend to the poisons that unleashed these furies in the first place. So in the best of cases—not the present world, I'm afraid—we attempt to deal with the way resentment has built itself into the community in order to remove its toxic effects and provide people with lives that don't lead to such vicious acts. We attempt to rebuild south central Los Angeles, to bring opportunities to the people whose lives have been blighted by the "It Was" as it manifests itself in their neighborhood; to the extent that we address the problems the people face, we can say that resentment has been an instrument of the good by calling attention to the blight of the past that unfairly bore down upon the people and stripped them of any possibilities for a fate they would love.

To move beyond this indirect form of good, however, is to arrive in a domain where death and destruction must be seen as part of the inevitable course of things within human communities, which are themselves defined by the unavoidable unfolding of the rhythms of the universe as they move through those communities. Here we are less happy with the notion that resentment is a good, particularly inasmuch as all of us remain acutely aware of what a negative force it is, in small ways and large. But if we are to take the consequences of *amor fati* where they go, we have to become aware of this dimension of the good as well, even if it is one we should prefer not to contemplate. Henderson's paean to rhythm is the most pertinent statement of the issue, for it makes it clear that the rhythms of life are not limited to the inhale and exhale of respiration or the movement in and out of heart muscle. If these are goods, and if the movements of the tides are good, then the rhythms that drive social systems must also be a part of the unfolding of the universe, must participate fully in the drift of the tides and the respiration of the planet.

This good is beyond good and evil as conventionally construed because it adopts what we might think of as a planetary view of value, at least insofar as humans are capable of imagining such a thing. To use the environmental example again: we are not the least bit interested in saving the planet—our concerns lie with trying to preserve a planet whose forces are amenable to the sustenance of human life. The planet existed for a long time without human beings, and it may well continue for a long time without us again. What we do or do not do to deal with the potential problems that come from overpopulation, carbon dioxide in the atmosphere, poisons in the ground, devastated forests and the like has nothing to do with saving the planet. But we assume that there is a rhythm to the activities of the planet that will sway against us if we push its processes past a certain point. At its most basic, the question is whether the accumulated effects of billions of people and technological manipulation are sufficient to create an earth that will no longer support human life. The planet has its own calibration of the good built into the rhythms that we sense when we find ourselves in the midst of beauty, but also when a hurricane looms on the coast or a tornado comes blowing down the road. For some reason this kind of good seems peculiar to us because we have linked the word *good* to only two contexts: the human community and the world of the gods. We have no problem thinking of the good of human societies, and for millennia we had no trouble thinking of the good when it came to whatever God we worshipped. Likewise, we had no fundamental difficulty imagining a God who was good who was also capable of bringing devastating floods and wiping out entire communities—one thinks of Sodom and Gomorrah—forcing His people to live in exile and slavery for many, many years. It did not seem incongruous to us that these acts of violence could be part of God's good, yet when we apply a similar perspective to the planet or the world as a whole, somehow it seems inappropriate, even if it remains the most logical extension of the good for us to consider when we begin to revise our relations with the world.

When we take this good of the planet and apply it in any way to an event like the riots in Los Angeles, things become even more problematic. It is one thing to assert that the good of the world includes the possibility that the one location that seems to recognize the possibility of the good—humans—should no longer find the earth a hospitable place, and it is another to imagine a scenario in which riots within social contexts are seen as part of the good of the planet. To begin with, if we were to assume such a vantage point, we would be forced to think of human behavior as far more determined than we have ever been willing to consider before. But we need assume no more than what we have already known for years: groups of humans adhere to fairly predictable patterns, and one of them is the riot, the stripping away of self-conscious civility, the loss of that self which construes things in terms of responsibilities and its replacement with a form of collective madness within which all rules are abrogated and anything goes. During the riots in Los Angeles commentators were given to complaining that many of the rioters didn't care a bit about Rodney King or the verdict in his trial, as though that should be the immediate concern of rioters and the only justification for their behavior. Other analysts pointed out that many of the people involved in the looting were taking advantage of the lack of order to steal whatever they could with impunity, again as though a riot couldn't entertain such heresies. Even some of the awful beatings that took place were construed as unrelated to the energies that started the riot in the first place. They were simply done by bad people who also used the riot as an excuse to do in broad daylight what they ordinarily only did under cover of darkness. Such criticisms miss the entire point of the riot, which hardly developed according to laws of propriety that keep people's rage focused on the abuse they feel themselves to have suffered. On the contrary, the resentment level of the people in the ghetto was at such a high pitch already that the King verdict simply provided the flashpoint for the furies that followed.

Were all those who participated in the riot working toward some good, reflecting the rhythms of the planet and helping to correct an imbalance in its patterns? It would seem not. Most rioters may have been expressing a sense of outrage over their dehumanizing conditions and the ways in which the police force of the area regularly contributed to their abjection, so one could argue that indirectly a kind of good was being asserted through the desperate lives that reflected its absence. And surely the planet itself didn't feel an imbalance in Los Angeles that needed to be corrected the way earthquakes resolve tensions along fault lines. But the natural dynamics of human communities *did* have everything to do with those riots, and from that perspective the only surprise is that it took so long for the country to have such a disturbance and that there weren't more mimetic appropriations of Los Angeles in the other big cities of the United States. Humans can be degraded to the point where they accept the futility of their lives, and they can even be pushed to the point where it doesn't occur to them anymore that their lives are truly debased, but in any circumstance in which it is apparent that others live better lives beyond the abjection and squalor of the ghetto, sooner or later the futility of such lives must gather strength and rise up on its own.

The facts of the ghettos were known fairly well a little more than twenty years ago when the last serious riots took place, and one of our best poets of the working class, Philip Levine, was masterful in his exposition of that which generates such outrages:

> Out of burlap sacks, out of bearing butter,
> Out of black bean and wet slate bread,
> Out of the acids of rage, the candor of tar,
> Out of creosote gasoline, drive shafts, wooden dollies,
> They Lion grow.[11]

These were the circumstances of the riots in Detroit, a context that actually had far more of humanity to offer than the ghettos of the nineties. Here at least the dehumanization comes about as a result of the abuses of industrialism, the "bearing butter," the gasoline, "drive shafts," and "wooden dollies" that steal the best energies of the people. Out of these debasements the "acids of rage" and the "candor of tar" "Lion grow" while the whites sleep in their bungalows. These forces don't need a leader to form any more than they require direction of some sort to explode. If they did, they wouldn't manifest themselves in riots but rather in collective acts of civil disobedience of the kind that Martin Luther King undertook.

No, the collective violence of people is a manifestation of forces that are as natural as the lion who has mutated his part of speech. They will flower under the conditions that develop out of the dehumanization of the ghetto regardless of who is in power and regardless of systems of welfare or housing programs for the poor. Levine's own sense of the outrage expressed through revolt, echoing Yeats's "Second Coming," seems as natural as the movement of a cold front across the land:

> From they sack and they belly opened
> And all that was hidden burning on the oil-stained earth
> They feed they Lion and he comes.[12]

There were no doubt rioters in Detroit who were looting just for the fun of it, and others probably beat up people just because they liked to do that sort of thing, and still others who could have cared less about Martin Luther King. But all that is beside the point. The riots themselves are a function of the rhythms of human communities, and those patterns involve the violent destruction of neighborhoods and people that emanate from the "oil-stained earth" in which they have been "hidden" for some time. The reason for their coming forth may be legitimate, as it was with Martin Luther King's assassination or the verdict in the Rodney King case, or it may be a mere pretext, but in any case the forces of revolt follow as naturally from the way people are ghettoized in this land as tornadoes are a function of extreme differences in air pressure.

There is no right and wrong to riots of the kind that occurred in Los Angeles, although we can easily enough establish both right and wrong. Surely the police in the area had done much to contribute to the dehumanization of the people, even as the rest of the Los Angeles area and the country in general has done much to ignore the plight of those whose lives take place in such terrible circumstances. Surely it is reasonable to watch the footage of the beating and conclude that King was no more in control of the situation than he deserved to be treated in such a barbarous fashion. Regardless of the concerns of the police about this large man, there can be little doubt that their excesses had something to do with their deeper fears about black people in general. It was an inhuman act regardless of how one construes it, and it was obviously hard for most people throughout the country to believe that the verdicts were just.

One can equally seize upon some of the greater outrages, from the beatings of people who were driving through to the abuses heaped upon Korean-Americans simply because they were Korean-Americans. There was much evil to be found in the riot. But these forms of good and evil have little to do with an event that is driven by the equivalent of the wrath of God. Fair play and decency may work on the cricket fields of England, but they don't apply in riots. They are totally irrelevant to such contexts except in the most obvious case: riots almost always are a function of a collective recognition of the gross injustice that is meted out to those who revolt. There was every justification for rebellion within south central Los Angeles, even if justification is also finally beside the point. At some fundamental level a great many of those who took part in the riot had to be driven by fierce resentment of their blighted lives, by the deep unfairness of a country that allows people to live in squalor, that, even worse, allows them to live in the midst of daily gunfire, horrific violence and endless gang activity that threatens the lives of many every day. These conditions are not a function of jobs or lack thereof, and they are a scandal regardless of the reasons for their existence. Revolt is the only thing that can come from collective dehumanization, and for this reason alone simplistic moralizing is beside the point.

In most cases, however, the rhythm of resentment doesn't come in such toxic forms. Baby Suggs wasn't murdered; she was simply excluded from the circle of the human for a moment, long enough for her life to be ruined. Dahfu wasn't killed directly; he was simply placed in a context where the game was fixed to encourage an unhappy outcome for him. Nietzsche wasn't pilloried for his work; he was simply ignored. Within their respective communities, these fictional and real figures each could be seen as having perpetrated some outrage, some excess, that threatened the stability of the group, and the reaction of the group is to eliminate that which causes the disturbance. This is most unfortunate in many respects, particularly inasmuch as each of these figures was potentially an agent for the good, for change that would have benefited the community. But the community itself determines these things according to its own tacit laws and doesn't ask what the benefits are of the intrusive figure. The dynamic unfolds according to its own logic, and if its effects are often pernicious, we cannot avoid recognizing that the community is indeed acting in terms of its own sense of its best interests.

The act of rioting is not a good, and the elimination of people with great hearts like Baby Suggs is not a good, yet these events take place according to a collective sense of what is fitting that cannot be denied, however much we may be outraged by the outcome, whether we protest the ruination of a great human's life or condemn the random violence of a riot. These are acts we should hope never happen even as they must also be seen for what they are: the collective expression of good on the part of the involved community. Resentment is part of the dynamic of the good whether we want it to be or not. It is not to be rooted out by strong self-discipline or the careful control of an intelligent leader. It can be dealt with only as part of the good of human communities as they move into ever new territory. The only question is about the degree to which we are aware of these rhythms and the ways in which we seek to allow their patterns to develop in nonviolent ways that contribute more constructively to community life. But they will contribute to the life of the community one way or the other, however horrified we are by that, however much we want to think of these rhythms as exclusively a function of some evil that intrudes itself unfortunately into a world that otherwise would be quite benign.

In smaller ways we see the effects of these rhythms in the development and dissolution of relationships between individuals. All relationships are predicated on a fragile set of circumstances because they depend on the contrary needs of identification and differentiation: one must see oneself as *like* the other even as one feels the need to retain one's difference from the person. There is a dynamic movement between identity and difference that goes on throughout a friendship of any quality, and one needs to be careful not to move too far in either direction. If one moves too close to identity, one risks losing one's sense of self and self-significance; if one moves too far away, there are no ties to hold the relationship together. In this respect, all good relationships are inevitably like excellent sporting events: they require an equal distribution of the qualities through which they are defined. If friendships are not contests, still they depend on both a likemindedness about fundamentals and an equal ability to express those fundamentals in everyday life. The movement between identity and difference can sustain itself in constructive ways only when these conditions are met.

At the same time, the circumstances of life are such that the dynamics change from year to year. Relationships become unbalanced because lives unfold in different ways, and if the differences become too great, the tensions in the relationship can build, leading to the dissolution of the connection. At some level these tensions are invariably a function of *ressentiment*, regardless of the good will that both parties might bring to the relationship. The tension itself is a manifestation of the perceived inequality in the distribution of goods within the relationship that can only be overcome by broadening the temporal horizon, by assuming that the rhythms will eventually move in the other direction as well, compensating in turn for the excessive differences of any particular moment. Unfortunately, unlike sound waves that can be mixed to generate silence, human relationships have two collateral difficulties to contend with: first, it is often extremely difficult to keep the larger temporal horizon in mind when the differences of a relationship expand and threaten it; second, there is never a guarantee within the human world that the rhythm will sway back as one hopes it will. Lives have different outcomes, move in different directions, and sometimes the return of the other rhythm does not take place. Even in the best of circumstances, where the parties involved give things time in the hope that the dynamic will swing the other way, sometimes it does not, and in such a case the dissolution of the cords of the relationship is finally a good, even if it doesn't feel that way to either of the people involved. It is a good because it is a function of the dynamics of human relationships that cannot be escaped, because when the carefully woven network of identity and difference gets pushed too far in one direction, the only result can be the negative accumulation of resentments, either expressed as envy in one way or another or reflected in a kind of servility or condescension that declares the relationship to be over. Again, it seems unfortunate that we are no more in control of the flows of friendship than we are of the collective forces that lead to riots. And it seems inappropriate to see these forces as a manifestation of the good, for the end of a relationship is an unhappy event. Nevertheless, in the larger scheme of things these processes are equally a manifestation of the rhythms of the universe, of the dynamics of the world as expressed through collective and personal human contexts, and they inevitably constitute that which is fitting to that which we have developed.

In the end, these forces of dissolution, the manifestation of a violence that ends things, are as much a part of the good as the rhythms that bring humans together and allow them to live through the beauty of the world. Many people are content to embrace the sublime moments of life as necessary and good parts of the rhythm of the world, those moments, as Dahfu put it, when "there is no old and no new, but only an essence which can smile at our arrangement" (296). Others are even more willing to argue that these moments when an essence smiles at our arrangement—the development of the natural rhythm we have allowed to unfold—are as much violent and destructive scenes as they are the site of our joy at being human. They are the Dionysian furies creating and destroying at the same time, destroying *because* they are creative, because the implementation of the new demands the destruction of the old. But there is another view, one which construes the smile at our arrangement as being one pole of a dynamic the other side of which is the wrath of God, the slap in the face that comes from having gone too far, the blow that is meted out as an inevitable part of a natural rhythm that is self-correcting. If our sense of fair play is that which allows us to think that the rhythm of the world hasn't moved in accord with our individual sense of what is fitting, the declaration of the value of the straight and narrow, the middle path, the golden mean is that which informs us of the dynamic between the smile and the slap, between the embrace and the blow, the sine and cosine of the natural world as it works itself out through the play within human societies.

5

Pride Goeth Before the Fall

If human existence develops its character through a dynamic that flows between the smile at our arrangement and the slap that disapproves, and if all cultures have evolved an ethic of the straight and narrow as a result, a prominent player in these systems of value has been pride. The straight and narrow demands humility, asserts that the proud will be struck down, and construes the particular relationship between the smile and the slap in these terms: if we are properly humble, the world smiles at our arrangement of its forces; if we are proud, it slaps us down. The univocity of voice leads to the Tower of Babel, the excesses of the community lead to the great flood, the continual violation of the laws of God lead to the destruction of Sodom and Gomorrah. In other contexts, we observe the fact that Socrates' assertion of his ignorance was a manifestation of his wisdom, and most religions have rituals that place their members in subordinate roles. The very act of prayer—whether it happen silently in one's head or with knees and forehead on the ground—is an act of humility that works against the flows of pride within the human world. In the secular world, we note the pleasure with which people anticipate the downfall of the arrogant, whether that person be Donald Trump or a president who lost sight of the limits of his power. However much the proud are inevitably a part of daily life, and however much there is a countermovement in some circles to stress pride of self, we as peoples have overwhelmingly come down on the side of humility even as pride threatens at any moment to break the bounds of propriety and lead to the slap that will put us back in our place.

As with the three manifestations of the good, however, there is a tangle of motives to be found in the midst of these condemnations of pride. Among the prominent expressions of the dangers of pride, we can find superstitions that are connected to a general fear of the wrath of God: one preaches against pride because one has seen or heard of others who have been struck down. One thus creates rituals to keep in check those tendencies that manifest themselves in pride, and these rituals can be either religious in nature—prayer, for example—or purely personal in nature, as in the person who crosses him or herself in the face of potential trouble or the individual who always gets up on a certain side of the bed because bad things have happened when she has gotten up on the other side. The accusation of pride is also quite clearly an instrument of social control: it is that which the community uses to deal with certain people in specific situations in order to address whatever excesses they seem to have introduced into the community. Sometimes this social control has a legitimate interest in dealing with the proud, and sometimes it accuses people of pride to hide from its own sins.

There is in turn the particular manifestation of pride that the Greeks called *hubris*, so-called overweening pride that shows itself as an attempt to usurp the place of the gods, to remove oneself entirely from the constraints of the human world. And finally, we might assume for the purposes of argument that there is a kind of pride or hubris that is a function of entire communities, either in their disregard of the laws of civility—one thinks again of Sodom and Gomorrah—or because of a cultural arrogance that leads to notions of racial superiority and delusions of grandeur. In each of these cases, we can find legitimate and illegitimate expressions of pride, particularly when we deal with specific situations. Each kind of pride has a real peril built into it, and each is also employed by humans to deal with other threats that have nothing to do with pride itself, unless it be the pride of the one who accuses the other of the same sin. Unfortunately, in everyday life it is often almost impossible to discern the legitimate and illegitimate uses to which notions of pride are put, but fortunately, great literature allows us to see the unfolding of the assertions of pride and the slap that it demands and thereby gives us the opportunity to understand better a dynamic that is so much a part of every community that it might lead us to think the whole world is a morality play to which we are supposed to attend with our humility clearly on display.

The superstitions and rituals that accompany human concerns about pride are usually a function of very real fears humans have about the risks of life. If we all know at some level that our life can disappear in a moment, none of us seems to be able to bear constantly facing that prospect, so even if we are always assessing the relative riskiness of our position in the world, we are also imposing structures that provide some degree of assurance that we are likely to survive to the next day. The prayer before bed, the same route to work that we take every day, the ritual gestures that are in place to deal with moments of uncertainty—even if they are as unconscious as lighting up another cigarette—all work to mitigate our sense that our life is always at stake in the world. These are humbling gestures in that they admit our lack of control over the disposition of our fate, but they also speak to our own potential pride and the fall that will come from it. We sense that as soon as we think we are in control of things we shall pay a price for thinking so. God will strike us down, and we shall learn again how puny a thing the human will is.

It may be that the superstitions we establish to deal with our fears about the stability of our lives are purely a function of the domestic environment of which we are a part. We have faced what seems to us to be the arbitrary wrath of parental power, we internalize it as superego, and we build structures that compensate for our ongoing awareness of this quixotic authority that can strike us down at any moment. Or contrarily, we can see the implementation of superstitions in individual lives to be a result of good fortune as well. We are equally aware of how little control we have over the good things that come our way, so when the world smiles at our arrangement, we seek to repeat the conditions that seemed to engender the smile in the first place. The most obvious examples have to do with ballplayers who will wear the same socks for days in the midst of a winning streak or the writer who always sharpens her pencils in the same way before sitting down to write in the hope that this will make the inspiration flow. Regardless of whether we seek to induce the good magic in our lives or to keep away the bad magic, we have all created circumstances that tacitly acknowledge our humble status and that just as tacitly seek to keep us away from the shores of pride that would prompt our good fortune to falter and push us into the abyss.

Most of us tend not to think of these prayers and other acts as superstitions that acknowledge our humble status and that work to keep us away from our inevitable propensity toward pride, but they are part of the dynamic we develop to keep ourselves on the straight and narrow as we imagine it. Their efficacy results from a combination of superstition and reality: they are fictions that also bespeak the truth, artificial structures we impose on our behavior that allow us to perform tasks we would otherwise be unable to complete. The mystery is why we need such ritual structures given the putative highly advanced nature of our civilization and why they work so well. One would think that at this point in our development we would be able to distinguish between those structures we establish to perform meaningful activities and those we create in order to keep the forces of pride at bay, but in fact it is often difficult to distinguish between the two.

If a novelist like Hemingway, for example, depended on a stack of newly sharpened pencils before he began to write, and if he always wrote standing up at a table, were these gestures essential parts of his creative routine or only superstitious attempts to woo the muse, to guarantee that something worthwhile would actually be written? It could be argued that they were indeed local fetishes with no intrinsic value to them, but one could also assert that they were a function of Hemingway's work habits. He knew that he could go through a good number of pencils in a writing session and didn't want to have to be bothered with sharpening any while he was in the midst of what he was doing, so he always made sure there were more than enough available for any work session. Likewise, his physiology may well have determined his manner of writing while he was standing up. In these cases, the structures he imposed upon his activities were common sense derived from years of writing on a regular basis.

We could just as easily imagine both gestures as attempts to woo the muse, though, the clean pencils reflecting a need for a pristine order at the beginning, a clean origin through which to evoke that which had yet to be discovered, and the standing writing position could have been a function of chance: Hemingway's back bothered him one day so he had to stand to write, and the writing went so well he stayed with that posture the way a baseball player stays with old socks on a winning streak. More than likely, these gestures were both practical means for undertaking the task at hand *and* developing superstitions that helped the writer achieve the quietude of mind he needed in order to get down to work. They may have started as superstitions, or they may have begun for practical reasons, but if they led to successful writing sessions, they were likely to become part of the future routine, fictions that were superstitions as well as pragmatic responses to the particular needs of a given writer.

If we imagine Hemingway in the midst of writing through structures that are both superstitious and pragmatic, we again do not assume that he is undertaking an act of humility by adopting them, nor do we suppose that he thought of these acts in this light. But the writer is aware of the fragility of his fate, of how easily words do not come, and so it is likely that these gestures did have something to do with inducing the muse to appear on a regular basis. We may not believe in the muse anymore, but anyone who has performed any activity well knows that there are some days when things work out as they should and other times when things do not go as well as one would like. Michael Jordan averages about 30 points a game, but there are games when nearly every shot he takes goes in and others when he misses two thirds of his attempts. In the case of someone like Jordan, we would assume that ordinarily he puts out his best effort every day—something of a fiction given the long basketball season, but a fiction that is truer for people like Jordan than others—yet even with the best intensity there are times when his body performs miracles on the court and occasions when it reflects the performance of an average player, at least when it comes to shooting. One can assume likewise that there are times when things don't go well and yet Jordan feels perfectly at home in his body, and other situations where he doesn't quite feel in sync, feels tired or a step behind his own sense of presence. Regardless of the reasons for being off a bit, Jordan would know that he had his off days and like Hemingway would doubtless undertake pragmatic and superstitious means to compensate for the knowledge. He would subordinate himself to his gift and to whatever dynamics there were that made it flow easily on one occasion and struggle for 50 percent shooting the next night.

These days, when basketball players hit a hot streak or have a good night they talk about being "in the zone," a reference to a magical region in which everything feels right and goes in without effort. They know as well as anyone who performs that they cannot place themselves in that "zone": they can only put themselves in a position where it comes to them. They are not likely to think of their superstitious and pragmatic practices as attempts to avoid pride, to assume erroneously that their gift in itself is enough, but the very fact that they speak of a zone rather than something they personally will shows how well they know that their good nights depend on flows outside of their own abilities. They may not think of their gestures as acts of humility, nor does the average fan see them in this way, but in fact that is what they undertake when they work through the structures that will bring them good luck on the court or a fine day at the writing table.

The proud person is the one who loses sight of several factors involved in his or her success: the first thing to go is the awareness that one's abilities are a function of something for which one can take at best partial credit inasmuch as they derive from genetics, domestic upbringing, cultural affairs, or the simple accidents of life. The second thing to depart is the understanding that the great moments are not under one's own control, that the gift is not sufficient in itself, requires a "zone" for its magic to take flight. Pride is not thinking too highly of one's own gifts in and of itself, although that is the way one is perceived by others: it is losing sight of one's dependence on the relations around one that provide a context for one's gifts meaningfully to express themselves. Those who are most aware of this fact are equally conscious of the fragility of what has been made available to them and treat it with the necessary humility. Those who lose sight of this fact tarnish their gift by placing their ego between the gift and the context that would most bring it to life. In doing so, they increase the likelihood that the zone of magic will never appear and thereby reduce the quality of their performance. Here too we seem to be in the midst of a dynamic that is part of the rhythms of the world, a pattern that works well only when one is aware at some level that one's performance does indeed depend on a dynamic and not on the assertion of will over a given set of circumstances.

At the level of individual performance, then, we could say that the universal condemnation of pride is justified. We simply need to qualify that statement by suggesting that this particular region of pride has nothing to do with the social evaluation of an individual's character. It cannot be determined by the society in which the person finds him or herself but is rather the result of his or her performance, something individuals are usually quite aware of themselves. There are circumstances that can prevent one from knowing how well one is expressing one's capabilities, but most often Michael Jordan knows when he is at his best even as Hemingway knew when he was at the peak of his powers. It is harder to tell the quality of one's performance when it is in the good rather than the sublime range because the sense of magic is not as much in evidence, and so there is a greater chance of delusion when evaluating what one has done. Hemingway's "shit detector"—his built-in sense of a good sentence—worked best at finding his truly distinguished moments; it was less successful at discerning those moments that were good from those in which he was merely repeating a routine he had already accomplished many times before. Jordan's gifts are such that he could easily enough coast through most games and look quite good to himself and to others, and given the comparative nature of his performance relative to the rest of his team, he might lose sight of how well he was in fact doing.

Distinguished work depends on the stretches of good performance that are as much a part of the activity as those sublime moments when there is only an essence that smiles at our arrangement, but those who do the work know that the essence cannot be faked, cannot be induced, cannot be willed in any particular way. Unless they lose sight of this fact, they also therefore know that pride is that which comes between one's gift and that which allows a fitting expression of it. It is not that God's wrath strikes down the individual who loses sight of the fact that the gift is indeed a gift and not something earned, for there is no outside agent involved in the process. Rather, the insertion of the self in the process as the central element disrupts the dynamic and one's understanding of it, thereby diminishing the quality of the performance. The reciprocity involved in this rhythm is not moral in the traditional sense, for it is not tied to the paymaster and his attempts to bring justice to the world or to even things out when humans lose perspective on their lives. It is simply that all great performances in life in whatever milieu depend upon the flows of a context, on the rhythms from which they derive their grace, and when humans forget that, they lose touch with the rhythms as well and therefore lose contact with that through which they can best express themselves. If the repetition of a person's bad self is the worst rhythm there is, that is because it keeps us focused on the person we are. The value of the rhythms is that they take us away from ourselves, keep us from focusing endlessly on our actions as discrete events with no linkages to anything outside of our own egos. When we filter everything we do through the grid of a fictive self we invent to control the flows around us, we guarantee a bad self that will repeat itself endlessly until we learn again that virtue inheres in the rhythms out of which our behavior takes on its grace and meaning.

If it is true that in everyday life it is often difficult to distinguish between those practices that provide a useful structure for focusing one's performance and those that are superstitions designed to keep the magic with us, we might assume that this wouldn't present any problem for the individual: whatever works works, we might think, and whether it is superstition or meaningful gesture should be beside the point. If a writer strokes a rabbit's foot before she starts to write and manages to produce good work, who is in a position to tell her that she is practicing a superstition that has no real relationship to the quality of her writing? And surely some of the superstitions we employ do have a benign character. They are harmless in nature and are simply a way for us to make our surroundings comfortable before we undertake meaningful activity. This may be particularly true of an athlete's dirty socks or a rabbit's foot or a favorite writing implement.

But superstitions are superstitions, are fictions devoid of contact with the real, and they need to be distinguished from practices that derive from a serious attempt to find structures that will best allow one to express oneself in the world. These too may be fictions in the sense that they are artifice, cultural contrivances we invent to locate ourselves comfortably in the world, but they also exist to provide the best linkage to the flows around us. If one writes at a table standing up because one's back aches when one sits down or even because one thinks one concentrates better in that position, the structure addresses the fit between body and context and therefore allows the site of one's activity to link itself to the rhythms that will give it grace. If one writes early in the morning rather than later in the day, that is because one senses that one's mental activity is most acute during that time and thereby provides structures that will allow that acuity the proper forum of expression. This may in turn call for additional regimes throughout the day that help to provide the clarity of mind one wants early in the morning, but these too, artificial though they be in some respects, are an essential part of the pattern through which one allows one's rhythms best to express themselves. As such, they are a part of the real rather than an attempt by the person to will the real into compliance.

Superstitions are unreal, have no intrinsic linkage to the rhythms that determine the outcome of our activity, and whereas they may be harmless in and of themselves, they can lead to practices that work against one's activities or that end up buffering one from the world through which one's skills must achieve expression. There is a big difference between the individual who washes his or her hands before an activity because the person wants to start "clean" and the person who compulsively washes his or her hands throughout the day. At the same time either act of hand-washing is based on the same superstitious relationship to reality: it assumes that that which comes between one and the world can be removed by washing one's hands. Washing hands might be nothing in itself, but there is always the tendency over time to develop more and more of these kinds of gestures until one's activity is beclouded by pointless acts designed exclusively to bring the magic one's way, having no relationship at all with one's skill or the body through which it will be expressed. At this point the superstitious behavior gets in the way of the performance of the activity, and the result is diminished capacity.

The more elaborate the regime we establish through our superstitions, the more likely we are to remove ourselves from the reality that is essential to successful actions in the world. For one thing, an elaborate structure of superstitions minimizes the contexts through which one can work: the more defined the routines are, the fewer places and times there will be where they can be performed. If one ends up with rituals that consume the better part of an hour and one requires at least three hours of clear space before one can think of undertaking the activity, one has added an additional hour to the time frame that is necessary before an activity is even contemplated. This in turn makes it less likely that one will find the necessary blocks of time. Likewise, if one insists on a regime that depends on specific items that are only present in one place, one arbitrarily limits one's work to that place. In most cases, a certain amount of this kind of restriction of activity is useful and largely irrelevant, but it can also lead to the continuing disuse of one's gift.

To take only one example, it is well known that it is often hard to sit down in front of one's desk and start writing, regardless of whether one is a student working on an essay or a novelist with a major reputation. It is therefore easy enough to find excuses to avoid sitting at the desk, particularly if it is a daily activity that demands one's best energies. One always runs the risk that nothing will happen, and the apprehensiveness that is an inevitable part of writing therefore prompts one to find excuses not to sit down at the desk. One didn't sleep well the night before, one is therefore not at one's best, so perhaps it is preferable to wait until tomorrow to do any writing. Or one has a big social event to go to in the evening with its usual complement of anxieties and other diversions, and one cannot keep one's mind on the task awaiting one at the desk, so perhaps it is best to wait until the next day. Or this or that or that. Any writer who has had to submit to the regime of writing can imagine a number of reasons for not undertaking the task on any particular occasion. One can in turn incorporate one's superstitions into the list of reasons for not sitting down to write, and the result is that one finds more and more superstitious reasons not to write and comes to write less and less, losing track of the gift upon which so much depended.

I remember well in my own case how much my writing before I had a child was based on certain superstitions about the metaphorical weather in my area. I needed, I *demanded*, absolute clarity of attention and established an order that allowed me to escape for the most part from those things I thought would hopelessly befog my mind: minimized social contact, no disruptions in the ordinary daily routine, a minimum of consumer activities of whatever sort, no strenuous physical activity, no conflicts with my wife (to the extent that was possible). I had a highly developed structure created that allowed me to sit down and write every morning and evening and do some good work. And it worked well until circumstances changed with the presence of my daughter, who created more and more disruptions to the routines I thought were essential to my writing as she started to grow up. By the time she entered school I was faced with the virtual ruination of my structures. I liked to start writing in May, but her school year didn't end until June, requiring regular trips to and from her classes to pick her up. The last month of her school year involved endless social activities, from field day to class picnic to numerous other special events, all of which involved me in the kind of social discourse I sought to minimize during my summer months so that I could write. I found myself wanting to do more and more with my daughter both during school and during the summer out of an acute awareness that she would not want to be doing these things with me for very many years. So I ended up being baked by the hot sun at a swimming pool or riding horses or playing baseball with her. The more of these things I did, the more I was pressed to find time to undertake my household chores, so I had to find ways of squashing them into still other places in my itinerary that had previously been devoted to quiet time. Where I used to spend an afternoon reading news magazines, I now went to the pool or pruned trees or waxed the car or mowed the lawn or performed some other task that diminished the amount of physical energy I had available for my writing.

Year by year the routines I had established to create a comfortable space for writing disappeared, and I was faced with a choice. Possessing the same anxiety in the face of the writing-yet-to-come (or-maybe-not), I was tempted at first to use these disruptions in my routines as excuses for not writing. If I had to go to the elementary school class picnic and devote hours to pointless banter, I would excuse myself from writing. If I baked myself in the sun at the pool, I would excuse myself from writing. The day eased up because I convinced myself that these were legitimate reasons for putting off that troublesome yet necessary act of writing. It didn't take me too long, however, to realize that at the rate the disruptions to the smooth flow of my life were increasing, it would be no trouble at all to avoid writing altogether, for I had arrived at a point where most of my days involved the kinds of disruption that I had previously thought were intrinsically inimical to my work habits and therefore harmful to my writing.

In effect, I came to see that my choice was to abandon writing during my daughter's childhood years—and perhaps forever given the possibility that the disruptions were less a function of a child than of the increasing responsibilities that come with age, and would not diminish once my daughter had moved up and out of the house—or to try to write in the midst of disruptions that seemed the worst thing for it. After all, the superstitious structure I had built up around my activity suggested to me that there was no way I could write with clarity of purpose while all these external pockets of turmoil existed. Fortunately, I discovered that in many respects the superstitious structures were indeed that rather than pragmatic patterns I had established to allow my activity to be caught by whatever flow was necessary for it to work well. True, I still worked best early in the morning because my mind was clearer. True, I still needed that space to be free of other encumbrances so I could give myself wholly over to whatever came next. But I learned that I could still have this clarity of purpose in the midst of an afternoon full of turmoil, that I could even return to my desk in the evening after too much in the way of gratuitous social activities or too much time in the sun. I didn't *need* all the structures I had thought were necessary to provide me with a context in which to write, yet I could just as easily have used the lack of space for those structures as a way of getting out from under the psychic burden of facing the as-yet-unwritten every day.

In this respect, although it is virtually impossible to undertake meaningful tasks without some superstitions blended into the practical structures one establishes to get the work done, it is necessary to find ways regularly to probe what structures are indeed superstitions—and hence relatively superfluous—and what structures are in fact necessary to establish the frame of mind one needs to express oneself. Otherwise, one might find oneself overwhelmed in the end by patterns that have little to do with the work one undertakes but which also finally undermine the likelihood that one will take up anything at all. This point is even more essential given the temporal nature of things, for structures that begin as pragmatic devices for work could lose their usefulness over time as circumstances change and thereby become part of the superstitious regime. Superstitions too can lose their effectiveness as we change in unanticipated ways, yet it is easy enough to keep maintaining them without thought to their usefulness.

The crucial point is that superstitions do require maintenance and therefore energy. They are not freely given gestures but rather activities that demand as much of us as most other things we undertake. The more we invest our energies in them, the less we have to give to the activities that they are supposed to create a useful context for. Just as important is the fact that superstitions are not a part of the real but an artificial structure we impose on reality to allow us more meaningfully to interact with it, and the more time we devote to the superstitions in our lives, the less time we spend with the flows of the real. In too many cases this means that we come to mistake the patterns of our own routines for reality, whether those superstitions be cultural conventions we subscribe to or idiosyncratic rituals we establish that allow us to get work done. Just as celebrities face the problem that their public persona detaches them from the world that usually provides the circumstances through which they achieve their special status—making it increasingly difficult for them to find the patterns that allowed their work to achieve grace—so too one can become absorbed into one's superstitions and lose sight of their unreality, losing in the process one's connection to the rhythms that made the activity possible in the first place. The dynamics between one's structures and the world at large then get out of whack, and the quality of one's work diminishes.

Pride may seem to have little to do with these potential pitfalls that are found in the superstitious and pragmatic structures we create to allow ourselves to do the work at hand, but in fact they are precisely that through which we measure the effects of our work and others'. The straight and narrow exists as a ruling motif because it cautions us about getting caught on these shoals, because it alerts us to the ways in which the self we create can be built out of structures that lead to obliviousness of the reality about us, for one reason or another. We may get a swelled head and lose sight of the context upon which our work depends, a kind of pride we all recognize easily enough. But we can just as easily relax in our efforts to determine what is real and what isn't, what is a useful structure through which our relationship with the flows around us can be established and what is superstition that leads to a forgetfulness of our relationship to those flows, and that too is a form of pride, albeit one that is seldom recognized. Both manifestations of pride have the same effects—the diminishment of the application of one's skills in the world at large—and so both are limits to the useful expression of the rhythms of the world from our locations within them.

The personal constraint of pride is an intrinsic part of the rhythms of the world. It is not something that humans add to the world in order to create a rough kind of justice, even if there may be some such principle inevitably at work in the dynamics of the universe as they flow through human activities. Practically speaking, the kind of pride we have been discussing has nothing to do with good and evil; it is simply the expression of a dynamic, of a pattern that unfolds according to its own logic: one stays on the straight and narrow, or one veers off and gets slapped down by the countervailing rhythm. This is neither good nor bad, fortunate nor unfortunate. It is simply the case. When Aristotle speaks of *hamartia* in tragic drama, we might think of it as this kind of pride: it is not that Oedipus is so full of himself that his swelled head creates obliviousness that prompts the gods to strike him down; rather, Oedipus has created certain superstitions that keep him from realizing fully what the dynamics of reality are all about and therefore a mistake is made. This is not an error for which Oedipus can be blamed, although he willingly takes responsibility nonetheless. It is a mistake that comes from the fact that human knowledge always only extends so far, and we don't consistently remember that the richness of a context requires careful assessments rather than sweeping gestures. One might say that Oedipus is so determined to find the truth—a noble quality of the highest order—that he loses sight of other essential aspects of governance: the politics of caution that might prompt him away from making the hunt for the truth such a public matter. Perhaps he should have told the people that he had undertaken some initiatives to find out what the problem was and that he would let them know what he discovered when he knew something more. He could have heard the counsel of the various individuals in private and then decided how best to present this information to the people. He could have done all of this in an honorable fashion, and the outcome might have been much different. But he made a mistake, he forgot about the requirements of politics or didn't adequately consider the relationship between those requirements and unanticipated outcomes that might result from his investigations. He made a mistake, and that was the root of the tragedy: human wisdom is always incomplete, can never wholly take in a situation, and when one combines that inevitable sense of incompletion with the delusions that can be engendered through social structures—people endlessly paying fealty to one, calling one their savior and so forth—one can get lost in the superstitions and exacerbate the effects of any mistakes that might come about as a result of one's good intentions. Neither good nor evil is found here, only a mistake with most unfortunate consequences.

The problem human communities face, though, is that the pride that has nothing to do with good or evil bears the same name as that pride which society makes use of in order to exert its own discipline upon those whom it feels have abused its privileges. Pride is an instrument of social control, a means of slapping down people who have grown too large, a way in which communities take upon themselves the wrath of God and use it for their own purposes. We recall that when Baby Suggs contributed to a feast that made the community feel shame over its excesses, they turned on her and accused her of pride: "Too much, they thought. Where does she get it all, Baby Suggs, holy? Why is she and hers always the center of things? How come she always knows exactly what to do and when. . . . Loaves and fishes were His powers—they did not belong to an ex-slave. . . ."[1] Baby Suggs has no more been prideful than she has gone out of her way to make others envious of her, but when people come to feel small about themselves, they need someone upon whom they can foist their shame so that they can feel better again. If the community thinks that it has gone beyond the bounds of propriety, it must be because some proud person overstepped the bounds ahead of them and led them to their shameful moment. So Baby Suggs must be the culprit. Lord knows they wouldn't have had a feast without her.

As with Oedipus, it could be argued that Baby Suggs was proud, did indeed overstep her bounds by making miracles when she was only human. She should not be creating food and feast when she has only her two small hands to work with and no magic, and if she does somehow manage to transform the threadbare lives of the community into something full of the richness of life, she must truly be usurping the powers of God. The people themselves were unable to do anything on their own to bring charm to their lives, and they had given up any hope of enjoying life. When the feast comes, then, its magic is more than they can bear, and they come to see it as a manifestation of evil rather than a spontaneous display of good. Shame goes to envy, and envy names the problem as pride, and the proud person pays a price for being who she is. So Baby Suggs is guilty without question.

One could also argue that the feast was a result of *harmartia*, of a mistake that might or might not be seen as a result of the limits of Baby Suggs' wisdom. In a world that is saturated with woe and slavery, it might not occur even to a wise person that there could be too much joy, too much life, and that people accustomed to woe would react negatively to what they would perceive as excessive. The feast was no more an excess of life than Baby Suggs was usurping the powers of God, but values are always contextually determined, and this is the way the community came to see the feast because it was too much for them. Baby Suggs was not blinded by pride, was not prevented from seeing this because she was convinced she always knew what was right and was overcome by her abilities to minister to the people. Unlike Oedipus, she never for a moment assumed the role of savior for the community and never once waxed poetic about all she had done for the people in the past. A mistake happened, but it was the kind of error that had nothing to do with good or evil or with any particular agent: the flow of the community went too far as a result of its own momentum on the day of the feast, and the excess caused a reaction in the people that they had to deal with so that their hearts would not rot with their own undignified behavior.

Still, from yet another angle Baby Suggs was a proud person who had usurped Christ's place in the scheme of things. It is not an accident that her sermon moved the people's faith away from a deity and toward themselves any more than it was coincidental that her remarks focused their minds on their *flesh* rather than their spirit. These were heretical statements that undermined the community's faith in Jesus and the other world. They may not have specifically doubted the virtues of faith in heaven, but they made the people responsible for their own grace. Yet the Bible asserts that grace must come from God. Like Jesus, Baby Suggs brought the community life, and like most of those who listened to Jesus, her words finally caused a reaction that led to her sacrifice. She had not simply violated the bounds of propriety; she had undermined the entire social fabric by preaching a message that was in direct opposition to the faith upon which the people's lives were based. If that isn't hubris, the term has no meaning.

Baby Suggs was no more interested in usurping the place of Jesus in the community than she hoped one day to be seen as a god. She was no more prideful in her relations to those around her than Stamp Paid or anyone else was. Ella was far more given to hubristic tendencies than Baby Suggs ever was. As we saw, Baby Suggs wasn't even the specific agent that engendered the feast: she was only one of many whose hearts transformed the day into something special. And on top of all those things, her sin was not the usual one, for it was not the destruction of the community with which she was being charged but the enhancement of it. Far from being responsible for a plague that imperiled everyone's life, she threatened everyone's death-in-life by reminding them that they were not really living, no more loved their flesh than took an interest in the gifts that were left to them in the midst of a highly impoverishing racist society. Baby Suggs was not the least bit proud, yet she had overstepped her bounds and was considered too proud. She was wise in her knowledge of how far her efforts could take her, yet she also usurped the place of God by preaching heresy to a community whose fragile sense of itself depended on an otherworldly form of grace and salvation that Baby Suggs tacitly destroyed by focusing on the flesh.

When a community settles on the notion that one of its members is guilty of pride, we are confronted with a complex event that defies logic: Baby Suggs is guilty of pride at the same time that she is the most humble person in town. How can she be both? Our tendency is to assume that the community is wrong, that Baby Suggs isn't proud, that the people only say she is so they can use her as a scapegoat for their own sins. And we are right in thinking so. But the community is also right in assuming that Baby Suggs is responsible in some respects for their shame. She has undermined their faith in the superstitions through which they have been preserving their fragile hold on life both through her sermons and through the feast that developed a life of its own. Surely a community has the right to preserve and defend itself when its tissues are threatened, and Baby Suggs was calling the people's morés into question. In this respect we could say that the feast was the flashpoint for the accusation of pride against Baby Suggs because it took the community that long to figure out the import of what she was saying. She didn't tell them not to listen to the Bible, nor did she say that Jesus had it wrong. She didn't create her sermons out of parallels that would have made the point clear: "The Bible tells you to have faith in God, but I tell you to have faith in yourself. The Bible tells you that grace comes only from above, but I tell you that you must make your own grace. The Bible tells you to love the spirit and spurn the flesh, but I tell you that you must love the flesh as much as the spirit." Such statements would have made clear to the people the stakes of Baby Suggs' sermon, for they express the gist of her message. She may not be specifically telling them to abandon their faith in another world and in the power of the Lord to take care of them, but these are among the implications in her words.

Still, like Jesus, Baby Suggs brings life to the people, provides a context in the clearing where they can feel joyful about their existence when they otherwise feel dead. So they give her the caress of *holy* and listen to her message. Then there is the feast, an excess of life that embarrasses them, and they come to understand through its extravagance precisely what Baby Suggs has been preaching. She wants to bring them back to life in *this* world when they have been patiently waiting for a spot in the *next* world. It is not the least bit extravagant for them to hurl these accusations at Baby Suggs, and the only reason this seems surprising is that it has taken them so long to realize the implications of what Baby Suggs has been saying that they were first caught up in adoration of her for her charming powers. They were captivated by her message because it felt *good* to be alive, if only for a few hours, and it was a *good* to celebrate the flesh and to be wholly human. Their captivation, their gratitude for having been brought to life, kept them from seeing what was at stake in their new existence: if they put off the old life, if they had been born again, they had tacitly abandoned their faith in the other world upon which their earlier sense of things depended. When they realize this finally, they turn on the person who had persuaded them to abandon that to which they were accustomed. And they had every right to do what they thought was necessary to preserve their existence. This too is part of the rhythm that slaps back at excess, that seeks to preserve the patterns that dominate the community by eliminating that which calls them into question.

From this perspective, the town's act of omission is relatively minor. The people performed no ritual act of murder or expulsion. They simply chose not to do something in a context where their insightful action might have saved a life and preserved the wholeness of Sethe and Baby Suggs. A small crime at best, and hardly one for which the people could be prosecuted, except in terms of their God's laws, which would prompt them to feel guilty about what they didn't do as much as what they did do. They know that they could have prevented the horrifying events at the center of their community, the unifying events that shroud their actions in silence for twenty years, and they realize that if Baby Suggs was proud because her sermons and her feast sought to usurp the place of God, they were proud because they had tacitly participated in the taking of a life, an act reserved for God alone. So they condemn themselves for what they have done, although they never publicly admit to the crime, and therefore are grateful when many years later Denver provides them with a context through which they can make amends for their sin. In doing so, though, they are taking responsibility for the grace in their lives; they are attending to Baby Suggs' message rather than the Bible's.

The condemnation of Baby Suggs is an act of social control, a way that the community attempts to reestablish its rhythms after they have been disrupted by her attempts to bring them back to life. But we who read the novel are inclined to side with Baby Suggs and condemn the community for what it has done. We see that she was celebrating a life that we ourselves more or less give praise to, and her paean to the flesh is far more consonant with our own views of things than it was for the community to which she spoke. So we praise Baby Suggs and revile the community, claiming along with Nietzsche that the strong always need to be defended against the weak because the weak have the numbers and will therefore rise up and snuff out the lives of their betters. So it was with Jesus, so it was with Baby Suggs. She brought them back to life, and they were so horrified by the prospect of living that they had to find a way to do her in. If they succeeded beyond their wildest dreams, they also realized that they were asking for precisely the kind of personal devastation they had inadvertently wrought in her life. Is the community therefore wrong to accuse Baby Suggs of pride? Is it wrong for them to seek to preserve their fragile hold on things with the prospect of a much richer life in the offing? Of course it is wrong from an individual perspective, but from a collective viewpoint that is precisely what communities are driven to do. Their actions are often dehumanizing at best and extremely violent at worst when they are faced with the dissolution of their structures, but it is as inevitable for a community to try to preserve itself from the disruption of an extravagant voice as it is proper for Baby Suggs to try to bring the people an awareness of the value of what they have, life.

We may side with Baby Suggs and feel the terrible injustice of the word *pride* as it is applied to her, for clearly from her own perspective—and from our view of her perspective—she is being charged with a crime that is not relevant to her life. Or if we are more conservatively inclined we may side with the community and argue that any apparent contradiction in its actions is a result of Baby Suggs' artful deceptions, of the fact that she doesn't make the stakes of her values clear to the people. It therefore takes a while for the implications of her words to sink in, and when they finally do the people choose to turn on her rather than abandon their current way of valuing their lives. From this perspective the community takes upon itself the rightful role as articulator of God's wrath, the force that legitimately strikes down she who would destroy the values of the community. This too is an act of pride, without question, an act which more clearly arrogates to itself the power of God than anything Baby Suggs proposes. She only wanted to give to the community a life they already had whereas they want to take a life, something far more serious and intrusive.

Unfortunately, we are faced with the fact that *pride* is a word that is used to focus certain social energies in negative ways. The forces that make use of the word may or may not be legitimate from the individual's perspective, but from the community's viewpoint they are almost always reasonable. Typical readers of Morrison's book may be inclined to think that Baby Suggs has become a scapegoat for the people's sins, and they are correct. Such individuals would also be right in distinguishing the use of community wrath in Baby Suggs' case from that which is employed when a society determines the fate of its murderers and thieves; in the one context the exercise of wrath is justified by law and in the other it is an arbitrary expression of the people's own resentment. But those forces operate under their own laws, and even if we don't choose to countenance them or seek to make use of their effects in our lives, the community itself doesn't distinguish between the tacit laws of *ressentiment* and the written laws of resentment; it doesn't assert that the killing of a murderer is a fitting action whereas the scapegoating of a good person like Baby Suggs is not. The law that operates in both cases is the same—the community's sense of its need to preserve itself—and the only difference is that one act is sanctioned by laws that people specifically develop to justify their acts whereas the other is dealt with outside of the written law.

If we ask why the community doesn't have laws for dealing with acts like Baby Suggs', we can only conclude that there are no rules for such cases because they are the very grounds of law, the context where the order of the community threatens to violate all the canons of respectability. It is out of shame for these acts that people institute laws to prevent themselves from arbitrarily acting in such a way in the future, yet they can never come up with a law that justifies scapegoating because the situations are always too overdetermined to be covered. Is Antigone right or is Creon? Should the domestic good be upheld or the good of the community? We are given to thinking that such tragic contexts only occur in the ancient Greek world. Surely today no one would be placed in Antigone's position, and if she were, we would attack Creon for violating the bounds of propriety. Yet a tragic vision of things is based on the fact that honorable people—through accidents of life and their own convictions—can end up in situations in which the goods do not come together, in which one good must inevitably be sacrificed to another, with total justification from the perspective that asserts its good over the other. We think all outcomes are determinable by law, yet we can only arrive at such a view by deliberately reducing the effects of the real to partial acts rather than whole ones.

Baby Suggs was right in her ministrations to the people, she was noble and good and caring and wise, and she did everything she could to give her community what it most needed: life. But she also threatened the community's life by these actions, and so the people took upon themselves the role of God and struck her down. They too were doing good by their own lights, even if buried within their actions would be found the guilt that also recognized that Baby Suggs was no more a demon than they were. In our own day when such events occur—and one can't help but think of the riots in Los Angeles—we, like Baby Suggs' community, tend immediately to reduce the situation to understandable terms: the rioters performed barbarously, or they had every right to do what they did given the barbarity of the verdict against Rodney King. Then opposing sides can talk to one another and moderate their views: maybe the rioters were barbarous, but given their debased lives, there was a certain amount of legitimacy to what they did; maybe the sense of outrage the rioters felt was justified to a certain extent, but still many of them were simply plundering and killing because it was a thrill to be able to do so with impunity. Then all sorts of pious statements will be uttered about the need to address the implications of the riot, to get to grips with the conditions that made such actions possible in the first place, and the horrific manifestation of good and evil will be reduced to a memory and a few social programs whose efficacy will doubtless be nugatory. We can assume this to be the case given the effectiveness of the social action following the riots of the sixties.

After all these millennia, we still do not possess a cartography that will allow us to deal with a context like a riot in any sensible way. And inasmuch as most readers of texts such as this would be all too willing to agree, it should be emphasized that although most of us would seek to distinguish the kinds of reactions we might have in the face of the violence of a riot from the silence that greets the work of a writer like Nietzsche, there are parallels between the two that speak none too well of our own lives or our ability to deal with the overdetermined nature of human activity. We might argue that Nietzsche was ignored because he was "ahead of his time," as indeed he was. He is ahead of *our* time. But for all practical purposes that simply means that people were unwilling to abandon their reductive visions of the world in order to confront the horrifying truths that Nietzsche presented them with. Nietzsche himself as a human being might or might not have been the best individual to be a spokesperson for his vision, but that aside, the fact is that our idea of what is ahead of its time and behind it seems always to be predicated on a notion of expanding contexts or changing situations or new developments or revisions of old ones, when for the most part there are only two kinds of developments, and there have *always* been only two kinds: the attempts to reduce the complexity of the world in ways that are more appropriate to the historical and social events that have taken place, and the attempts to make people see that these reductive visions always succeed in burying that which most needs to be dealt with in an honorable way every day: the complex, overdetermined site of human action that cannot be reduced so quickly to law or principles of resentment without guaranteeing further problems in the future. Nietzsche was ahead of his time only to the extent that in his day—as in ours—people were unwilling to look at the world as it is and were reluctant to confront the overdetermined nature of their own behavior. We have heard about shooting the messenger many times, but we have failed to acknowledge that there are many ways to shoot one. In the intellectual world that is sometimes done by bringing out the attack dogs, but it is also done by silence. So nobody read Nietzsche. He was ahead of his time, still is, and may always be. But the silence that greeted Nietzsche's work is no different than the silence that greeted Baby Suggs on the morning when her fellows failed to announce the arrival of the slaveowner and his self-righteous crew.

To extend the example in one further way, we might briefly bring to the fore the context through which Jacques Derrida has made his way in the world, at least in the United States. He was greeted more by the attack dogs than by silence, and when that failed, we domesticated him and turned him into a practitioner of circus tricks for the elite. But at first he was a demon to be dealt with, an overturner of the sacred values of the academy and all humanity. He was someone whose threatening vision had to be eliminated before the entire community went up in flames. And of course many other people who sided with Derrida went along with him precisely because he had been demonized into someone who was going to torch the town: they *wanted* to burn everything down, were ready for a riot, and Derrida provided them with a context to express their own resentment at the way they had been unfairly treated. So Derrida came to be defined by the excesses of those forces that gathered around him, the demonizers on the one hand and those who were looking to do a little violence on the other. Those in the middle who did what they could to make sense out of difficult work were swamped in the end, and the entire process was finished off by the total domestication of Derrida's product. He was a performer, and a good one, but nothing to get all worked up about. We put a few such performers in each department and redefine the academy in terms of deconstructionist jugglers and new historical firebreathers and feminist trapeze artists. It all becomes a show in the end because it is too much for us to deal with it in its raw indeterminacy. Human action is always overdetermined, so we individually and collectively are determined to reduce it to grids that will allow us more comfortably to contain it. Yet we persist in thinking that the community was wrong to do in Baby Suggs.

❦

Strictly speaking, pride and hubris are distinguishable terms, although our discussion of Baby Suggs' pride shows that the one term easily slides over into the other. The community only accuses Baby Suggs of pride, not hubris, but the people would be unaware of the word *hubris* given their cultural circumstances, so they could hardly accuse her of it. We think of pride as a mark of an individual's overestimation of his or her abilities whereas hubris is an extreme version of pride, a context in which the individual seeks to usurp the role of God. Such people may not intentionally be trying to become God and may not even recognize that their actions are an attempt to do so, but at least from the community's perspective that is precisely what they are doing. Baby Suggs at no point realizes that she is trying to usurp the role of God. She recognizes that she has gone too far, but that is the limit of her assessment: "Her friends and neighbors were angry at her because she had overstepped, given too much, offended them by excess."[2] Baby Suggs never acknowledges that she is ministering to the people in ways that usurp the place of Jesus, nor does she see that her life-affirming message is—at least from the people's eyes—incompatible with Jesus' message of life. Her only sin in her own eyes is to have given too much to people who weren't ready to take as much as she had to offer them.

There are, to be sure, megalomaniacs who are truly convinced that they are Christ incarnate or a manifestation of God, and whereas I don't wish to minimize the importance of such figures—who are significant precisely because all too many people are so desperate for a savior that they will countenance the words of such crazed individuals—it is most often the case that hubris is just a shade away from pride, and sometimes, though not always, that shade is a matter of community interpretation more than anything else. From a secular perspective, Baby Suggs' words have no hubris in them, but from within a community that embraces the word of God, her remarks do smack of hubris, of an attempt to take away the powers of grace from God and give them to the people instead. In many respects, however, even if *hubris* is not among the favored few thousand words that people most often use, it tends to cover those situations when the community determines that an individual has acted out of pride. The specific cases when we take upon ourselves the evaluation of our friend's or neighbor's actions are most often thought of as prideful situations, for it is a rare middle-class person who seeks to usurp the role of God in any compelling way. When he or she does, it usually is cause for concern by the entire community and requires a collective response.

In order to bring the dynamics of hubris more specifically into play, I want to look briefly at one of the Greek dramas whose strength is its exposition of overweening pride, and for that Aeschylus's *Agamemnon* is most fitting. This is a play that demonstrates the pride of humans even as it presents circumstances that could in another case fully justify the acts of the major characters. Agamemnon's choice, for example, is clearly put by the chorus of the play when they state:

> and I still can hear the older warlord [Agamemnon] saying,
> "obey, obey, or a heavy doom will crush me!—
> Oh but doom *will* crush me
>   once I rend my child,
>   the glory of my house—
>   a father's hands are stained,
> blood of a young girl streaks the altar.
> Pain both ways and what is worse?
> Desert the fleets, fail the alliance?
>   No, but stop the winds with a virgin's blood,
>   feed their lust, their fury?—feed their fury!—
>   Law is law!—
>   Let all go well."[3]

Agamemnon sees himself faced with a terrible choice: he can kill his daughter to get his ships moving, or he can allow her to live and fail to answer the call of war. In his mind this appears as a question of personal good against civic good, but he also knows that there is "Pain both ways and what is worse?" In accord with that logic, he decides that it is worse to "desert the fleets, [and] fail the alliance" and so agrees to "stop the winds with a virgin's blood," but even though he also prays "Let all go well," he understands that "a father's hands are stained" with the "blood of a young girl." He risks outrage and violation of the good regardless of what he does, and realizing this, he claims to support the alliance in spite of the need to kill his own daughter to do so. He takes on this burden knowing full well that there will be consequences.

The chorus also makes clear to us how horrifying such an act is, should we need any instruction in Agamemnon's rough choice:

> And once he slipped his neck in the strap of Fate,
> his spirit veering black, impure, unholy,
> once he turned he stopped at nothing,
> seized with the frenzy
> blinding driving to outrage—
> wretched frenzy, cause of all our grief! (110)

Agamemnon's spirit has become "black, impure, unholy," and he has brought a curse upon his people, has become the "cause of all [their] grief." He didn't want to curse his home, yet his choice led him to such a pass, we are told, because "once he slipped his neck in the strap of Fate. . . he stopped at nothing." He was "seized with the frenzy / blinding driving to outrage." Once Agamemnon has made the decision to kill his daughter, he loses his gauge of what is fitting; he will stop at nothing to achieve his goals, and he is therefore perceived as someone who is driven by a "wretched frenzy" that will destroy the community.

Seen exclusively in this light, Agamemnon is faced with a horrible choice, and he will lose no matter what he does. He will perpetrate an outrage that will cause much grief in either case, and he knows this before he makes up his mind. If we look at his situation without regard for other circumstances, we can say that in some ways his choice makes sense: there is nothing more horrific than sacrificing one's own child, but strictly in terms of numbers, his act can be seen as serving the greater good, for more lives will theoretically be preserved through this act of sacrifice than would be if his ships remained stuck at home because of the ill winds. The act seems to demand the vengeance of a divine force, the Furies, in the chorus's eyes, because the codes of the community are based on specific prohibitions against such crimes. So, we might think, it is the chorus who determines that this initial act leads to a "wretched frenzy" that overwhelms all. They need to have a cause-and-effect sequence that will further demonstrate the bad blood that drives Agamemnon to his awful deeds so that future condemnation will be more than justifiable. It is also possible that Agamemnon does lose all moral perspective once he kills his daughter, figuring that he has so outraged the gods by the initial act that there is little point in trying to accommodate their wishes afterward. One way or the other, a trail of destruction follows from the first act, and both Agamemnon and the chorus expect the worse.

Why then does Agamemnon perform the sacrifice? If it is wrong not to help the alliance when he knows a way he can, still that seems to be a lesser crime than sacrificing his own daughter. That act is more heinous, cries out for retribution by the Furies in a way that the failure to perform the act would not. Yet Agamemnon's remarks do not suggest this differential. On the contrary, he equates the two acts, simply telling us that pain will be the result in either case. This could be the proper choice on his part, or it could be a mistake, part of the *hamartia* that moves the action of the play forward. But it could just as easily be a mark of Agamemnon's manipulation of the horrible choice in an attempt to make it work to his advantage. He is clearly playing to the audience, for otherwise the chorus would not have known of these words, so he is just as clearly thinking that maybe he can do his awful act and *not* be attacked by any divine form of justice. Therefore he seeks to placate the social forces that the chorus represents, for they could easily end up being the expression of the divine frenzy that destroys Agamemnon's life, or they could simply seek to do him in out of outrage for what he has done, for the way he has violated a fundamental law. Agamemnon's choice is based on the assumption that he might escape the consequences of his act and live to lead his people after everything is done. His hubris comes in thinking that it is possible to outwit a fate that he knows is woven into his initial act.

If that were all, we would at least have compelling evidence of the complex network of relations through which hubris revealed itself to the Greeks, but there is also the fact that Agamemnon's decision is not as neutral as he makes it out to be. Wonderful though his daughter is, she is only a daughter, and in the social context that must count against her. There are laws against sacrificing one's own children, but we might think that Agamemnon would be less likely to do the deed if his child were a son rather than a daughter. It is not that he doesn't love Iphigeneia but rather that she is less important as a human than a boy would have been. And it is not that Agamemnon specifically makes that fact known, for it wouldn't occur to him to do so. Nor is this all, for even if the sacrifice involved a son rather than a daughter, Agamemnon would still have much to gain personally by sacrificing his own child, not because he would eliminate his successor—that is part of his heritage that he should doubtless wish to live on, particularly if it were a male—but rather because fame and glory are to be won in the war, and shame can be the only result of failing to send the fleet. The other tribes would not be satisfied if Agamemnon sent a messenger telling them that he could not help them out because the winds have kept his ships on shore and he is unwilling to do the only thing that will change their direction. They would see this as subterfuge, as a means of escaping the obligations of the war as they imagine them, and that would be the end of Agamemnon's reputation as a warlord.

Even though Agamemnon doesn't tell us, then, he has much to gain by sacrificing his daughter. Glory is available to him only if he does so, although a crabbed kind of honor might belong to him if he chose otherwise. In this economy of action, Agamemnon must think that if he faces potential horrors no matter what he does, he at least has a chance to achieve great power by killing his daughter whereas only a local ethic would be upheld if he were to restrain his hand, and even then his own people might well later condemn him for not coming to the aid of the alliance. Agamemnon's acts are overdetermined, even if like most humans he seeks to hide those motivations that seem self-serving. He may well have acted as honorably as he thought possible in the midst of an awful choice, but how could he deny that he also stood to achieve personal gain through the slaughter of his own child? How could his cries of woe be more than at least partially hypocritical as a result? If personal gain weren't also at stake, part of the nature of hubris would be lacking, for if extreme pride is a result of taking upon oneself the acts of a god, part too is thinking that one can manipulate the gods for one's own ends. Agamemnon seeks to straighten out his own motivations and hide the obvious element of self-interest in his act to make it seem more justifiable to any gods who might be watching. And having committed one act in this guise without immediate consequences, he might think that he can control the gods through such manipulations, leading to a frenzy that knows no ethical bounds.

In this respect, Agamemnon's public choices are not much different from the acts of the Wariri tribe in *Henderson*, for even though the novel presents its subject matter in a comic format, there can be little doubt that what the tribe does is akin to what all who undertake acts of hubris do. The rain ceremony itself—the symbolic attempt to move the clouds over the mountain to get the rain the Wariri so desperately need—may be seen as an act of obeisance too, but like Agamemnon's sacrifice, it is an act designed to get one's way, an attempt to manipulate the gods. And like Agamemnon's act, the rain ceremony violates the order of the gods even as it tries to manipulate it: its cruel treatment of the symbolic gods manifests a resentful violence that is clearly proscribed by the gods even as Agamemnon's sacrifice of his daughter violates the prohibition against such acts. Why should Agamemnon's act be one of hubris whereas this collective rain ceremony—or any other superstition that is taken up both to violate the social code and yet seek justification for it at the same time—not be? Even more pertinently, we see the Bunam, the high priest of the Wariri, deliberately manipulating for his own ends the sacred ceremony through which Dahfu is supposed to capture his lion father and thereby legitimately become king. From altering the symbolic colors to create bad omens to tinkering with the mechanism of the hopo so that it will lead to Dahfu's death, the Bunam typically shows the hubris of one who thinks he can take the materials of the sacred and make them work for his own bloody and self-serving ends. If the Bunam could argue that his actions are necessary because Dahfu has violated the codes of the tribe by having an evil lion in the palace, Agamemnon has justification for his act as well.

In a world in which there are always multiple motivations for whatever one does, there are always reasons for undertaking bloody acts that make them seem to reflect the will of the gods, regardless of whether they do or not. This is why Agamemnon's choice is finally more interesting than the equivalent decision of someone like Abraham in the Bible, for even though Abraham is faced with a horrifying conundrum, his burdens are lessened. They may be greater to the extent that he is asked to kill his only son, a violation of the moral code even more heinous than killing one's daughter, but God makes it clear to him that this is an act he must perform and therefore specifically legitimizes it, however much Abraham himself might be torn by the act in a personal way. Abraham, at least theoretically, has much to gain by the act, but that motivation is never specifically presented in the text. We could argue that he is given the choice of being the origin of a great people who loses his more tangible genetic origin when he kills his only physical link to the future, Isaac, or that he could contrarily choose his genetic immortality over political and historical immortality, but there is little in the account in the Bible to suggest such a reading. Abraham's decision is an awful one, but the lines of authority are clear and his act is justified by God. This is to say nothing for the fact that he was allowed to escape from the sacrifice of his son in the end and thereby avoid a terrible fate. Agamemnon was not, and so the psychology and politics of human events are more graphically presented in his case even as the linkage of such acts to hubris, to a pride that would allow one to deny one's connection to the morality by which humans are supposed to live, gives us a code through which to understand the limits of human choices.

As in the case of *Oedipus Rex*, *Agamemnon* also involves us in the perspective of the chorus or the society as a whole. We are given the weather report of the kingdom through the agonizing the chorus goes through over the acts of its leader, and in both plays we see how much the Furies and the fury of the people seem to be one and the same force:

> The people's voice is heavy with hatred,
> now the curses of the people must be paid,
> and now I wait, I listen . . .
> there—there is something breathing
> under the night's shroud, God takes aim
> at the ones who murder many;
> the swarthy Furies stalk the man
> gone rich beyond all rights—with a twist
> of fortune grind him down, dissolve him
> into the blurring dead there is no help.
> The reach for power can recoil,
> the bold of god can strike you at a glance. (120)

In every tragedy, it seems, there must be a crowd clamoring for the death of the great one even as it takes upon itself the mantle of the divine through its bloody assertions. The chorus here clearly thinks that "the curses of the people must be paid" and is more than willing to anticipate the moment when "God takes aim / at the ones who murder many." They themselves will make sure that "the swarthy Furies stalk the man / gone rich beyond all rights," and in this way take up their own form of hubris, a collective mania rather than the individual variety that appears through Agamemnon's act. Both forces are divine in nature, and both are self-serving, for if Agamemnon stands to gain by achieving glory in a war that he can only reach by killing his daughter, the chorus will achieve peace of mind and restored order through the expression of its own divine frenzy. What it wants above all is to avoid feeling threatened. Like the community in *Beloved*, it seeks to escape the full risk of being alive and will do anything to put that possibility out of play, even taking upon itself the role of the divine and assuring the death of its leader, if that should be necessary.

In one respect, the chorus is simply asserting the law of human societies: "The reach for power can recoil, / the bolt of god can strike you at a glance." At the same time, however, it reveals through a voice that is heavy with hatred that it relishes the possibility that the Furies would "stalk the man / gone rich beyond all rights"; the people embrace the thought that the Furies will "with a twist / of fortune grind him down, dissolve him / into the blurring dead." If there is reciprocity here, if the rhythms of the universe work themselves out through such acts of retribution, they are divine regardless of whether they express the will of a god or merely account for the inevitable way the patterns of human relations lead to social furies that grind down and dissolve those who exceed the social bounds. We have been inclined in our secular era to assume that hubris only makes sense in a context in which there is a divine source whose will one can seek to usurp; contrarily, we reduce the social furies that engender their own horrible responses to the arrogance of power to petty motives and small selfishnesses. They may be that in some ways, but they remain attached to divine furies regardless of the pettiness of the motivation. There may be no god, but there are furies even in a purely secular world.

So, as in *Oedipus*, we find a chorus that both takes upon itself the furies of the gods and explains to itself that it has no desire for anything more than a modest life. If it anticipates with great relish the destruction of Agamemnon, it also hides from its own hubris and its hope for omnipotence. Far from wanting to be wealthy and powerful, the chorus prays:

> Make me rich with no man's envy,
> neither a raider of cities, no,
> nor slave come face to face with life
> overpowered by another. (120)

Wealth and power are too risky to be worth having, for hubris waits for any raider of cities or rich person who loses sight of the consequences of his acts. Envy is recognizably present here, and it is envy that takes up hubris to do away with it in the wealthy and the powerful. So one should choose to be neither a wealthy person nor a slave, one who comes "face to face with life / overpowered by another." Rather, one should hope for the middle path, the straight and narrow, the mean where all excesses are out of the question and so need not be a concern. The regulative force of all social desire is on display here, and it is just as inevitable a manifestation of the rhythms of human existence as are the arrogance and hubris that both Agamemnon and the Chorus take upon themselves when it suits their needs. Just as Agamemnon speaks from self-interest as well as from the perspective of one who must make hard choices, though, we should not ignore the fact that the chorus speaks truth even in the midst of its own self-interest. If its expressions of the simple life are attempts to hide from its own deep outrage and need for blood, they are also assertions of the truth at the center of human relations, the need for the golden mean, the more or less equal reciprocity between people. Excesses lead to excesses, engender hubris and the furies of the gods that destroy the social fabric and ruin many lives. This is no more a self-serving observation than it is dependent on an otherworldly ethos or a god. The recoil is a necessary and essential force, the collective bad self of a people coming back and slapping down that which has violated the bounds that would allow reciprocity to be the mean through which things are gauged.

I want to look at this rhythm of reciprocity through one more statement by the Chorus only because we tend to make either too much or too little of these forces that are so essential to the maintenance of social life. When driven to fury, people can also be given to eloquence, and they can turn their sense of outrage into the poetry of divine law, as the Chorus does here:

There's an ancient saying, old as man himself:
men's prosperity
never will die childless,
once full-grown it breeds.
Sprung from the great good fortune in the race
comes bloom on bloom of pain—
insatiable wealth! But not I,
I alone say this. Only the reckless act
can breed impiety, multiplying crime on crime,
while the house kept straight and just
is blessed with radiant children.

But ancient Violence longs to breed,
new Violence comes
when its fatal hour comes, the demon comes
to take her toll—no war, no force, no prayer
can hinder the midnight Fury stamped
with parent Fury moving through the house. (131)

Such "ancient sayings" exist among all peoples because they express a fundamental understanding of the dynamics of power, of the rhythms that determine who shall have how much for how long, that establish how much is too much and how the too much should be taken away. Prosperity, it would seem, leads to excess, which engenders "bloom on bloom of pain" as a result of "insatiable wealth." Wealth itself is insatiable, desires to breed more, not the possessor of it, who is only an agent through which wealth can breed. Wealth becomes an organism in its own right, a cancer that threatens to take over everything if it is not held in check by something. Inasmuch as the Chorus is seldom willing to admit that *it* is precisely that which is outraged by the excesses it demands must be dealt with, that *it* is that which marks out the space of impiety and takes on the robes of the Furies, it must come up with a demonology to cover its own acts in a cloak of respectability, beyond responsibility, beyond good and evil.

The Chorus explains that "Only the reckless act / can breed impiety" and contrasts the impious with "the house kept straight and just" which is "blessed with radiant children." The one counterbalances the other, establishing the possibilities for any human and suggesting a fair outcome for all. The reckless act leads to impiety, and "ancient Violence longs to breed" until eventually "new Violence comes" to reciprocate the initial act, to match it and modulate the rhythms of society so that the straight and just house is seen to be more in accord with the forces of the divine. When "the demon comes / to take her toll," when the Fury moves through the house and destroys all, then the blooms of pain will cease, at least temporarily, until the next excess leads to another act of impiety, which adds in turn to the crimes that require once again the power of the Furies.

What should be amazing to a reader in 1994 is how perfectly applicable such a statement is to our own time, how well it accounts for the excesses of our own era, whether they be the dissolution of Yugoslavia, the riot in Los Angeles, or the ever-increasing crime that overtakes cities, suburbs and rural areas alike. These "random acts" are seldom seen as part of a pattern, as a function of violence that breeds slowly until bloom on bloom of pain leads to larger explosions that threaten total destruction of the kingdom. We are told that poverty breeds crime, and that ghettos are breeding grounds for all sorts of evil. We speak of the decay of the "family unit" and explain how the decline of that order contributes to the violence that haunts all lives in the United States in one way or another. And we endlessly agonize in public over our own fascination with violence, as seen in movies and sports and most of the other recreational activities we take up. Yet we don't really believe in the Furies and see nothing in the way of divine justice at work in such contexts. We may have occasional feelings of dread through which we get a sense of the horrific possibilities of the future if all of these blooms of pain are not dealt with in some way, yet we seem like Agamemnon to think that somehow we are not responsible for these excesses ourselves, that they have come about as a result of other people's actions, that therefore any divine retribution will fall upon other people's heads.

The virtue of the word *hubris* is that it allows us to distinguish between common pride and that state which marks out—if too often only in retrospect—the fundamental violation of the middling rhythm of social communities. As a rule we don't necessarily believe that a person who has an exaggerated sense of his or her importance will get some kind of comeuppance at a later date, for there are enough experiences in life to suggest that such an economy doesn't prevail. But *hubris* marks a threshold that goes beyond a simple misapprehension of one's capabilities and their value and carries us into that ever-threatening domain in which the reciprocal ties between humans threaten to dissolve the entire community. We cover this ground on the one side with commentaries about the Ten Commandments and the seven deadly sins and the moral code of God, and on the other we poke around in the psychological dark with discussions of envy and greed and the politics of resentment, but we fail to acknowledge the middle ground between these two positions, the one that assumes that the rhythms of the universe are expressed in these patterns, that asserts that the patterns of the universe are both the moral law of God and the psychological expression of such basic human attitudes as envy and pride and greed and resentment. This seems to be too large a leap into the void, too much an anthropomorphization of the laws of the universe, when in fact it is the opposite: it is an assertion of the laws of the universe in a context we have been unwilling to find them. So our Chorus in 1994 and the one in Agamemnon's world assert that "Justice shines in sooty hovels, / loves the decent life" (131), and we go about our business as best we can, hopeful that this simple creed will keep the furies away from our own door.

Within *Agamemnon*, we see the dynamic of social disorder taking place as a result of hubris, but the continuation of that pride in Clytaemnestra adds one more element to the mix, for she is aware of the ways in which the Chorus makes use of the Furies of divine vengeance to suit its own purposes, and she employs that knowledge to justify her own excesses. In defense of her own horrific violation of the social code, she claims to be indifferent to the will of the people. She has gone one step further than Agamemnon by not even showing the barest pretence of being interested in their "petty" complaints about her immorality:

> And you,
> you try me like some desperate woman.
> My heart is steel, well you know. Praise me,
> blame me as you choose. It's all one.
> Here is Agamemnon, my husband made a corpse
> by this right hand—a masterpiece of Justice.
> Done is done. (162)

Clytaemnestra considers the murder of her husband "a masterpiece of Justice" and is proud of having committed the act. If the Chorus chooses to praise her for putting to death the man who brought the vengeful Furies into their lives, that makes no difference to her. If they blame her for committing an act that is as heinous as killing one's child, she doesn't mind that either. Agamemnon at his worst never succumbed to this kind of excess, for he knew full well that "The voice of the people—aye, they have enormous power" (138). Clytaemnestra is full of contempt for the people and thinks that the magnitude of her sin is a matter that should have nothing to do with them.

Even worse, Clytaemnestra will point out to the people the hypocrisy of their own actions by demonstrating the parallel between her act and Agamemnon's and then reminding them of the difference in treatment they received:

> And now you sentence me?—
> you banish *me* from the city, curses breathing
> down my neck? But *he*—
> name one charge you brought against him then.
> He thought no more of it than killing a beast,
> and his flocks were rich, teeming in their fleece,
> but he sacrificed his own child, our daughter,
> the agony I laboured into love
> to charm away the savage winds of Thrace. (162)

The Chorus may have been unsettled in all sorts of ways by Agamemnon's crime, but they let him get away with it out of fear. Yet now they proceed to condemn Clytaemnestra because she tries to undo Agamemnon's deed with another crime. She at least attempted to eliminate the fire of the Furies, and she suggests that Agamemnon might have first tried sacrificing one of his sheep to the gods "to charm away the savage winds of Thrace" rather than his own daughter. Logically speaking, much of what Clytaemnestra says makes sense, for there is no consistency in the way the people act. On the other hand, her words are also a cover for a crime that was undertaken at least as much for power as it was for divine retribution. The Furies didn't appoint her the instrument of their vengeance. Rather, she saw an opportunity to make use of them for her own purposes and exploited it well.

Nevertheless, Clytaemnestra is right to ask the Chorus:

> Didn't the law demand you banish him?—
> hunt him from the land for all his guilt?
> But now you witness what I've done
> and you are ruthless judges. (162-63)

Agamemnon should have been dealt with according to the law, and he was not. Given that, the ruthlessness of the people's acts toward her, a woman, makes no sense, violates their own past inaction, and gives Clytaemnestra all the more reason to think that she will be able to escape from both the wrath of the people and the violence of the Furies. Her blood crime is nothing because her steel heart will allow her to best any opponent.

The grave social problem facing the people is that Clytaemnestra is correct: their actions have not been in accord with their own law, and the inconsistency is such that it leaves room for those in power to exert leverage where they should not be able to. If people simply want order returned to their lives and make use of the law to bring this about as much as they can—just as the Wariri move wooden statues about to urge the clouds to come over the mountains and bring rain—their failure to act in one case has guaranteed them more disorder later on, and they have no legitimate way of dealing with the problem:

> Each charge meets counter-charge.
> None can judge between them. Justice.
> The plunderer plundered, the killer pays the price.
> The truth still holds while Zeus still holds the throne:
> the one who acts must suffer—
> that is law. Who can tear from the veins
> the bad seed, the curse? The race is welded to its ruin. (167)

Social order dissolves once "charge meets counter-charge" and "None can judge between them." If Agamemnon can strip his overdetermined act down to a single strand and argue that he killed his daughter because he needed to answer the call of the alliance, Clytaemnestra can construe his act another way, as a brutal murder of a child by a father, an act of incredible arrogance that violated all the laws of blood and that consequently brought the wrath of the Furies down upon the family. Given this, Agamemnon should have been killed or banished.

In turn, Clytaemnestra can take her own overdetermined act, one that is far more obviously the manifestation of her greed for power and her wish to be done with Agamemnon, and strip it down to a single strand as well, asserting that she was only trying to put an end to blood crimes through one of her own, simply carrying out the will of the gods herself when the people were too cowardly to do so. No one can argue with her because all know that they should have done something about Agamemnon's crime but did not. Caught in a mess that is partially made by their own lack of will, they are reduced to the statements of the impotent: "the one who acts must suffer—that is the law." It may be the law, but they haven't acted on it in Agamemnon's case, so it is pointless to hold it up as a requirement once Clytaemnestra doubles his deed. Knowing its own complicity in the crimes, the Chorus can only ask with helplessness: "Who can tear from the veins / the bad seed, the curse?" And their answer is compelling: "The race is welded to its ruin." Their resolve to eliminate the curse has been sapped by Clytaemnestra's cunning argument and by her indifference to their wishes. She has grown to be like a god in her power and cruelty, so they can only conclude that her hubris means that ruin is the only course for the race to take. They are doomed, and there is nothing they can do about it.

Clytaemnestra manifests her ignorance and her hubris at the end of the play when she foolishly asserts that she really believes that her blood crime will be the last and will somehow not receive its own recompense. Aegisthus is concerned about the people's reaction to their crime, and Clytaemnestra once more seals their deed with complete contempt of the Chorus:

> Let them howl—they're impotent. You and I have power now.
> We will set the house in order once for all. (172)

On the one hand, the cries of the Chorus are met with disdain because they have no power, or so Clytaemnestra thinks. Therefore, there is no reason for her to attend to their complaints about blood crimes and vengeance any more than she needs to address the justice that should follow from her deed. On the other, she believes that she and Aegisthus "will set the house in order once for all." Like most who commit horrible acts in the name of justice but whose main interest is power instead, Clytaemnestra somehow thinks that her blood act will not be met with another, that the violence will stop with what she has done and will not call forth a counterblow. She senses no rhythm to these crimes and thinks that the law of vengeance is a fiction that societies establish in order to control their leaders and those who would perform these terrible acts on others. Like most in our own world, her contempt is a result of her ignorance of the rhythms of the universe, for she thinks that declaring the laws of the people and the gods to be fictions will put an end to the powers of the Furies rather than guaranteeing their return.

If blow leads to counterblow, and if one immoral act leads to a greater immorality down the road, that is never better demonstrated than in *Agamemnon*, where Agamemnon at least acted with self-awareness of the magnitude of his crime and the potential consequences. When the consequences are not forthcoming in the way that people suspect, however, such acts can lead to dismissal of the law at all levels and still greater acts of hubris, as Clytaemnestra's bloody hands testify. We ourselves no more believe in the laws of the gods as they measure out acts of vengeance through the hounding of the Furies than we have faith in the will of the people. Our own contempt for the rhythms of the universe is collectively as strong as Clytaemnestra's. We too think vengeance is a personal act with no consequences beyond the individual upon whom it is inflicted; we too fail to realize that hubris is not a specifically Greek concept but rather an expression for one of the most powerful manifestations of the rhythms of the universe in human societies.

❦

The pride of people and the wrath of God meet in at least one other representative situation as well, and that is the collective manifestation of hubris. One thinks of Sodom and Gomorrah, twin testaments to a social mania that runs its course only to receive divine obliteration as a result. What such communities reveal to us is that here too we are inclined to think that the laws that govern social networks are fictions designed to impose an artificial order upon people in order to constrain their desires and prevent bloodshed. If there are millions and millions of citizens who adopt a fundamentalist view of morality, this voice is not really ours and doesn't reflect the spirit of the intellectual world of the late twentieth century. We are imbued with a vision that registers contempt for the fundamentalists because we see their narrow and intolerant view of human behavior as repressive and superstitious in the extreme. I believe we are right in thinking so. But it is one thing to condemn narrow and intolerant views of human behavior and another to assume that the social codes that govern collective situations are fictions of arbitrary value. We may be inclined to see the story of Sodom and Gomorrah as an anecdote that deals more with Abraham's negotiations with God than with the high immorality on display, but in working the material around in this direction we lose sight of the larger point, which at least from a biblical perspective has to do with hubris: those communities whose social order has been corrupted by decadence of one kind or another will come to ruin. Few in the academic world today would be willing to argue that God has a similar plan for our own society, and we can be grateful for that. But if God's wrath is not laying in wait to strike a slothful and decadent society to its knees, it doesn't follow that there aren't other rhythms that will achieve the same ends.

If we assume that Clytaemnestra's acts can occur only in a society that is taken over by its own lack of will, by its inability to act in a meaningful way, by its unwillingness to see the applicability of its own order any more, there are certainly parallels in our own day. It is not an accident that our problems seem to mount even as we find no leaders fitting enough to propose useful solutions or even viable ways of thinking about what ails the body politic. If our leaders do not lead, we give them no real authority to do so. If they fail to act, that is because we have no idea what we want them to do. If we are increasingly haunted by the threat of violence and the sense that something is deeply awry with the economic system to which our lives are welded and the morality that links the two together, we are also accustomed to the comforts that our laissez-faire attitudes have provided for us, and they are an integral part of the economic and ethical systems that have led us to an impasse.

We are inclined to see decadent societies as ones where immorality dominates every act, but at the same time it is difficult to imagine such a society from a liberal Western perspective anymore because the definition of immorality has become so attenuated that virtually nothing qualifies.

Regardless of that problem, the larger difficulty is that the only fitting definition of a decadent society that is overcome by its own self-indulgence is that it is incapable of making distinctions. The people of Sodom and Gomorrah couldn't make distinctions, for they had abandoned themselves to all sorts of excesses that their own laws prohibited, and these excesses in turn led to the total breakdown of order: they are more than ready to violate the sacred laws of host and guest and attack Lot's divine visitors and sexually molest them, so much so that Lot has to devise his own evil ways of dealing with their insatiable appetites by offering his daughters to them. The people are unwilling to make distinctions, and the result is that their community burns to the ground.

We are also at the point where we can no longer make distinctions, even if the context of our decadence differs in some respects from Sodom and Gomorrah. We have unquestionably been unable to distinguish between a compassionate tolerance for the inherent differences within all human communities and the breakdown of all distinctions of value, and the result is that there are no meaningful distinctions left to speak of. The fundamentalist community will rise up against this immorality and claim that it will call the wrath of God down upon us, and the liberal community will attack the fundamentalists for being narrow and intolerant, but the ultimate effect is that we as a society have arrived at a point where we can no longer make distinctions of value, yet we know that social systems are a function of precisely this ability. One side may argue that we can escape the wrath of God because He no longer exists while the other side maintains that He has already begun to strike us down, but neither side seriously undertakes the necessary inquiry into how we are to learn to weigh the value of things anew in an era when the old distinctions need to be reassessed. One side wants to return to the very distinctions that the other side no longer finds applicable, and the other seems uninterested in any distinctions whatever.

If it is hard to find pride in this mess of indistinction, it is nevertheless located in the notion that somehow the lack of distinctions is not a problem, that our unwillingness to assess the nature of order in our lives is an isolated act with no consequences bound up in it. Every social history that we have evaluated from our own context has demonstrated that decadence is a function of an unwillingness to make distinctions and an indifference to the idea that the Furies will overrun a community that fails to create a system of values, yet we seem to think that our own society can escape from these laws. We are sophisticated enough to draw distinctions within history that demonstrate how the codes of a given people are less a function of a particular god or gods and more a function of the way order works itself out in aggregates of humans, and we can also see that when the distinctions upon which the code is based no longer function, the society dissolves under its own weight, but we aren't wise enough to recognize the same processes within our own society.

Not that there aren't always more than enough doomsayers who are willing to declare that the end is near, either as a result of religious zealotry or simply out of concern for the lassitude that dominates the system. There are always Cassandras who come straight from *Agamemnon* to tell us of our impending doom (and like Cassandra, they may be right). Clytaemnestra and the people pay no attention, and life goes on as well as it can. What is in question here is not whether our system is on the edge of doom but rather the arrogance of a people who have come to define everything by nurture rather than nature, who have concluded that there is nothing nature has done that humans cannot undo, who have decided that all social codes are arbitrary implementations of power designed solely to keep those with power in power. In the best of cases it is always difficult to know from within a given social system the mechanisms that drive it. It is impossible to be aware of all the implicit biases in one's own system just as one can never know all of the unconscious prejudgments through which one's daily life is construed. It is extremely difficult to be self-aware of the perspectival lines that establish themselves within our individual and collective ways of looking at things long before we are aware we have a perspective. But it is one thing to concede that we shall never know all of the lines of sight that determine the way things look to us and another to fail to undertake on a regular basis the essential scrutiny into these mechanisms that acknowledges both their power over our lives and their inevitable link to the rhythms of the universe. America in particular has always prided itself on its anti-intellectualism, and in this respect the only thing that has changed in the last generation is that now even most of those in the academic world are anti-intellectual, are unwilling to undertake the scrutiny into their own distinctions that most needs to be worked through.

At any given moment within a community, there is always the danger of collective hubris. If we were to look for that threat within our own society at the end of the millennium, there would be more than enough evidence to convict us of the kind of hubris that will invariably guarantee the reciprocal slap of a universe that strikes extremes down in order to modulate its own rhythms. If we were to look elsewhere, we could find the same possibilities in other cultures. Indeed, we would have an easier time of it precisely because they weren't our own. It would be a simple task to reduce the Japanese to some of the strains that become visible in our interactions with them, and we could then think that their tendency toward a sense of racial superiority, their arrogance in the face of what they perceive to be lazy American workers and the like come together into a picture of a culture whose rhythms are still on the upswing, who have yet to realize that they are indeed a part of a rhythm. When the wave is still cresting, few contemplate the nature of waves. Only when the curl of the wave sparks the foam that foretells the crashing of the water do people usually begin to realize that one state inevitably oscillates into another. So we who elected a leader twelve years ago in part because he was given to saying repeatedly that our society represented the last best hope of the world are now more and more inclined to think that the Japanese are driven by cultural arrogance, are so full of their ability to confect technological devices that they cannot see the dependence of their own rhythms on those of other cultures. We may be right about this, but even if we are, such assertions ignore our own cultural arrogance, a pride so strong that it assumes our society can suffer any abuse and recover without difficulty.

The point of Sodom and Gomorrah or late, decadent Rome or any other example of a society that has been swallowed up by its own puffed-up sense of self-importance and self-indulgence is not to hurl imprecations at any particular society or to lament the passing of humane systems of order or to proclaim the second coming of Jesus but rather to suggest that pride is not always a local effect in an individual life, to remind us that hubris is a constituent element of all social systems that can potentially lead to their dissolution and decay. If the house of Atreus falls under the weight of its accumulated sins—and out of its deliberate unwillingness to address the relationship of those sins to the distinctions upon which it was based—it conjures up possibilities for our own societies as well. We who live in so-called individualist societies have regularly tended to reduce tragic drama to a contest between an individual and his or her fate, thereby losing sight of the more powerful drama that is going on at the social level. Yet both Thebes and Argos are in the grip of plagues that define the individual, are contesting with their own dissolution, thereby threatening the disposition of individual fates as well. If in some respects both plays also display the move from barbarity to civilization, they equally show that barbarity is a constituent element of those civilizations that doesn't go away with the implementation of order. Cultural arrogance in this sense is the tendency to assume that one has bested the barbarity out of which one's society has been constituted, that one has killed off the Furies of blood lust and violence. Instead of recognizing that one can at best hope to chain the Furies and contain their vicious energies, those who have been fortunate enough to emerge into a stable social order lose sight of the yapping at the edges of the community and within themselves. Those who think they have buried the Furies forever have lost all perspective on the patterns of social life and have forgotten their own origins as well. One of the virtues of living in the house of Atreus is that it is hard to deny one's own violent origins, though Agamemnon and Clytaemnestra do their best. But if the blood that has colored the earth differs from society to society, each violent event begins with the house of Atreus, or with the Titans whose bloody battles established the original order of the world.

From a slightly different angle we could say that the implementation of individualist societies in itself is an act of hubris that loses sight of the essential relations out of which everything in the world, including individuals, is constituted. This is most obvious in our attempts to distance ourselves from the rest of the animal kingdom, something we have worked very hard to do. There may be much to recommend in any effort that seeks to discern what most distinguishes us from other animals, for we are innately curious about that which gives us our distinctive features, but when such an effort veers into an attempt to deny our links to the other animals on the planet, we begin to imagine ourselves in a different hierarchy from them, one that approaches the separateness of the kingdom of God. The species may have needed a civilization like ours that denied the relations between humans and other living things on the planet, for without the attempt to differentiate ourselves in this way we would have never learned how irretrievable our connections to other life are.

But the side effects of our denial of a common heritage with the other animals were a general loss of the body and an exacerbation of our sense of homelessness. We were unwilling to consider the earth our home, yet we could find no other fitting place no matter how hard we tried. Henderson's deep restlessness makes this point very well, as does Dahfu's attempt to get him to imitate the lion, a task that seems both absurd and frightening to Henderson (as it would to us). He assumes on the one hand that he could learn nothing from such a brute species and on the other that his very life would be at stake. And his sense of his life was in the balance, for he needed to learn specie-beauty; the only way he could do that was by imitating the lion successfully enough to recognize that Atti truly did possess specie-beauty in every whip of her tail, that he too had specie-beauty in his own rhythms, and that those rhythms were as much a part of the world of the lion as they were a function of the human world. Henderson is forced to give up his otherworldly position when he stoops to Atti's level and therefore must abjure the species-arrogance that has carried him through 55 years of life, but what he gets in return is more valuable: a proper sense of how his own bodily nature fits within the rhythms of the world.

The simplest yet most profound truth of all of these rhythms remains the same: they are the most fundamental aspect of our relationship to the world and therefore that which links us to everything else we come in contact with, and they are that which assures the appropriateness of our individual and collective actions. They don't manifest self-awareness in themselves, so they do not thoughtfully gauge the quality of a culture and determine how well it works within the rhythmical nature of existence. Nor do they slap societies down out of a sense of vengeance or retribution—we added those human poisons onto these forces and turned them into the fury of God because the world originally made more sense to us this way. But these forces have nothing personal against us even as they are the most intimate and personal forces in the lives of individuals and the societies in which they live. Humans either learn to live within their flows or feel the slap of the counter-rhythm somewhere along the way.

In the case of our relationship with animals, it is worth remembering that we have not treated the other species of the planet in a fitting way. Even today we have people in governmental agencies who claim the right to eliminate species without a thought for our own petty uses, assuming the kind of species-arrogance they think devolves upon us from the biblical injunction to have dominion over the life forms in our midst. But our willingness to overrun every other species is distasteful because it reflects our attitude toward the creatures whose lives are related to ours: if we are barbaric to them, what is to keep us from being barbaric to our own species? The answer, clearly, is nothing, and our barbarity shows itself in our attitude toward all human life. We may think along with the early Henderson that it is better to inflict our blows on animals than on people—though Henderson preferred the inanimate to other animals—but that would be true only if we weren't in crucial ways kin to them, part of the same pattern of life they are. Since we cannot escape our relations with them either through the blows we pass on to them or through the total elimination of them from our purview, we should long ago have come to the conclusion that there is something essential in our relationship to the other life on the planet that every human needs to consider on a regular basis.

Milan Kundera has best expressed our collective hubris toward the animal kingdom in *The Unbearable Lightness of Being* when he makes our relationship with the rest of the species the measure of our virtue: "True human goodness, in all its purity and freedom, can come to the fore only when its recipient has no power. Mankind's true moral test, its fundamental test (which lies deeply buried from view), consists of its attitude towards those who are at its mercy: animals. And in this respect mankind has suffered a fundamental debacle, a debacle so fundamental that all others stem from it."[4] We have slaughtered the animals and hidden them from view; we have done everything we can to remove them from human consciousness altogether because they tell us what we don't want to hear: we share their animalhood, we have lives that greatly resemble theirs in their patterns of development, in the rhythms of daily life, in the features that root us to a planet we are most uncomfortable with, and in the brevity of our lives. If our goodness is a reflection of how we have treated these creatures that we can blow away as easily as flies, we have indeed suffered "a fundamental debacle," for there is no goodness to be found in what we have done to the animals we have been able to reach.

These days we are more willing to pay lip service to other species for all sorts of aesthetic and economic reasons, and we have even come to realize that the sense of the living world must extend past the animals and the plants and embrace the earth itself, a living critter if ever there was one, with a dynamic all its own that billions and billions of people have some effect on. One might hope that all our facile talk about the environment will translate into a more enduring relationship with its various elements once we realize the fatuousness of our notions of separation from the rest of the life on the planet. At present we are still governed by the debacle to be found in our dealings with what little is left of the original growth forests in North America. We have an economic obsession that impels us to believe that 30,000 jobs are worth more than the one or two percent of first-growth wood loggers can still get their hands on, ignoring the fact that once that one or two percent is gone those jobs will be lost in any case. The only question is whether they are preserved for a few years while we destroy what is left to be cut. Jobs for trees is the way the matter is presented to us, as though there is an easy and obvious reflection to be found in the equation that will inevitably come down on the side of jobs. What are trees anyway? They may have lived hundreds and in some cases even thousands of years, but what is that to a living wage for a single human for a year or two?

In the year of the planet or whatever special ecological year we will imagine ourselves living through next, there is always someone who will point out that in the end our economic systems must embrace a larger field of action than they have so far. They construe human interest too narrowly and reduce the time frame of human choice so much that they allow the destruction of most everything on the planet for short-term gain. We need to remember that the word *economy* originally referred to the disposition of the activities of the household, and we need to realize that our household is not contained in the square footage of that brick edifice an individual lives in any more than it is circumscribed by the governmental agencies that distribute our relations to the rest of the world. The earth is the only logical horizon for our household at this point, and it too has suffered from a fundamental debacle that makes our relations to the animals look almost decent. The only economics worth having—because it would be the only system that was capable of construing the dynamic relationship of the species to the rest of life on the planet over the long term—would be one that broadened the household to include the earth, that was based on the rhythmical relations we adopt to the rest of the living matter on the planet, and that determined economic matters on the basis of these relationships. The very fact that we have come to conclusions of this sort demonstrates how the rhythms of our own activities in conjunction with the effects they have on the world around us have brought us back to this much larger economy of life, the one with which we began, the one we lost sight of when we determined that individuals weren't constrained by their location on the planet, by their bodily natures, or by their relationship to the rest of the living members of the earthly community. We might think of our embryonic understanding of these relations at the moment as the return of the wave, the countermovement to the rhythm we asserted a few hundred years ago. We might also think of this understanding as the rhythm that calls us before the slap of its edge knocks us back within the flows of the natural world.

The collective hubris of the West has allowed many humans to ignore their rootedness to the planet even as it has given them an arrogant sense of the power they wield over their own lives and the lives of other species. But our attempt to break the bonds that tie us to the earth and to other living creatures also sought to remove the constraints that the social world placed upon us. If we forgot that we have a rhythmical relationship with the other animals, if we ignored the patterns that tied us to the earth as well, we also sought to deny the flows of communities. We lost sight of the fact that communities are organisms in their own right composed of the tissue of individual humans in consort with those about them. The ever-increasing world of demographics reminds us more and more insistently of the organic nature of communities and their rhythms and unfolding patterns, but we have yet to find a way to relate to this on an individual level. As with our relationship to the animals and the earth, the notion that the communities of which we are a part are also organisms is something too disconcerting for us because it constrains our behavior in ways we find unappealing. After all, demographics demonstrates how people move back and forth and in and out without great thought for what they are doing, and we don't like the idea of being part of a pattern that is unfolding without specific input from us, failing to realize that naturally enough our choice to move with or against any particular pattern is precisely the input we desire. The only problem is that our choice is collated along with millions of other people's and thus has what seems to be a nugatory effect. But if great waves of people move north and then back south, if they migrate to the cities and then to the suburbs and then to the exurbs, these patterns have powerful effects on the disposition of our own lives. At the most basic level, one either moves with the flows or gets stuck on the prairie by oneself, and each choice carries with it a system of values that determines one's general attitude toward one's life. Just as important, however, is that these flows and our participation in them reflect at the mass level our individual responses to the rhythms of the planet and the community of which we are a part. They are instrumental in effecting the outcome of our life in relation to these communities even as they have effects upon both our society and the planet as a whole.

We can easily trace many of the "causes" of the demographic shifts we have begun to notice, and usually we find specific human and cultural reasons for the movements of populations. People move north because of the increase in manufacturing in the big cities, or people move south because companies have moved to areas where wages are lower, or people move north to extricate themselves from a static way of life, or people move south to escape from the crime and the degradations of life in the city. As always, our tendency is to reduce large shifts to simple explanations. Just as the multiple effects that go into each of our own actions are often reduced to one specific thing in order to make sense of what we have done, so we are inclined to account for these migrations as though there were specific answers to each shift in population. There is always truth to be found in these explanations, for at any given moment most people do want decent jobs and decent lives, and many will move to a different region if they think they can find their own definition of the good life. We are even getting better at seeing the ways in which ongoing changes in the definition of the good life come about in reaction to the excesses of the prevailing definition: if life in the big city was at one time thought to be good because of all the benefits to be found there, the collateral effects of so many people choosing that good life turned out to revise our idea of what was essential to the life we thought was good. We could sacrifice the great variety of cultural events for a neighborhood that wasn't threatened by crime; we would trade higher wages for a less frenetic life. These changes too are rhythmically determined by the patterns of community organisms, and our last step into the world of demographics will come about when we find ways of construing these shifts in terms of the organismic movements of the community itself.

In the end, the collective manifestations of hubris are as compelling as those to be found at the individual level, and in our own age they might be more intriguing because our own collective hubris has been under serious revision for a century and more now and continues to undergo interesting changes. The very fact that we can begin to imagine again our relationship to the animals and to the earth, the fact that we can think of a community as an organism in its own right, the possibility that our actions are enhanced by an understanding of these emerging relations give us prospects for the future that were unavailable within the prevailing arrogance of the West. In increasingly coming to the conclusion that life is relational from bottom to top rather than a series of discrete events, we have responded to the rhythm we developed in reaction to an earlier view of individuals and the communities of which they were a part and the environment that sustained those communities. We thus can imagine a new set of coordinates through which to construe our relations to things even as we can see that the consequences that would follow from a continuing denial of our links to the life around us may well be the wrath of God we once thought came from an other world altogether. It may be that these prospects are in play at any given moment within all cultures and are thus not a function of a privileged moment in the history of the planet, but it is hard to imagine a time when the stakes of our future were so large, when the prospects for humans and the world they know as home were so clearly defined, when the choice between hubris and wisdom was so compelling.

Conclusion: On Virtue

In seeking to determine the parameters of the golden mean at the end of the twentieth century, and in assessing the concomitant relations between the three goods through which our specific sense of the straight and narrow makes itself apparent to us, I have proceeded under the assumption that there is increasing agreement about our need to find a way of thinking of ourselves that avoids the pole of absolutism on the one hand and relativism on the other, that absolutism and relativism express the extremes through which the middle path establishes itself in our lives. Having lived under the good of God and the wrath of God for so long, we might not find it altogether to our liking to think of our lives in relation to natural rhythms that greatly affect the sway of everyday life and the course of events in the world, but this is where our thinking has brought us, and we might find this view preferable to the notion that we ourselves freely determine the course and outcome of our lives. It doesn't matter in the end whether we find this vision of things appealing or not, for it will have its day regardless of our preference for or revulsion to it. And it will engender revisions in the relations between humans and the other species as well, which is as it should be.

But one of the challenges of the revisions in thinking of ourselves that are currently under way concerns our relationship to what we might call *virtue*, if we understand that word to embrace the possibility of living a life of moral excellence in accord with all three of the goods we have discussed. More to the point, we might ask the question Plato has Menon put to Socrates: "Can you tell me, Socrates—can virtue be taught"?[1] This is a question we often lose sight of today because we are more concerned with an education that is suitable to the jobs we need to sustain our standard of living, but the best debates about the way we should instruct our children invariably raise the same question: can virtue be taught? Meno's collateral questions are also worth raising at this point: "Or if not, does it come by practice? Or does it come neither by practice nor by teaching, but do people get it by nature, or in some other way"? (28) Meno pretty well seems to cover our potential relations to the good and our possibilities for achieving a life defined by excellence, so our only duty is to attend carefully to his questions and to consider them afresh given the new relations with the world we are in the process of establishing.

It is worth remembering that Plato's dialogue leads to a conclusion few of us would be satisfied with today, that essentially virtue cannot be taught because it is a function of divine dispensation: "Then we should be right in calling these [men] we just mentioned divine, oracle-chanters and prophets and the poets or creative artists, all of them; most of all, the politicians, we should say they are divine and ecstatic, being inspired and possessed by the god when they are often right while they say grand things although they know nothing of what they say" (67). Inasmuch as there is no specific brand of knowledge or wisdom that can be declared the domain of virtue, this is the only conclusion Socrates can come to: those who have virtue are inspired and possessed, and therefore there is no way to teach that which we all most need to know, how to be virtuous and how to pass that wisdom on to our children. Socrates has already concluded that such a thing cannot be taught by example because many of the most virtuous statesmen have been unable to pass their best quality onto their children, and surely they would if they could, either through example or specific teachings. As the other possibilities are eliminated one by one, the only conclusion left is that virtue is a function of divine possession, not a conclusion we ourselves are likely to come to on our own.

Socrates ends the dialogue by restating his assessment of the relationship between divine inspiration and virtue, although he leaves the testing of this proposition to a future discussion, thereby undermining our full confidence in it. He suggests that "from this our reasoning, Menon, virtue is shown as coming to us, whenever it comes, by divine dispensation; but we shall only know the truth about this clearly when, before enquiring in what way virtue comes to mankind, we first try to search out what virtue is in itself" (68). As usual, even the tentative proposition is put in quotation marks for further study, and future inquiry will conclude that virtue in itself cannot be pinpointed. Nevertheless, it is notable that Socrates finds the site of virtue to be one that is inhabited by all those who manifest excellence in their lives, at least at particular moments when they are inspired. He emphasizes the politician in his remarks, but he includes the oracle-chanters, the prophets, the poets, and the other creative artists.

Socrates' conclusions about the relationship between virtue and possession echo the assessments he has made in the *Ion* about the rhapsode and his craft: "For the poet is an airy thing, a winged and holy thing; and he cannot make poetry until he becomes inspired and goes out of his senses and no mind is left in him; so long as he keeps possession of this, no man is able to make poetry and chant oracles. Not by art, then, they make their poetry with all those fine things about all sorts of matters . . .

not by art, but by divine dispensation. . . ."[2] In linking the poet and the person of virtue, Socrates is working from the same region that allows me to assert that there is an essential relationship between the aesthetic good and the other two goods, that one should be able to derive from those sites of excellence within one's life a pattern and a sense of what makes one's actions fitting in a particular context. Virtue is nothing more or less than that, though Socrates himself may be unwilling to go so far as to define it in this way. In this respect, although his own remarks are couched in the hypothetical, he is right to find the origin of virtue in that which cannot be taught: the divine inspiration that takes us out of ourselves and places us wholly within the rhythms of the universe, thereby rendering for us the proper sense of our activities and their relationship to the patterns of which they are a part. This is the site of the poem, of the great play in basketball, of the great political speech that sways people's minds, and of the quiet moment when we find ourselves alone in the midst of wonder. Virtue is not to be discovered only here, but if it is to be found, it will have taken root as a result of ecstatic moments through which the parameters of life are made available to us, and as anyone knows who has experienced such moments, they are decidedly not teachable.

In asserting this, we need to distinguish once again between the programmatic expression of the good and the expression of virtue. There are many people in the world who have been brought up well within the normative vision of the good and who are wholly capable of acting most of the time on the basis of this good. They obey the Ten Commandments and avoid the seven deadly sins and are unquestionably nice people. In and of itself, this kind of life cannot be said to be virtuous because it has never tested the nature of the propositions on which it is based. That is not to say that it is a bad life, for it is not. Nor is it to say that this expression of the good is one we should hope to eliminate, for it has its own value and is obviously preferable to those lives that are dominated by self-indulgence and thoughtless behavior.

Virtue, however, is not a result of making the right choices according to the code of one's community, although it is often found there as well. It is marked by the careful resolve of one who questions the code of the community too, who risks his or her sense of what is good and places the future on the line through the assessment of each particular case. Hypothetically, we might say that Socrates is virtuous, and he dies as a result of his virtue. There are other ways of looking at his behavior, and we could easily conclude that he is a threat to the community as well because he fails to note the subversive effects of his questions on the body politic. It might be that like Baby Suggs, Socrates doesn't know how much is too much in all cases and occasionally gives people more than they are capable of taking in. Regardless, his virtue is manifested in his questions and his willingness to question, in his self-proclaimed ignorance in the face of matters that exceed the grasp of any particular individual, and in his willingness to contemplate the possibility that the most important aspect of a good life, virtue, is not something that can be taught but rather something that comes by divine dispensation.

Socrates tells us that it may be that virtue is found at the site of divine possession, the ecstatic moment when we are not ourselves in particular but assume an aesthetic vision that places us in a relational context to the rest of the world. The dialogues themselves are relational machines through which Socrates can measure his sense of things as it relates to the community and to that which is being pursued. Socrates molds the structure of the dialogue to invent a literary form through which virtue can be the focal point. The poets focus on *arete* in other domains: the greatness of the hero, the wonders of the poet. The essayist, the one who speaks not through the rhythms of the poem but through those of the dialogue, devotes himself to an inquiry into the nature of pattern itself, that through which virtue manifests itself and is gauged, that through which all human activity finally expresses itself in one way or another. The dialogue in and of itself is never enough, just as Michael Jordan's whole life cannot be basketball, for Socrates goes off to dinner with the rest of his interlocutors. But the dialogue lays bare the aesthetic rhythms that human actions depend on, and it demonstrates the way in which excellence is always a function of a particular site through which those rhythms are made available to oneself and to others.

We can assume that in this very narrow sense virtue cannot be taught. None of us can instruct another in how to be divinely inspired any more than we can easily find the pattern of the possessed in our own lives. Michael Jordan can no more guarantee that he will have a sublime night on the basketball court than we can rely on such divine dispensations coming to us when we most need them. We work out patterns of our own that seem to place us in the right region for aesthetic experiences, but we can do no more than that. We can study the nature of relations and rhythms, and we can work to create contexts that allow these relations to make their appearance in our lives, but we can never be sure of their arrival. For us the notion that these experiences are a function of divine inspiration is problematic inasmuch as we no longer tend to locate the source of their energy in an otherworldly dispensation, but that shouldn't keep us from realizing the centrality of these kinds of experiences in most people's lives.

These days we are more inclined to talk about the flow of endorphins in the brain than to speak of divine possession, but the specific nature of our descriptions of aesthetic events is less important than an awareness of what is involved in them. Whether we speak of not being in our right mind, of ecstatic states, or of particular hormones pulsing through the brain, the main point is an understanding of the relational nature of the universe. In an ecstatic state we are not outside of ourselves so much as we are ourselves in a different way: we are a site within relations rather than a self that imagines itself above the relations that determine it. In this respect we are outside of that self which is preoccupied by its own specific interests and that sees those interests in discrete terms, but there are other dimensions to who we are that can never be accounted for in this definition by self-interest and self-possession. The most profound dimensions of our selves are those that reveal to us the way the curve of our own life moves in accord with the flows around it, those through which we see that the pattern of our own existence is bonded onto the universe and its rhythms in ways we can never wholly chart. We can discern over time how a life unfolds according to certain patterns, just as we note on an ongoing basis how our choices and actions are based on an always-unfolding sense of the appropriateness of what we do with where we are allowed to do it. The ecstatic moments, those times when these rhythms are most apparent to us, are the crucial events in our lives through which the rest of the relational choices we make are gauged, through which their adequacy to what is is measured, and as such they are both the most profound situations we ever find ourselves in—and thus wholly deserving of the term *divine inspiration*—and the most straightforward moments we ever experience in the world.

Virtue cannot exist without an aesthetic context. It is not to be found outside of a particular human being's understanding of the relational patterns of the world of which he or she is a part, and such knowledge can never be taught. It is something that happens to one rather than something one can hope to learn in school or through the example of one's parents. But if virtue cannot be taught, this aesthetic site also suggests that theoretically everyone is capable of virtue, for most humans have such charmed moments on and off throughout their lives. Most pertinently, we might assume that the virtuous person is one who has found ways of teaching himself about the nature of these patterns as a result of the charmed moments in his life. Individuals may or may not get help from others in their ongoing quest to achieve virtue, but regardless of such help, they must have found ways on their own to arrive at a better understanding of the virtue inherent in their lives. This is most apparent in that those who have charmed moments seek out similar events, and most learn over time the parameters of those kinds of experience. They can figure out easily enough that for them the aesthetic is to be found in their grace in an athletic contest or in their ability to paint or in the way they cultivate the local spaces of their yard or in countless other cultural contexts each society provides for the expression of such virtue. Most of us are capable of discerning over time that which we have a facility for, and this is only another way of speaking about the ways in which we learn more about the sites through which we are most likely to be able to have a graceful relationship with the rhythms of the universe. If virtue depends upon the possession of specific abilities and uncanny moments when these abilities seem to express the beauty of the world on their own, we can all learn enough from these events to find ways of making them happen again.

The easy part of the virtuous equation is to be found here, in our ability to sort out those contexts that are most likely to provide fitting expressions of who we are from those in which we shall always be a little off the prevailing rhythm. The harder form of instruction is the one we contemplated when we thought about the ways in which Michael Jordan's grace on the basketball court could be translated into virtuous action in everyday life: through one's understanding of pattern and rhythm in one context, one comes to discern equivalent patterns in other situations, thereby spreading the effects of grace from a context where one naturally expresses it to one where it is more difficult to find one's place within meaningful patterns. Strictly speaking, we might say that this kind of transference of pattern cannot be taught either, although it is the site where most teaching takes place. The presentation of information, the usefulness of exemplification, and models of human behavior all possess strength as modes of instruction only to the extent that the student becomes aware of the nature of the rhythm through which the exemplary life is lived. And in some respects these things can never really be taught. In a fundamental way the use of example, the presentation of specific models of behavior, and the attempt to reduce a particular kind of wisdom to a phrase are all efforts that depend on something beyond teaching as we know it, even if in some ways they are all employed when teaching at its best takes place.

To use a common example, I can say without question that one of the most frustrating tasks I face as a teacher throughout any given semester is giving my students a proper idea of what I want them to do on their papers. It is impossible for me adequately to convey through language alone just what I mean. I always begin by telling them that I simply want their papers to demonstrate to me that the texts they are working with have had an effect upon them. I tell them that all distinguished work is a function of a context that has redefined one's sense of things, and that that is what I look for in their work. But of course this makes no sense to them, so I have to anticipate the kinds of context they bring to my remarks. Thus, I tell them that I am not interested in a summary of the work, nor do I want them to reduce the text to a theme—indeed, I insist that no worthy piece of literature ever has a theme as they have been taught to think of it. Likewise, I insist that I don't want them to spout back what has been said in class, though they are always free to make use of whatever comes up there.

I have also learned that I must proceed to talk at length about the question of originality, for that word is the one students tend most immediately to associate with my demands on them. They assume that I am asking them to be original, and they are right, yet their sense of what being original means invariably differs from my own. So I must tell them that originality is not a function of a gimmick or the equivalent of a sound bite or an astonishing reading of a work that overturns every earlier reading of it, but they don't believe me and then begin to think that I am saying one thing—be original—and meaning another—spout back on your paper what you heard me say in class. So I explain that originality is not a function of thought—let's see now, how can I be original, how can I impress the teacher with my originality?—but rather what I told them at the beginning: it manifests itself in their genuine willingness to let the text have an effect upon them and will be seen in the ways in which they find their own modes of expression to talk about what changes the text brought about within them.

This never has the proper effect, for the students are now more befuddled than they were when we started out. They seem to feel that I am speaking out of both sides of my mouth and don't know where else to look, so I proceed to talk about divine inspiration, explaining that all of us have had the good fortune to have come upon things in our writing that we never expected, that those things were invariably accompanied by powerful emotions, and that most of us continued to write precisely because the activity placed us in the way of these experiences. Call it divine inspiration, call it the bubbling up of the unconscious, call it what you will, the wisdom to be found in such sites, the virtue that is located there, is the reason why people undertake the arduous journey that writing involves. And then I will bring in examples from collateral domains, usually sports and music, to talk about the transformative effects these moments can have in lives, and by then most students have a fair idea of what I am talking about. They have almost always had such powerful moments in their lives, and they understand their importance.

Most often, however, none of this has the proper effect, at least not the first time through. I will repeat such a discussion on one or two other occasions before the first paper is due, and I will gladly look at rough drafts and seek within them places where this grace manifests itself and then point to it and say *There!* And then the papers will come in, they will be graded, and the students will revise their sense of my requirements on the basis of how well they did. Sometimes students "get it" and become inspired to write what they should. Other times they never figure out what I am talking about and give up in frustration and settle for a programmatic essay that manages to oblige me by saying all the usual things about a work. And sometimes students think they know what I am talking about and then don't get the grade they want and conclude that I was really asking them to repeat my own ideas. In a sense, of course, they are right, for I do insist that an "inspired" paper is the only kind worth writing, and that definition of a good paper is by no means universal. So in asking for this kind of essay, I am essentially requiring them in one way or another to write the kind of paper that will reveal the relational nature of the universe, that will establish the nature of the rhythms through which writer and text interact to inform them and me of that which we most need to know.

Can virtue be taught? Can virtue be taught when one can't do any better than this when one is seeking to establish the parameters of one of the most routine exercises that a student ever undertakes? If I cannot be more successful in explaining to students what to write on than this—a flawed and incomplete description of a good paper at best, and one that probably depends more on the inspiration of the moment and the divine possession that will overtake me while I get worked up about these things in class—how could virtue ever be taught? But clearly the problem is that I am trying to teach virtue in telling them how to write a paper. I am explaining that half-hearted repetitions of others' ideas are not virtuous, that the callow recollection of the teacher's words is even worse, that the restatement of key ideas in others' work is not sufficient, that their own subjective wandering in the text is no good either. And that usually gets to them, for they have been defining originality in terms of "subjectivity" for a long time. They have great trouble getting past the point where they can see that originality is never an expression of their subjectivity but rather an aesthetic expression of their relation to the universe as measured through a discussion of a text or some other event in the world. So I could tell them that I am trying to teach them virtue, and that virtue is to be found in the ecstatic transformation of their subject matter in a paper—or in class—that is no more a function of their subjective impressions of the universe than it is derived from an objective discussion of the "facts" of the text or the world. But they would still be stumped, and I would be close to concluding that virtue cannot be taught.

Strictly speaking, it would seem that virtue cannot be taught. One can go the negative way. One can say: virtue is *not* this and it is *not* that just as I tell my students that their papers depend on originality, but originality is *not* this and it is *not* that. Even if I can come up with a pithy expression of originality on the spur of the moment, a bon mot that will encapsulate my own sense of it as the happy marriage of speaking and hearing (to steal from Faulkner), the students will either "get it" or they will be stuck back there with all the *nots* and thus still be looking for a point of entry into the paper and into the virtuous life. My example as a teacher isn't worth much in this respect either, for even if they can see my enthusiasm for the subject matter, for literature, and for the virtuous life, still they get caught up in all the wrong things and focus on the specifics of my person rather than the patterns that my specificity expresses. They are as given to fetishization as are most other people in the world, and fetishization, we know, is nothing more than mistaking the particular manifestations of beauty for the patterns of the aesthetic, losing sight of the rhythms by reducing them to the specific activities of the enthusiastic event that is taking place in front of one. I cannot provide by example that which I cannot give through instruction, yet it may be that example is useful if one can find ways of stripping it of the fetishistic tendencies that are found in the same neighborhood.

Strictly speaking, I cannot teach virtue in my classes even though that is the only thing worth teaching in *any* class as far as I am concerned. It is not a fact to be learned, alas, but an event that is found, an experience that wells up and will have its moment, and something whose effects one hopes will spread throughout the life to engender a genuinely virtuous human. But in other respects, it is as possible to teach virtue as it is to explain what I expect of a student on a paper. What is hard to figure out is the particular strategy that will work for each individual student. Anyone who has taught reasonably intelligent people for any length of time becomes convinced, rightly or wrongly, that there is a point of entry into each of those lives through which one can articulate the nature of the virtuous life. The problem is getting to it. This is why in some respects my own teaching reflects the "kitchen sink" approach: I throw as many different strategies at the problem as I can in the hope that most of my students will latch on to at least one of them as the path through which their own thinking about the matter can take root. I would be lying if I stated that all of my students had a proper sense of virtue at the end of the semester, particularly inasmuch as on any given day I remain uncertain of my own relations to the virtuous life, but I would like to think that I have at least given most all of them some hints and guesses about where virtue might be found, and I have seen a good number of manifestations of that virtue in their work as well. Like all teachers, I then simply hope that other classes open up whatever links the students might have discovered during the previous fourteen weeks. Nevertheless, in some respects one is left with the conclusion that virtue cannot be taught.

❦

If virtue both can and cannot be taught, and if instruction in it should be the foundation of education in all countries, it is striking that so few people are willing to talk about it anymore. *Virtue* is unquestionably an old-fashioned word, and one would likely get hooted out of any large gathering of academics if one were to speak on the nature of virtue and the question of whether it can be taught. It is even more striking that we have an educational apparatus that pays great lip service to Socrates and his cunning questions and yet is not at all interested in the words through which he probed the relations between humans the the world about them. Virtue indeed! In a pragmatic culture like the one in the United States, virtue hardly seems to be a useful notion, even if it is situationally defined (of necessity, it is *always* situationally defined). We have classes devoted to ethics, but almost invariably they hover around the "big" questions: should women be allowed to have abortions or not? Should we have a death penalty or not? At best they manage to work their way around to the bigger issues, like the question of how one can live honorably in a world in which one cannot simply dismiss the other side of these questions. Even so, the idea that virtue ought to be the central matter of all curricular decisions is decidedly out of place in today's world, even if it is also true that we seem to be in the midst of a major sea change and feel as though we have lost our way. The very lack of direction that characterizes so many individual attitudes toward the present moment in our culture might lead people to think that more instruction in virtue is precisely what we need. But then virtue will be chopped into something else: either the right-wing insistence on the necessity of the Ten Commandments, the importance of the work ethic, the need for the family unit, and the elimination of all government programs that attempt to address the lives that don't measure up to these standards; or the left-wing insistence that tolerance is the only virtue, that undifferentiated acceptance of all ways of life is the only honorable path, that one must stop discrimination of every sort. Where is there room for virtue in this mix?

If the instruction of virtue requires as much of the negative way as it involves the presentation of the wonders of the aesthetic, there are other impediments as well, most notably the fact that virtue seems to be a function of a kind of discipline we thought unrelated to the one we took up to lead honorable lives. Our normal understanding of virtue is that it is based on a discipline which excludes, and there is some truth in that. But it is also true that the discipline of virtue is based on the simple willingness to see what is there, to look at what is the case and embrace it regardless of one's attitude toward it. The power of human desire is great, and it often makes it difficult for us to know whether we are seeing the world through the lens of that desire or in fact seeing what is there. We do not so much need to discipline our desire in order to overcome the excesses to which it might lead as we need to keep it from overrunning our understanding of the world. Just as Henderson went through most of his life thinking that he loved reality only to discover in Africa that unreality had always been his favorite location, so too we tend to have our sense of things clouded by that which we want to be the case, and the sincerity of will that is required always to see only what is there is hard to master and even harder to keep in place all the time.

We also fail to consider the great impediments in the way of this virtuous willingness to see only what is there, although each of us knows well enough the power of the everyday codes that restrict our vision to the virtues society deems the normative ones. Walt Whitman focuses our attention on this problem when he explains his own relationship to society at the beginning of "Song of Myself":

> Houses and rooms are full of perfumes, the shelves are crowded
> with perfumes,
> I breathe the fragrance myself and know it and like it,
> The distillation would intoxicate me also, but I shall not let it.[3]

As a rule, people tend to move in two directions when it comes to houses and rooms and their social perfumes: they either want to embrace and be embraced by the social milieu, or they scorn the roles upon which all community activity is based. Whitman is that rare Romantic writer who both loves social discourse and yet realizes its perils. He admits that he could very easily become "intoxicated" by these social perfumes "also," suggesting that we already have, but he disciplines himself and refuses to let the mixture overtake him. His act of discipline is the "I shall not let it" that acknowledges both the power of the perfume to overwhelm his own good sense and his equal determination not to let that happen.

Humans tend to underestimate the force of perfume in their lives, fail to realize that its smell is so intoxicating that it is almost impossible for them to remember the pure odorlessness of simple air. Within it own flows, social reality seems so plausible and compelling that it is often difficult for one to realize that its structures are often arbitrary and unreal, often deliberately devoted to the cultivation of the unreal and the human desire that seeks it out. We all have a great need to be respected, to achieve the recognition that Hegel knew was at the heart of the human enterprise, and we forget the changes in our vision we adopt in order to be seen in a proper light by others. Even when we come to realize how much society feeds our resentments in order to train our desire in accord with the necessities of its own play, it is difficult to resist its pressures because we are always one against everyone else. Certainly by the time a writer like Ralph Waldo Emerson came to write "Self-Reliance," he was fully aware of the costs involved in seeing the world as it is rather than through the eyes society wants one to have. On the one hand, he will urge upon us the sincerity of heart we need to see things as they are—"Trust thyself: every heart vibrates to that iron string"[4]—and on the other he is just as clear about the penalty: "For nonconformity the world whips you with its displeasure" (136). One must come to rely upon one's ability to see things as they are, one must approach the world with sincerity, and yet one will be whipped by the world's displeasure if one does so because one's sense of things will be at odds with the prevailing wisdom of the culture of which one is a part. Whitman's discipline is necessary to keep to the middle path that allows one's sincerity to confront what is in the face of the world's displeasure, knows the imperatives that are required of us if we are to be as virtuous as we would like to be.

Emerson's vision of society is far more hostile than Whitman's, so it is perhaps better to see this part of the world through Whitman's eyes because most of us are more interested in the recognition of the other than Emerson admits to being, but he at least has the virtue of putting the difficulty of the task in straightforward terms. He tells us about our intuitive sense of the world and encourages us to explore it, yet he also realizes that "These are the voices which we hear in solitude, but they grow faint and inaudible as we enter into the world. . . . Society is a joint-stock company, in which the members agree, for the better securing of his bread to each shareholder, to surrender the liberty and culture of the eater. The virtue in most request is conformity. Self-reliance is its aversion. It loves not realities and creators, but names and customs" (133). Emerson is certainly right that the difficulties in the way of the sincere heart are related to the fact that what can be easily heard in solitude tends to get lost in the noise of society: he refers to the sounds of social voices where Whitman speaks of the intoxication of the social perfumes, but both understand how hard it is to hear the nature of what is in the midst of social customs that train us to see other things. Emerson is also doubtless right that conformity is that which is most in demand in society. Whatever lip service we pay to the independent person in our culture, we are just as committed to names and customs—as opposed to realities and creators—as any other society. We may mask our desire for conformity by the rhetoric of individualism, but this only makes the pressure to move away from self-reliance all the greater. Virtue may be something one can at least nudge along within another, but no one can help someone else deal with the pressures to reduce the world to the social perfumes that are always much more in evidence than the wonderfully odorless smell of the outdoor air.

If the sound of our own voice in private is that to which we should attend, we easily lose track of its music and forget what it wants to tell us. We are swamped by the social codes that dominate the everyday world and snuff out the silence that would be necessary for us to hear our own voice and to learn from it what was actually the case. At the same time, we all always already know what we need to know and always already have within us that voice which is too seldom heard and even less often attended to. Our own sense of what is, that understanding of the world through which virtue manifests itself in ways large and small, is in the end not really a private preserve at all but the voice of the earth as it is filtered through our own joy and sorrow. This is why a poet like Whitman can tell us with confidence in the midst of his own great poem that:

> These are really the thoughts of all men in all ages and lands, they are not original with me,
> If they are not yours as much as mine they are nothing, or next to nothing,
> If they are not the riddle and the untying of the riddle they are nothing,
> If they are not just as close as they are distant they are nothing.[5]

Whitman's song may be his in the sense that it achieves utterance through him, but that which he expresses must necessarily be "the thoughts of all men in all ages and lands." His originality doesn't come from what he has to say, for that is a communal possession that anyone can conjure up by listening to his or her own voice. On the contrary, what distinguishes Whitman's work is the manner in which he modulates these thoughts through his own particular orientation to the rhythms in the midst of which he finds himself. He therefore realizes that he is giving us nothing we don't already have. Just as Socrates seriously considers the possibility that virtue is something inherent in each person, something that cannot be taught because it is innately present from the beginning, so too Whitman asserts that we already have the song that we need, the voice that will allow us to express life through virtuous action in the world. He is simply calling that voice forth from within us through the bold pronouncements of his poem.

Whitman's democratic faith is based on the belief that his thoughts are really the thoughts of all people in all lands and times, his conviction that it is only because we have lost the sound of our own voices in the din of society that it might appear otherwise to us. We become intoxicated by the perfumes that hide the world and thereby lose track of the thoughts with which we began. Whitman also understands the dynamic inherent in his thoughts of the real, for he acknowledges their curious condition by asserting that they must be both the riddle and "the untying of the riddle." We are not accustomed to seeing code and decoder in the same place and believe in utterances that need a hermeneutic machinery applied to them in order to probe their inner meanings. For Whitman, the utterance is both what is and an explanation of what is: it occupies the space of the real even as it expresses that state through a social code that links it to the rules of the community. If it can't do both of these things at the same time, it fails to express that which Whitman thinks it should.

Likewise, Whitman tells us that if these thoughts "are not just as close as they are distant they are nothing," once more establishing the problematic nature of that region through which virtue expresses itself in human life. If these thoughts are to be found in all of us, they are clearly as close as they can be, for they inhabit the same space as the rest of us. If they are distant, that is because we are distanced from ourselves, caught up in the mediations of society and incapacitated by our intoxication with the social perfumes that prod us to see the world through desires that blind us to what is real. Whitman, then, needs to bring out that which is close, even as he points to the distance from ourselves that we have moved in order to bend to the call of the social world and achieve recognition. The "near and the far" place us in the midst of this tension because we all want recognition even as we cannot hope to hear our own voice when we enter into the contract that distances us from what we hear in private. Our discipline comes not from cutting out desires we need to train, but rather in cutting to the desire at the center of our lives, the desire to see what is and embrace it.

If virtue is to be found in a sincere willingness to look at what is the case, we realize the difficulties we have in focusing on the world with the necessary intensity and clarity to achieve this kind of vision, and the modern world has made our task all the more difficult because our knowledge has become fragmented. We are given to thinking of the various features of human life as separable elements: there is abstract thought, reasoning; there is emotion, the affectional orientation we have to the world; there is need and desire as expressed through our attempts to obtain food, water, sexual activity and the like; and there are instruments through which these characteristics find expression, whether they be language or some other medium of communication. These splits we perceive within us prompt us to construe virtue in erroneous ways, for we come to imagine it as an abstract consideration of what is that is stripped of all emotional ties to the world, or as an intuitive response to things that is rooted in the earth rather than based on high abstraction, or as an immediate kind of emotional tie to the world that has nothing to do with society at all. Whitman's strength as a poet is that he sees virtue as an expression of all of these things: the medium is that which is as much as it is a medium, and it expresses affect, thought, intuition and bodily nuance as well. It is filtered through the body that is located firmly in a physical world, and it expresses the one thing we most want: a virtuous relationship to the world, a full participation in the three goods that manifests the affirmation of life we all desire more than anything. Although this is as close as it is distant, although it is hard to recognize at times, when we find it we all see it for what it is and embrace it on the same terms. We are glad to be in its presence and hope to find ways of making it stay. Henderson complained about the fact that beauty would come into his life and then leave too quickly without explanation, and he defined his quest as a path whereby he could make beauty remain. But if he finally found what he was looking for, that was because he came to see that he was always in the midst of the beauty he sought, that it was always as close as Whitman says it is. Its distance is a function of our inability to attend to what is, our willingness to stray from the middle path and move into the intoxicating world of social desire where reality is a construct that is designed by human will. Henderson achieves virtue by agreeing to see the world as it is and accept its terms, and that is what is demanded of us all.

Socrates' dialogic inquiry into the nature of virtue shows that the subject has always been an elusive one, so it is not that the modern world has moved us away from a clarity of vision that earlier eras possessed. Nevertheless, we may have created a world in which the knowledge of virtue is more fragmented than it once was, and we get a glimmer of our distance from that which is when we contemplate briefly the central word of our tradition: *logos*. We know that this word has a range of meanings that cannot be encapsulated by any single one of our own, yet we perhaps mistake the reasons for this broadness of applicability. If *logos* seems to move in so many directions, perhaps that is because the early Greeks were more adept at discerning the complex relations to the planet we have, were better able to assess the nature of what is because they saw its multifarious rootedness in their own lives in a way that we seldom do. It is not that they all possessed virtue with ease whereas we have great difficulty in achieving it, for Socrates makes it clear that there was never a time when virtue was easy, and certainly less civilized societies aren't by any means inclined to act in the world on the basis of virtue. But there is something in the magic word *logos* that manages to achieve the knowledge that we all seek and possess at the same time, and it is found in the range of application the word has. We can get a sense of its range by looking at G. B. Kerferd's definition of it in his study of the sophists:

> What we are confronted with is not strictly speaking one word with a number of different meanings, but rather a word with a range of applications all of which relate to a single starting point. . . . In the case of the word logos there are three main areas of its application or use, all related by an underlying conceptual unity. These are first of all the area of language and linguistic formulation, hence speech, discourse, description, statement, arguments (as expressed in words) and so on; secondly the

> area of thought and mental processes, hence thinking, reasoning, accounting for, explanation. . . ; thirdly, the area of the world, that *about* which we are able to speak and to think, hence structural principles, formulae, natural laws and so on, provided that in each case they are regarded as actually present in and exhibited in the world-process.[6]

Logos is a word that marks the intersection of world, thought, and speech, embracing all the effects of the human world, taking up the social conventions through which our relations to the world are manifested, and allowing the rhythms of the world to make themselves apparent to us as well. When we talk about that which is included in *logos*, we tend to move in one direction or another and forget about the essential connections among world, thought and speech; if we are going to retrieve that logic that is both close and distant, both clear and maddeningly diffuse, we must insist on the interrelatedness of these elements of *logos*.

We must find a way of integrating this *logos* into our everyday lives, and we can do so only by looking to our own voice as an expression of what is, regardless of whether we are poets or not, regardless of whether we like the sound of our voice, are too much taken with it, or are too timid to let it achieve utterance in public or private. Virtue is to be found in those who agree to express the *logos*, who take upon themselves the complex relationship that is endlessly worked out through the movement in and between world, thought, and language, and it can be found only where the relations between these three sites are fluid and evenly distributed. A balance of these areas is necessary because in the end the *logos* is rhythm, is pattern, is the measure of the world as it expresses itself in humans through the sounds that bring together the world, our thought about it, and the language through which both are articulated. This is that magnificent region through which the wonders of the world are made manifest to us and through which the richness and fortuity of our lives become apparent to us, and it is always the only place we want to be, even if we have great difficulty in finding it and even greater difficulty in remaining under its sway once we locate it. It may not be a place we can be taught to find in the strictest sense of the word, but we learn over time how to sniff it out and recognize it precisely because its odorlessness is so intoxicating.

At the same time, virtue is seldom to be found in the grand events of life simply because there are so few of them. We need to attend to the everydayness of poets like Whitman, and we must listen to Wordsworth when he tells us with great feeling how the sublime moments of the kind he found at Tintern Abbey

> have no slight or trivial influence
> on that best portion of a good man's life,
> His little, nameless, unremembered, acts
> Of kindness and of love.[7]

For the most part, the three goods come together in our lives through such nameless, unremembered acts, the pure expression of generosity that declares through its interest a belief that the world is good, that we are touched by the beauty of things, that we wish to pass it on, to keep it circulating, to find ever-new ways of articulating our relationship to everything that lives. We may be instructed in the discipline of virtue by the likes of Whitman and Wordsworth, or we may teach ourselves through experiences that allow us to approach the golden mean that becomes clearer and clearer as we learn what to look for in the specificity of our own particular circumstances in life. Whatever the means, we all arrive at the same place, at the world we were meant to embrace even as we continue to wrestle with it and struggle for the Blessing of life.

Notes

CHAPTER ONE: THE THREE GOODS

1. *Ralph Waldo Emerson*, ed. Richard Poirier (Oxford: Oxford University Press, 1990), 18.

2. *The Random House Dictionary of the English Language*, Second Edition, Unabridged (New York: Random House, 1987), 826-27.

3. Wallace Stevens, "Of Modern Poetry," *The Collected Poems* (New York: Vintage Books, 1982), 239.

4. Stevens, 240.

CHAPTER TWO: THE STRAIGHT AND NARROW

1. *The Wisdom of Confucius*, ed. and trans. Lin Yutang (New York: Modern Library, 1966), 138-39.

2. Wallace Stevens, "The Snow Man," *The Collected Poems* (New York: Vintage Books, 1982), 9.

3. Toni Morrison, *Beloved* (New York: NAL, 1988), 87. Subsequent quotations from the novel will be from this edition and will be noted parenthetically with page numbers in the text.

CHAPTER THREE: MAN WANTS TO LIVE

1. Harold Bloom, *The Book of J*, translated by David Rosenberg and interpreted by Harold Bloom (New York: Grove Weidenfeld, 1990), 210. Subsequent quotations from this text will be noted parenthetically with page numbers in the text.

2. Saul Bellow, *Henderson the Rain King* (New York: Penguin Books, 1959), 85. Subsequent quotations from the novel will be noted parenthetically with page numbers in the text.

3. Toni Morrison, *Beloved* (New York: NAL, 1988), 268.

CHAPTER FOUR: THE FAIR PLAY OF THE WORLD

1. Herman Melville, *Billy Budd, Sailor and Other Stories*, ed. Harold Beaver (New York: Penguin Books, 1970), 306.

2. Friedrich Nietzsche, *Thus Spoke Zarathustra*, trans. R. J. Hollingdale (New York: Penguin Books, 1969), 117. Subsequent quotations from this work are from this translation and will be noted parenthetically with page numbers in the text.

3. Alexandre Kojeve, *Introduction to the Reading of Hegel*, assembled by Raymond Queneau, edited by Allan Bloom, translated by James H. Nichols, Jr. (New York: Basic Books, 1969), 7. Subsequent quotations from this work are from this translation and will be noted parenthetically with page numbers in the text.

4. René Girard, *"To double business bound": Essays on Literature, Mimesis, and Anthropology* (Baltimore: Johns Hopkins University Press, 1978), vii.

5. Saul Bellow, *Henderson the Rain King* (New York: Penguin Books, 1959), 213. Subsequent quotations from the novel will be noted parenthetically with page numbers in the text.

6. Friedrich Nietzsche, *Thus Spoke Zarathustra*, as quoted in Fred D. Wieck and J. Glenn Gray's translation of Martin Heidegger's *What Is Called Thinking?* (New York: Harper and Row, 1972),

93. Although both Kaufmann's and Hollingdale's translations of these lines are perfectly serviceable, I prefer the translation to be found in this work because it uses the word "revulsion," which carries with it a tone of physical and innate response at the deepest levels of human existence. Hollingdale"s "antipathy" and Kaufmann's "ill will" do not sufficiently convey the instinctiveness that "revulsion" covers.

7. Toni Morrison, *Beloved* (New York: NAL, 1988), 87.

8. Friedrich Nietzsche, *Ecce Homo*, trans. Walter Kaufmann (New York: Random House, 1967), 303-44.

9. Nietzsche, 303.

10. Friedrich Nietzsche, *Thus Spoke Zarathustra*, in *The Portable Nietzsche*, trans. Walter Kaufmann (New York: Viking Press, 1968), 211.

11. Philip Levine, "They Feed They Lion," *Selected Poems* (New York: Atheneum, 1984), 81.

12. Levine, 81.

CHAPTER FIVE: PRIDE GOETH BEFORE THE FALL

1. Tony Morrison, *Beloved* (New York: NAL, 1988), 137.

2. Morrison, 138.

3. Aeschylus, *Agamemnon*, trans. Robert Fagles (New York: Penguin Books, 1977), 110. Subsequent quotations from the play are from this translation and will be noted parenthetically with page numbers in the text.

4. Milan Kundera, *The Unbearable Lightness of Being*, trans. Michael Henry Heim (New York: Harper, 1984), 289.

CONCLUSION: ON VIRTUE

1. *Meno, Great Dialogues of Plato*, trans. W. H. D. Rouse (New York: NAL, 1956), 28. Subsequent quotations from this edition will be noted parenthetically within the text.

2. *Ion, Great Dialogues of Plato*, trans. W. H. D. Rouse (New York: NAL, 1956), 18.

3. Walt Whitman, *Leaves of Grass*, ed. Sculley Bradley and Harold W. Blodgett (New York: Norton, 1973), 29.

4. Ralph Waldo Emerson, *Ralph Waldo Emerson*, ed. Richard Poirier (Oxford: Oxford University Press, 1990), 132. Subsequent quotations from Emerson's work are from this edition and will be noted parenthetically within the text.

5. Whitman, 45.

6. G. B. Kerferd, *The Sophistic Movement* (Cambridge: Cambridge University Press, 1981), 83.

7. William Wordsworth, "Tintern Abbey," *Poetical Works*, ed. Thomas Hutchinson (London: Oxford University Press, 1969), 163.